# THE SOUL

## A Translation of
## St. Thomas Aquinas' *De Anima*

*By*

## *John Patrick Rowan*

**ASSISTANT PROFESSOR OF PHILOSOPHY**
**DE PAUL UNIVERSITY**

WIPF & STOCK · Eugene, Oregon

Wipf and Stock Publishers
199 W 8th Ave, Suite 3
Eugene, OR 97401

The Soul
A Translation of St. Thomas Quinas' De Anima
By Rowan, John Patrick
ISBN 13: 978-1-60608-256-0
Publication date 01/30/2009
Previously published by Herder, 1951

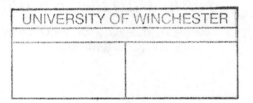

*To*
*CHRISTENA*

# TRANSLATOR'S PREFACE

The purpose of this translation is simply to make St. Thomas Aquinas' *Disputed Questions on the Soul* available to English-reading students who are interested in the philosophy of man. I have tried to render the Latin text into intelligible English without sacrificing, in any way, the teaching of the Angelic Doctor. This is a difficult task since many philosophical terms in the Latin have no adequate English equivalents. On the other hand, a verbatim translation often fails to convey to the reader the exact meaning of the original text.

To the best of my knowledge there is no critical edition of the *De anima*. In making this translation I have used the following editions of the work: Marietti (Turin, 1942), Hédde (Paris, 1912), and Vivès (Paris, 1872–80).

According to the best authorities [1] the *De anima* is an authentic work of St. Thomas and was written during his sojourn in Italy under the pontificate of Clement IV. The date of its composition is between 1266 and 1270. [2]

The title of this work is to some extent misleading, because St. Thomas' treatise *On the Soul* is primarily a treatise on man. The soul is the ultimate principle whereby man lives and understands, but it is man himself that is the ultimate subject of operation. Man is not his soul nor is he an accidental unity of an intellective soul and a body, but is one being substantially; for, while the soul is the mover of the body, it is primarily the formal cause of that body, giving it its proper existence. This

---

[1] See P. Mandonnet, O.P., *Des écrits authentiques de S. Thomas d'Aquin*, 2nd ed. (Fribourg, Switzerland, 1910), p. 130; also M. Grabmann, *St. Thomas Aquinas* (London, 1928).

[2] According to Grabmann, 1266; according to P. Glorieux, 1269–70. See "Les questions disputées de S. Thomas et leur suite chronologique," *Recherches de théologie ancienne et médiévale*, 1932.

is the nature of man which St. Thomas has in mind, and in light of it all the arguments in the present work are conducted.

All footnotes are by the translator. The problem discussed in each article of the *De anima* is treated in various other works of St. Thomas. References to works containing discussions paralleling those in the different articles of the present work are given in the first footnote of each article. The purpose of the other footnotes is to give additional information on different points of doctrine mentioned or discussed in the text; to identify different persons to whom reference is made; to acquaint the reader with certain of the physical and astronomical views of the Middle Ages to which St. Thomas refers in the *De anima;* and to supply in full the references to the works of the various authors cited in the text. In the references to Aristotle, Roman numerals are used to designate the book, Arabic numerals to designate the chapter. Numbers in parentheses are those of the Bekker edition of Aristotle, Berlin, 1831.

I wish to acknowledge express gratitude to Dr. James F. Anderson, Notre Dame University, for his valuable assistance. I owe thanks also to Rev. Bruno Switalski, S.T.D., for his helpful suggestions, and to two of my students, Miss Mary Hagman and Miss Irene Pass.

J. P. R.

# CONTENTS

vii

# CONTENTS

## ARTICLE I

## WHETHER THE SOUL CAN BE A FORM AND A PARTICULAR THING

In the first article we examine this question: Whether the human soul can be a form and a particular thing.[1]

Objections. 1. It seems that the human soul cannot be a form and a particular thing.[2] For if the human soul is a particular thing, it is a subsisting thing having a complete act of existing (*esse*) in virtue of its own nature. Now whatever accrues to a thing over and above its complete [substantial] existence, is an accident of that thing, as whiteness and clothing are accidents of man. Therefore, when the body is united to the soul, it is united to it accidentally. Consequently, if the soul is a particular thing, it is not the substantial form of the body.

2. Further, if the soul is a particular thing, it must be an individuated thing, for a universal is not a particular thing.[3] Now the soul is individuated either by something other than itself, or by itself. If the soul is individuated by something other than itself, and is the form of the body, it must be individuated by the body (for forms are individuated by their proper mat-

---

[1] See also *Summa theol.*, Ia, q.75, a.2; q.76, a.1; *Contra Gentes*, Bk. II, chaps. 56, 57, 59, 68, 69, and 70; *De potentia*, q.3, a.9 and 11; *De spir. creat.*, a.2; *Comm. in De anima*, Bk. II, lect. 4; Bk. III, lect. 7; *op.* XVI, *De unit. intell.*

[2] The term *hoc aliquid* (a particular thing, or this particular thing) is the literal translation of the Greek term τόδε τι. Aristotle uses this expression to designate *a* substance. St. Thomas discusses the various uses of the expression *hoc aliquid* in the answer to this article. See also *Summa theol.*, Ia, q.75, a.2, ad 1 um.

[3] Individual things alone exist in the natural order; a universal as such has existence only in the intellect. See *Summa theol.*, Ia, q.85, a.3, ad 1um, for St. Thomas' treatment of the universal.

ter).[4] And thus it follows that when the body is separated from the soul, the latter loses its individuation. In that case the soul could not subsist of itself, nor be a particular thing. On the other hand, if the soul is individuated by itself, it is either a form in its entirety (*simplex*) or is something composed of matter and form. If it is a form in its entirety, it follows that one individuated soul could differ from another only according to form. But difference in form causes difference in species. Hence it would follow that the souls of different men are specifically diverse; and if the soul is the form of the body, men differ specifically among themselves, because each and every thing derives its species from its proper form. On the other hand, if the soul is composed of matter and form, it would be impossible for the soul as a whole to be the form of the body, for the matter of a thing never has the nature of a form. It follows, then, that the soul cannot be at once both a particular thing and a form.

3. Further, if the soul is a particular thing, it follows that it is an individual. Now every individual belongs to a species and a genus. Consequently the soul will have a proper species and a proper genus. But a thing possessing its own species cannot have anything else superadded to it in order to give it its species, because, as the Philosopher [5] points out,[6] the forms or species of things are like numbers whose species change if a unit is added or subtracted. Matter and form, however, are united in order to constitute a species. Therefore, if the soul is a particular thing, it is not united to the body as a form to matter.

4. Further, since God made things because of His goodness, which is manifested in the different grades of things, He insti-

---

[4] In the *De ente et essentia*, chap. 2, St. Thomas explains that matter is the principle of individuation. This matter is not "prime matter," but "signate matter" (*materia signata*), i.e., what has extension, and an order of parts, and is considered under its "determinate dimensions." See also *Summa theol.*, Ia, q. 29, a. 1.

[5] The Philosopher is Aristotle.

[6] *Metaph.*, VIII, 3 (1043b 36).

tuted as many grades of beings as nature could admit. Hence, if the human soul can subsist in itself (which must be maintained if it is a particular thing), it would then constitute a distinct grade of being. But forms without matter do not themselves constitute a distinct grade of being. Thus, if the soul is a particular thing, it will not be the form of any matter.

5. Further, if the soul is a particular thing, subsisting in itself, it must be incorruptible, for neither has it a contrary, nor is it composed of contraries.[7] But if the soul is incorruptible, it cannot be proportioned to a corruptible body such as the human body is. Now every form is proportioned to its matter. So if the soul is a particular thing, it will not be the form of the human body.

6. Further, the only subsisting being that is Pure Act, is God. Therefore, if the soul is a particular self-subsisting thing, it will be composed of act and potentiality, and thus will not be a form, because no potentiality is an act. Consequently, if the soul is a particular thing, it will not be a form.

7. Further, if the soul is a particular thing capable of subsisting in itself, it would need to be united to a body only for a good accruing to the soul, either for an essential good or an accidental one. Not for an essential good, however, because it can subsist without the body. Nor even for an accidental good; for the knowledge of truth which the human soul can acquire through the senses (themselves incapable of existing without bodily organs) is evidently a pre-eminent good of this sort; but some hold that the souls of still-born infants have a perfect knowledge of things, and these certainly never acquired that knowledge through their senses. Consequently, if the soul is a particular thing, there is no reason why it should be united as a form to the body.

8. Further, a form and a particular thing are distinguished

[7] A thing can be corrupted if it has a contrary, or is composed of contrary things. "Corruption is found only where there is contrariety, because generation and corruption are from contraries into contraries" (*Summa theol.*, Ia. q.75, a.6).

from each other as opposites; for the Philosopher says in the *De anima*,[8] that substance has a threefold division: the first is form, the second, matter, and the third, this particular thing. But opposites are not predicated of one and the same thing. Therefore the human soul cannot be a form and a particular thing.

9. Further, it belongs to the very essence of a particular thing to subsist of itself. But it is proper to a form to exist in something else. These seem to be contradictory. Consequently, if the soul is a particular thing, it is apparently not a form.

10. But it might be said that when the body corrupts, the soul still remains a particular self-subsisting thing, but then loses the nature of a form. On the other hand, whatever can exist apart from a thing and retain the nature of a substance, exists in that thing accidentally. Therefore, if the soul continues to exist after the body corrupts, the soul ceases to have the character of a form; and thus the nature of a form belongs to it only accidentally. But it is only as a form that the soul is united to the body in order to constitute a man. Hence the soul is united to the body accidentally, and thus man will be a being *per accidens*. This is incongruous.

11. Further, if the human soul is a particular self-subsisting thing, it must have an operation of its own, because a thing that exists of itself has its own proper operation. But the human soul does not have its own proper operation, because the act of intellection itself, which seems to be proper above all to the soul, is not an activity of the soul, but that of a man through his soul, as is stated in the *De anima*.[9] Therefore the human soul is not a particular thing.

12. Further, if the human soul is the form of the body, it must depend in some way on the body, for form and matter depend on each other. But whatever depends on something

[8] III, 2 (414a 15).
[9] I, 4 (408a 14).

else [in this way] is not a particular thing. Therefore, if the soul is the form of the body, it will not be a particular thing.

13. Further, if the soul is the form of the body, there must be one act of existing (*esse*) common to the soul and the body; because from the union of matter and form there results a thing having one act of existing. But there cannot be one act of existing common to the soul and the body, since they are generically diverse; for the soul belongs to the genus of incorporeal substance, and the body to that of corporeal substance. Hence the soul cannot be the form of the body.

14. Further, the body's act of existing is a corruptible one resulting from quantitative parts. The soul's act of existing, on the other hand, is incorruptible and simple. Therefore there is not one act of existing possessed in common by the body and the soul.

15. But it might be said that the human body itself has the act of existing of a body through the soul. On the contrary, the Philosopher says [10] that the soul is the act of a physical organic body. Therefore that entity which is related to the soul as matter to act, is now a physical organic body; and this body can exist only through a form whereby it is placed in the genus of body. Consequently the human body possesses its own act of existing distinct from that of the soul.

16. Further, the essential principles of matter and form are ordered to the act of existing (*esse*). But whatever can be brought about in nature by one principle, does not require two. Therefore, if the soul has in itself its own act of existing because it is a particular thing, then the body by nature is united to the soul only as a matter to a form.

17. Further, the act of existing is related to the substance of the soul as its act. Hence the act of existing must be supreme in the soul. But an inferior being is not related to a superior one with respect to that which is supreme in the superior, but

[10] *Ibid.*, II, 1 (412b 5).

rather with respect to that which is lowest in it. For Dionysius says [11] that divine wisdom joins that which is highest (*fines*) in primary things [i.e., those having less perfection] to that which is lowest (*principiis*) in secondary ones [i.e., those having greater perfection]. Therefore the body, which is inferior to the soul, does not attain to that act of existing which is supreme in the soul.

18. Further, things having one and the same act of existing, have one and the same operation. Therefore, if the act of existing of the human soul, when joined to the body, belongs also to the body, the act of understanding, which is the operation of the soul, will belong both to the soul and the body. This is impossible, as is proved in the *De anima*.[12] Consequently there is not one act of existing for both the human soul and the body. Hence it follows that the soul is not the form of the body and a particular thing.

On the contrary, a thing receives its species through its proper form. But man is man because he is rational. Hence the rational soul is the proper form of man. Moreover the soul is a particular self-subsisting thing because it operates of itself; for its act of understanding is not performed through a bodily organ, as is proved in the *De anima*.[13] Consequently the human soul is a particular thing and a form.

Further, the highest perfection of the human soul consists in knowledge of truth which is acquired through the intellect. Moreover the soul must be united to the body in order to be perfected in knowledge of truth, because it understands through phantasms which are non-existent without the body.

---

[11] Dionysius the Pseudo-Areopagite is an unknown Christian writer of the fifth century. For a long time he was considered to be Dionysius or Denis, a convert of St. Paul. His writings had considerable influence on the Middle Ages. The text which St. Thomas refers to is found in the *De divinis nominibus,* VII, 2 (*PG*, III, 872).

[12] III, 4 (429a 18).

[13] III, 4 (429a 24).

Consequently the soul must be united as a form to the body and must be a particular thing as well.

I answer: "A particular thing," properly speaking, designates an individual in the genus of substance. For the Philosopher says, in the *Categories*,[14] that first substances undoubtedly signify particular things; second substances, indeed, although they seem to signify particular things, rather signify the specific essence (*quale quid*). Furthermore, an individual in the genus of substance is capable not only of subsisting of itself, but is also a complete entity belonging to a definite species and genus of substance. Wherefore the Philosopher, in the *Categories*,[15] also calls a hand and a foot, and things of this sort, parts of substances rather than first or second substances. For although they do not exist in another as a subject (which is characteristic of a substance), they still do not possess completely the nature of a species. Hence they belong to a species or to a genus only by reduction.

Now some men have denied that the human soul possesses these two real characteristics belonging to a particular thing by its very nature,[16] because they said that the soul is a harmony,[17] as Empedocles [18] did, or a combination [of the elements], as Galen [19] did, or something of this kind. For then the soul will neither be able to subsist of itself, nor will it be a com-

---

14 V (2a 10), The *Categories* is the first work in Aristotle's collected writings on logic.

15 *Ibid.*, V (3a 28).

16 In order to be a particular thing, i.e., an individual substance (*hoc aliquid*), a thing must subsist of itself and be a complete thing belonging to some species or genus of substance.

17 That is, a skillful blending of the elements.

18 Empedocles of Agrigentum, Sicily, an early philosopher of the fifth century B.C. According to Empedocles, all things are composed of different proportions of the four elements: earth, water, air, and fire. For St. Thomas' criticism of the soul as a "harmony," see *Contra Gentes*, II, 64.

19 Galen (A.D. 131–201), a physician of considerable importance in the early development of medicine. For criticism of this position, see St. Thomas, *Contra Gentes*, II, 63.

plete thing belonging to a species or genus of substance, but
will be a form similar only to other material forms.

But this position is untenable as regards the vegetal soul,
whose operations necessarily require some principle surpassing the active and passive qualities [of the elements] [20] which
play only an instrumental role in nutrition and growth, as is
proved in the *De anima*.[21] Moreover, a combination and a
harmony do not transcend the elemental qualities. This position is likewise untenable as regards the sentient soul, whose
operations consist in receiving species separated from matter,
as is shown in the *De anima*.[22] For inasmuch as active and
passive qualities are dispositions of matter, they do not transcend matter. Again, this position is even less tenable as regards
the rational soul, whose operation consists in understanding,
and in abstracting species not only from matter, but from all
individuating conditions, this being required for the understanding of universals. However, in the case of the rational
soul something of special importance must still be considered,
because not only does it receive intelligible species without
matter and material conditions, but it is also quite impossible
for it, in performing its proper operation, to have anything
in common with a bodily organ, as though something corporeal
might be an organ of understanding, just as the eye is the organ
of sight, as is proved in the *De anima*.[23] Thus the intellective
soul, inasmuch as it performs its proper operation without
communicating in any way with the body, must act of itself.
And because a thing acts so far as it is actual, the intellective
soul must have a complete act of existing in itself, depending
in no way on the body. For forms whose act of existing depends

---

[20] According to the classical physics, all corporeal things were composed of
different proportions of the four elements or simple bodies: earth, water, air,
and fire. These four elements possessed certain fundamental qualities which
were divided into two groups: the active qualities (hot and cold) and the passive qualities (moist and dry). See Aristotle, *De gen. et corr.*, II, 3 (330a 30 ff.).

[21] II, 4 (415b 28 ff.).

[22] II, 12 (424a 16).

[23] III, 4 (429a 24).

on matter or on a subject do not operate of themselves. Heat, for instance, does not act, but something hot.

For this reason the later Greek philosophers [24] came to the conclusion that the intellective part of the soul is a self-subsisting thing. For the Philosopher says, in the *De anima*,[25] that the intellect is a substance, and is not corrupted. The teaching of Plato,[26] who maintains that the soul is incorruptible and subsists of itself in view of the fact that it moves itself, amounts to the same thing. For he took "motion" in a broad sense to signify every operation; hence he understands that the soul moves itself because it moves itself by itself.

But elsewhere [27] Plato maintained that the human soul not only subsisted of itself, but also had the complete nature of a species. For he held that the complete nature of the [human] species is found in the soul, saying that a man is not a composite of soul and body, but a soul joined to a body in such a way that it is related to the body as a pilot is to a ship, or as one clothed to his clothing. However, this position is untenable, because it is obvious that the soul is the reality which gives life to the body. Moreover, vital activity (*vivere*) is the act of existing (*esse*) of living things. Consequently the soul is that which gives the human body its act of existing. Now a form is of this nature. Therefore the human soul is the form of the body. But if the soul were in the body as a pilot is in a ship, it would give neither the body nor its parts their specific nature. The contrary of this is seen to be true, because, when the soul leaves the body, the body's individual parts retain their original names only in an equivocal sense. For the eye of a dead man, like the eye of a portrait or that of a statue, is called an eye equivocally; and similarly for the other parts of the body. Furthermore, if the soul were in the body as a pilot in a ship, it would follow that the union of soul and body would be an

[24] Those who came after Empedocles, i.e., Socrates, Plato, and Aristotle.
[25] III, 5 (430a 24).
[26] *Phaedrus*, XXIV.
[27] *Alcibiades*, XXV and XXVI.

accidental one. Then death, which brings about their separation, would not be a substantial corruption; which is clearly false. So it follows that the soul is a particular thing and that it can subsist of itself, not as a thing having a complete species of its own, but as completing the human species by being the form of the body. Hence it likewise follows that it is both a form and a particular thing.

Indeed, this can be shown from the order of natural forms. For we find among the forms of lower bodies that the higher a form is, the more it resembles and approaches higher principles. This can be seen from the proper operation of forms. For the forms of the elements, being lowest [in the order of forms] and nearest to matter, possess no operation surpassing their active and passive qualities, such as rarefaction and condensation, and the like, which appear to be material dispositions. Over and above these forms are those of the mixed bodies,[28] and these forms have (in addition to the above mentioned operations) a certain activity, consequent upon their species, which they receive from the celestial bodies. The magnet, for instance, attracts iron not because of its heat or its cold or anything of this sort, but because it shares in the powers of the heavens. Again, surpassing these forms are the souls of plants, which resemble not only the forms of earthly bodies but also the movers of the celestial bodies [29] inasmuch as they are principles of a certain motion, themselves being moved. Still higher are brute beasts' forms, which now resemble a substance moving a celestial body not only because of the operation whereby they move bodies, but also because they are capable of knowledge, although their knowledge is concerned merely with material things and belongs to the material order (for which reason they require bodily organs). Again, over and

[28] The "mixed bodies" or "minerals" are the inanimate bodies composed of a mixture and union of the four elements. The elements themselves are "simple bodies."

[29] The movers of the celestial bodies are certain of the pure intelligences or separate substances.

above these forms, and in the highest place, are human souls, which certainly resemble superior substances [30] with respect to the kind of knowledge they possess, because they are capable of knowing immaterial things by their act of intellection. However, human souls differ from superior substances inasmuch as the human soul's intellective power, by its very nature, must acquire its immaterial knowledge from the knowledge of material things attained through the senses.

Consequently the human soul's mode of existing can be known from its operation.[31] For, inasmuch as the human soul has an operation transcending the material order, its act of existing transcends the body and does not depend on the body. Indeed, inasmuch as the soul is naturally capable of acquiring immaterial knowledge from material things, evidently its species can be complete only when it is united to a body. For a thing's species is complete only if it has the things necessary for the proper operation of its species. Consequently, if the human soul, inasmuch as it is united as a form to the body, has an act of existing which transcends the body and does not depend on it, obviously the soul itself is established on the boundary line dividing corporeal from separate substances.

Answers to objections. 1. Although the soul has a complete act of existing of its own, it does not follow that the body is united to it accidentally: first, because the same act of existing that belongs to the soul is conferred on the body by the soul so that there is one act of existing for the whole composite; secondly, because, while the soul can subsist of itself, it does not have a complete species, for the soul needs the body in order to complete its species.

2. The act of existing (*esse*) and individuation (*individuatio*) of a thing are always found together. For universals do not exist in reality inasmuch as they are universals, but only

30 That is, the pure intelligences or angels.

31 A thing's operation is proportionate to its mode of existing. Hence a thing's mode of existing may be known from its operations.

inasmuch as they are individuated. Therefore, although the soul receives its act of existing from God as from an active principle, and exists in the body as in matter, nevertheless the soul's act of existing does not cease when the body corrupts, nor does the soul's individuation cease when the body corrupts, even though it has a relationship to the body.

3. The human soul is not a particular thing as though it were a substance having a complete species in itself, but inasmuch as it is part of a thing having a complete species, as is clear from what has been said. Therefore the conclusion in the objection is false.

4. Although the human soul subsists of itself, it does not have a complete species in virtue of its very nature. Consequently souls existing apart from bodies cannot constitute a distinct grade of being.

5. The human body is the matter proportioned to the human soul, for the body is related to the soul as potentiality is to act. However, as regards its capacity for existing the soul need not be on a par with the body, because the human soul is not a form totally embraced by matter. This is evident from the fact that one of the soul's operations transcends matter. However, another explanation can be given in accordance with the position of faith, namely, that in the beginning the human body was in some way created incorruptible and incurred the necessity of dying through sin, from which necessity it will be freed once again at the resurrection. Hence it is accidental that the body does not share in the incorruptibility of the soul.

6. Since the human soul is a subsisting being, it is composed of potentiality and act. For the substance itself of the soul is not its own act of existing [32] but is related to its act of existing as potentiality is to act. However, it does not follow that the

---

[32] The soul's essence and its act of existing (*esse*) are really distinct from each other. The real distinction between essence and act of existing in created things is one of the central doctrines of St. Thomas' metaphysics.

soul cannot be the form of the body, because, even in the case of other forms, whatever is like form and act in relation to one thing is like potentiality in relation to something else; just as transparency [33] is formally present to the atmosphere, which is in potency in relation to light.

7. The soul is united to the body both for a good which is a substantial perfection, namely, the completion of the human species; and for a good which is an accidental perfection, namely, the perfecting of the soul in intellectual knowledge which it acquires from the senses; for this mode of understanding is natural to man. Nor is this position rendered untenable if the separated souls of infants and those of other men employ a different mode of understanding, for these souls are capable of such intellection rather by reason of being separated from the body than by reason of their human species.

8. It is not of the very nature of a particular thing to be composed of matter and form, but only to be capable of subsisting in itself. Consequently, although a composite [of matter and form] is a particular thing, this does not prevent other beings [i.e., those not composed of matter and form] from being particular things.

9. For a thing to exist in another as an accident in a subject, prevents that thing from having the nature of a particular thing. However, for a thing to exist in another as part of it (and the soul exists in man in this way) does not altogether prevent a thing having such an existence from being called a particular thing.

10. When the body is corrupted the soul does not lose the nature which belongs to it as a form, despite the fact that it does not actually perfect matter as a form.

11. Intellection is the operation proper to the soul, if the soul is considered to be the principle from which the operation flows, for this operation is not exercised by the soul through some bodily organ as sight is exercised through the eye. Never-

[33] See Art. IV, note 17.

theless the body shares in this operation on the side of the object, for phantasms,[34] which are the objects of the intellect, cannot exist without bodily organs.

12. Although the soul has some dependence on the body inasmuch as the soul's species is not complete without the body, the soul does not depend on the body in such a way that it cannot exist without the body.

13. If the soul is the form of the body, the soul and the body must have one common act of existing which is the act of existing of the composite. Nor is this prevented by the fact that the soul and the body belong to two different genera, for the soul and the body belong to the same species or genus only by reduction, just as the parts of a whole are reduced to the species or genus of the whole.

14. The thing that is properly corrupted is neither the form nor the matter nor the act of existing itself but the composite. Moreover, the body's act of existing is said to be corruptible inasmuch as the body by corrupting is deprived of the act of existing which it possessed in common with the soul; which act of existing remains in the subsisting soul. The same thing is to be said also for the parts composing the body, because the body is constituted of its parts in such a way that it can receive its act of existing from the soul.

15. Sometimes in the definitions of forms a subject is considered independently of its form (*informe*), as when it is said that motion is the act of a being in potentiality. Sometimes, however, the subject is regarded as informed (*formatum*) *as* when it is said that motion is the act of a mobile thing, just as light is the act of that which is transparent. Now it is in this way that the soul is said to be the act of a physical organic body, because the soul causes it to be a physical organic body just as light makes something to be lucid.

---

[34] In *Summa theol.*, Ia, q.84, a.6, ad 2um, St. Thomas defines a phantasm as "a movement produced in accordance with sensation." Hence a phantasm is a sensible likeness of a thing.

16. The essential principles of a species are not related merely to an act of existing, but to the act of existing of this [particular] species. Consequently, although the soul can exist of itself, it cannot be complete in its species without the body.

17. While the act of existing is the most formal of all principles, it is also the most communicable, although it is not shared in the same measure both by inferior beings and by superior ones. Hence the body shares in the soul's act of existing, but not as perfectly as the soul does.

18. Although the soul's act of existing belongs in a certain measure to the body, the body does not succeed in sharing in the souls's act of existing to the full extent of its perfection and actuality; and therefore the soul has an operation in which the body does not share.

# ARTICLE II

## WHETHER THE HUMAN SOUL, SO FAR AS ITS ACT OF EXISTING IS CONCERNED, IS SEPARATED FROM THE BODY

In the second article we examine this question: Whether the human soul, so far as its act of existing is concerned, is separated from the body.[1]

Objections. 1. It seems that it is. For the Philosopher says in the *De anima*,[2] that no sentient power exists without a body. But the intellect is separate and the intellect is the human soul. Therefore the human soul, so far as its act of existing is concerned, is separated from the body.

2. Further, the soul is the act of a physical organic body inasmuch as the body is its organ. Hence, if the intellect, with respect to its very act of existing, is united as a form to the body, the body must be its organ. This is impossible, as the Philosopher proves in the *De anima*.[3]

3. Further, a form is united to matter more intimately than a power is to an organ. But the intellect cannot be united to the body as a power is to an organ, because the intellect is simple.[4] Consequently it is even less capable of being united to the body as a form to matter.

[1] See also *Summa theol.*, Ia, q.75, a.4; *Contra Gentes*, II, 57; *Sent.*, Bk. III, dist., 5, q.3, a.2; dist., 22, q.1, a.1; *op.* XXX *De ente et essentia*, chap. 2; *op.* XVI, *De unit. intell.; Comm. in Metaph.*, Bk. VII, lect. 9.

[2] III, 4 (429b 4).

[3] *Ibid.*

[4] That is, the intellect, or intellective principle, is simple because it has neither essential parts nor quantitative parts. See *Summa theol.*, Ia, q.75, a.2 and 5.

16

4. But it might be said that the intellect, that is, the intellective power, does not have an organ, but that the essence itself of the intellective soul is united as a form to the body. On the other hand, no effect is simpler than its cause. Now a power of the soul is an effect of its essence, because all powers of the soul flow from its essence (*esse*). Consequently no power of the soul is simpler than its essence. If, then, the intellect cannot be the act of the body, as is proved in the *De anima*,[5] neither can the intellective soul be united as a form to the body.

5. Further, every form united to matter is individuated by matter.[6] Therefore, if the intellective soul is united to the body as the form of the latter, the soul must be an individuated [form]. Then the forms received in the soul are individuated forms.[7] Consequently the intellective soul will be incapable of knowing universals; which is clearly false.

6. Further, a universal form does not acquire its universality from the thing existing outside the soul, because all forms existing in such things are individuated. Thus, if the forms in the intellect are universal, they must acquire this universality from the intellective soul. Consequently the intellective soul is not an individuated form, and therefore is not united to the body so far as its act of existing is concerned.

7. However, it might be said that inasmuch as intelligible forms inhere in the soul they are individuated; but as the likenesses of things they are universals representing things according to their common nature [8] and not according to their individuating principles. On the contrary, since a form is a principle of operation, an operation proceeds from a form in accordance with the manner in which that form inheres in a subject. For instance, the hotter something is, the more it is

---

[5] III, 4 (429a 24; 429b 4).

[6] Signate matter is the principle of individuation. See Art. I, note 4.

[7] In the act of knowing, the forms of individual things exist in the mind intentionally.

[8] That is, the nature common to the entire species as distinct from the individual nature of this or that particular thing.

capable of heating. Therefore, if the species of things in the
intellective soul are individuated because they inhere in the
soul, then the knowledge which results will be knowledge only
of the individual [as such] and will not be universal.

8. Further, the Philosopher says in the *De anima*,[9] that just
as the triangle is contained in the quadrilateral and the quadrilateral in the pentagon, so also is the nutritive part of the
soul contained in the sentient part and the sentient in turn
contained in the intellective.[10] However, the triangle is not
contained actually in the quadrilateral, but only potentially;
nor is the quadrilateral contained actually in the pentagon.[11]
Therefore, neither is the nutritive nor sentient part of the soul
contained actually in the intellective. Consequently, since the
intellective part of the soul is united to the body only through
the intermediary of the nutritive and sentient parts, because
the sentient and nutritive parts of the soul are not actually contained in the intellective part, the intellective part of the soul
will not be united to the body.

9. Further, the Philosopher says in the *De generatione
animalium*,[12] that a man is not at once both an animal and a
man, but first is an animal and then a man. Consequently the
principle whereby he is an animal and that whereby he is a
man are not one and the same. But he is an animal because of
his sentient part and a man because of his intellective part.
Therefore the sentient and intellective parts are not united
in one and the same substance of the soul. Hence the conclusion is the same as the foregoing.

10. Further, a form belongs to the same genus as the matter
to which it is united. But the intellect does not belong to the

[9] II, 3 (414b 27).
[10] A higher order of life contains virtually the perfections of a lower order
of life.
[11] The triangle is present potentially in the quadrilateral, because the latter
can be divided into triangles. The quadrilateral is present potentially in the
pentagon for a similar reason.
[12] II, 3 (736b 2).

genus of corporeal things. Therefore the intellect is not a form united to the body as to matter.

11. Further, one being does not result from the union of two actually existing substances. But both the body and the intellect [i.e., the intellective soul] are two actually existing substances. Hence the intellect cannot be united to the body so that one being results from their union.

12. Further, every form united to matter is given actual existence by moving and changing matter. But the intellective soul is not given actual existence [by being educed] from the potentiality of matter, but receives its act of existing from an extrinsic agent, as the Philosopher says in the *De generatione animalium*.[13] Therefore the soul is not a form united to matter.

13. Further, a thing operates in accordance with its nature.[14] But the intellective soul has an operation of its own without the body, namely, the act of intellection. Therefore, so far as its act of existing is concerned, the intellective soul is not united to the body.

14. Further, even the slightest impropriety is impossible for God.[15] But it is improper for an innocent soul to be united to a body which is like a prison.[16] Therefore it is impossible for God to unite an intellective soul to a body.

15. Further, a wise artifex does not place an obstacle in the way of his work. But the body is the greatest obstacle to the intellective soul in acquiring knowledge of truth, in which its perfection consists, according to that text in the Book of Wisdom: "The body which is corrupted, weighs down upon the soul" (Wisd. 9:15). Therefore God did not unite the intellective soul to the body.

16. Further, things which are united one to another have an

---

[13] *Ibid.* (736b 27 ff.).

[14] A thing's mode of existing is made known by its activities.

[15] See Art. XXI, note 7.

[16] According to Plato a man is his soul, and in this earthly life the soul is enclosed in the body as in a prison.

affinity for each other. But the intellective soul and the body are opposed to each other, because "The flesh desires the opposite of the spirit, and the spirit, the opposite of the flesh" (Gal. 5:17). Consequently the intellective soul is not united to the body.

17. Further, the intellect is in potency to all intelligible forms having none actually, just as prime matter is in potency to all sensible forms having none actually. But it is for this reason that there is one prime matter for all things. Therefore there is also one intellect for all men. Hence it is not united to a body which would individuate it.

18. Further, the Philosopher proves in the *De anima*,[17] that, if the possible intellect had a bodily organ, it would have a certain determinate sensible nature, and thus could not receive and know all sensible forms.[18] But a form is united to matter more intimately than a power is to an organ. Therefore, if the intellect is united as a form to the body, it will have a certain determinate sensible nature, and thus will be incapable of perceiving and knowing all sensible forms. This is impossible.

19. Further, every form united to matter is received in matter. But whatever is received in a thing exists therein in accordance with the mode of the recipient. Therefore every form united to matter exists in matter according to the mode of matter. But the mode of sensible and corporeal matter is not the one that a thing receives through an intelligible mode. Consequently, since the intellect has an intelligible mode of existing, it is not a form united to corporeal matter.

20. Further, if the soul is united to corporeal matter, it must be received in it. But whatever is received in a thing that has received its act of existing from matter, is received in matter. Therefore, if the soul is united to matter, then whatever

17 III, 4 (429a 18).
18 That is, the intellect would be like those powers which operate through organs and thus would be limited in its cognition.

is received in the soul is received in matter. But the forms of the intellect cannot be received in prime matter. On the contrary, they are made intelligible by abstraction from matter. Consequently, a soul which is united to corporeal matter is not capable of receiving intelligible forms, and thus the intellect, which is capable of receiving intelligible forms, will not be united to corporeal matter.

On the contrary, the Philosopher says in the *De anima*,[19] that it is unnecessary to ask whether the soul and the body are one, just as it is unnecessary to ask whether the wax and its impression are one. But with respect to its act of existing, the impression cannot be separated in any way from the wax. Consequently, with respect to its act of existing, the soul is not separated from the body. But the intellect is a part of the soul, as the Philosopher says in the *De anima*.[20] Therefore the intellect, so far as its act of existing is concerned, is not separated from the body.

Further, so far as its act of existing is concerned, no form is separated from matter. But the intellective soul is the form of the body. Therefore, with respect to its act of existing, the soul is not separated from matter.

I answer: In order to settle this issue we must take into consideration that, whenever a thing is found to be sometimes in potency and sometimes in act, there must be some principle by which it is in potency; just as a man is sometimes actually sensing and sometimes only potentially. Now on account of this it is necessary to maintain that in man there exists a sentient principle which is in potency to sensible things; for if he were always actually sensing, the forms of sensible things would always actually exist in his sentient principle. Similarly, since a man is found sometimes to be actually understanding

[19] II, 1 (412b 6).
[20] III, 4 (429a 15).

and sometimes only potentially, it is necessary to maintain that in man there exists an intellective power which is in potency to intelligibles; and the Philosopher, in the *De anima*,[21] calls this principle the possible intellect. Consequently this possible intellect must be in potency to all things intelligible to man; it must be capable of receiving them and therefore must be devoid of them, because anything capable of receiving other things is in potency to them inasmuch as it lacks them; just as the pupil of the eye, which is capable of receiving all colors, lacks every color. Now man is determined by nature to understand the forms of all sensible things. Therefore, by its very nature the possible intellect must be devoid of all sensible forms and natures, and so also must have no bodily organ. For if it had a bodily organ, it would be limited to some sensible nature, just as the power of vision is limited to the nature of the eye. By means of this proof we exclude the position of the ancient philosophers,[22] who held that the intellect did not differ from the sentient powers, as well as the position of those who maintained that the principle by which a man understands is a certain form or power which is united to the body as other material forms or powers are.

But certain other men avoiding this position, fall into the opposite error.[23] For they think that the possible intellect is devoid of every sensible nature and that it is not present in the body, because it is a certain substance which exists in separation from the body and is in potency to all intelligible forms. But this position cannot be maintained, because we acquire our knowledge of the possible intellect only so far as a man understands by it.[24] Indeed, this is the way Aristotle obtains his knowledge of it, as is evident from what he says in the *De*

---

[21] III, 5 (430a 15).

[22] That is, the Ionian philosophers.

[23] The first error is to consider man a purely sensory being. The opposite error is to regard man as an intelligence.

[24] Faculties are known by their operations. Hence we acquire a knowledge of the possible intellect by considering its act of intellection.

*anima,*[25] when he begins to discuss the possible intellect: "Concerning that part of the soul by which the soul knows and perceives . . . it must be considered . . ."; and in another place he says: "I speak of the possible intellect by which the soul understands." [26] But if the possible intellect were a separate substance, it would be impossible for a man to understand by means of it; because, if a substance performs an operation, that operation cannot belong to any other substance than the one performing it. For although one of two substances can be the cause of the other's operation, as the principal agent is the cause of the activity of the instrument, nevertheless the action of the principal agent is not numerically the same as that of the instrument. For the action of the principal agent consists in moving the instrument, whereas that of the instrument consists in being moved by the principal agent and in moving something else. Consequently, if the possible intellect is a substance existing apart from this or that particular man, it is impossible for the possible intellect's act of intellection to be the act of any particular man. From this it follows that no man understands anything, because the act of intellection is not attributed to any principle in man except the possible intellect. Hence the same manner of arguing is opposed to this position and to those who deny its principles, as is evident from Aristotle's arguments against them in the *Metaphysics.*[27]

Now Averroes,[28] who is a follower of this position, intending to avoid its incongruity maintained that, although the possible intellect existed apart from the body, it must be united to man through the intermediary of phantasms. For phantasms, as the

[25] III, 4 (429a 10).
[26] *Ibid.* (429a 22).
[27] IV, 3 (1005b 25 ff.).
[28] Averroes (1126–98) was the most important Arabian philosopher of the Spanish school and the greatest commentator of Aristotle among the Arabs. Averroes maintained that there was one intellect for all men; that this intellect was a pure intelligence existing apart from man; and that a man understands by means of it when it is joined to the phantasms in the human mind. Averroes' position is discussed in Art. VI of the *De anima* and in the work *De unitate intellectus contra Averroistas.*

Philosopher says in the *De anima*,[29] are related to the possible intellect as sensible things are to sense, and colors to sight. Thus an intelligible species has two subjects: one in which it exists with an intelligible mode of existing, and this is the possible intellect: another in which it exists with a real mode of existing, and this subject is the phantasms. Therefore [according to Averroes] there is a certain union of the possible intellect with the phantasms inasmuch as an intelligible species exists in a certain manner in each of these subjects; and a man understands through the [supposedly separate] possible intellect as a result of this union with the phantasms.

However, this union is still not sufficient [to account for man's knowledge], for a thing is capable of knowing, not because intelligible species are present to it, but because it possesses a cognitive power. Now evidently, from what has been said, intelligible species alone will be present to man, whereas the power of understanding, that is, the possible intellect, exists in complete separation from him. Therefore it does not follow from the aforesaid union that a man will have what is necessary for understanding, but only that a species or something in that intellect will be understood. This clearly appears to be the case from the simile introduced above. For if phantasms are related to the intellect as colors are to sight, the union of the [supposedly separate] possible intellect with us through our phantasms, will be the same as that of sight with a wall through its colors. Now it does not follow that a wall sees because it has colors, but only that it is seen. Nor, similarly, does it follow that a man will understand because phantasms are present within him, but only that he will be understood.

Furthermore, a phantasm is not the subject of an intelligible species inasmuch as the latter is actually understood. On the contrary, an intelligible species is made to be actually understood by abstraction from phantasms. Moreover, the possible intellect is the subject of an intelligible species only inasmuch

29 III, 5 (430a 14).

as an intelligible species is now actually understood and abstracted from phantasms. Therefore the species existing in the possible intellect, and that existing in the phantasms, through which the [supposedly separate] possible intellect is united to us, are not one and the same.

Furthermore, if anyone understands through intelligible species only when they are actually understood, it follows, according to the aforesaid position, that we are incapable of understanding anything in any way, for then intelligible species would be present to us only inasmuch as they exist in phantasms, and here they are only potentially understood. Consequently it is evident on the side of our human nature that the above-mentioned position is impossible. This is also apparent from the nature of separate substances. Since these are most perfect, it is impossible for them in their own operations to stand in need of the operations of material things; nor need they be in potency to any things of this kind, for not even the celestial bodies, which are below the separate substances, require things of this sort. Hence, since the possible intellect is in potency to the species of sensible things, and since its operation may not be completed without phantasms, which depend on our operations, it is impossible and inconceivable for the possible intellect to be one of the separate substances.

Consequently, we must say that the possible intellect is a certain faculty or power of the human soul. For although the human soul is a form united to the body, it is not embraced completely by the body as though immersed in it as other material forms are, but transcends the capacity of the whole of corporeal matter. And so far as the soul transcends corporeal matter, the potentiality for intelligibles exists in the soul and this [potentiality] belongs to the possible intellect. Certainly the soul, so far as it is united to the body, has operations and powers in common with the body; such, for example, are the powers of the nutritive and sentient part. Thus the nature of the possible intellect is as Aristotle proves it to be,[30] for the possible intellect is not a power rooted in any bodily organ. However, a man understands formally by means of it inasmuch as it is rooted in the essence of the human soul, which is the form of man.

Answers to objections. 1. The intellect is said to be separate but not the senses; because the intellect remains in the separated soul when the body has corrupted, whereas the senses do not. Or a better way of stating it is to say that the intellect is said to be separate because it does not employ a bodily organ in its operation as the senses do.

2. The human soul is the act of an organic body because the body is its organ. However, the body need not be the organ of all the soul's active and passive powers, since the human soul exceeds the capacity of the body, as we have explained.

3. The organ of a power is the principle of that power's operation. Hence, if the possible intellect were united to an organ, its operation would also be the operation of that organ, and thus it would be impossible for the principle by which we understand, to lack every sensible nature. For this principle by which we understand would then be the possible intellect together with its organ, just as the principle whereby we see, namely, the power of vision, exists concurrently with the pupil of the eye. However, even though the human soul is the form of the body and the possible intellect is one of the soul's powers, it does not follow that the possible intellect is limited to some sensible nature; because the human soul transcends the capacity (*proportionem*) of the body, as we have explained.

4. The possible intellect belongs to the human soul inasmuch as the soul is elevated above corporeal matter. Consequently, because the intellect is not the act of an organ, it does

---

[30] Aristotle proved that the intellect is "separate," not in the sense of existing apart from man, but as being free from matter in its operation.

not follow that it completely exceeds the essence of the soul, but only that it is supreme in the soul.

5. The human soul is an individuated form and so also is its power which is called the possible intellect, as well as the intelligible forms which are received in the possible intellect. But this does not prevent these forms from being actually known, for a thing is actually known because it is immaterial, not because it is universal. Indeed, the universal is intelligible because it is abstracted from material individuating conditions. Moreover, it is evident that separate substances are actual intelligibles and yet are certain individual entities; just as Aristotle says in the *Metaphysics*,[31] that the separated forms which Plato claimed to exist, were individual things. Therefore if individuation is incompatible with intelligibility it is evident that the same difficulty remains when the intellect is considered to be a separate substance; for then the possible intellect would be individuated as well as the species which are received in it. Consequently we must understand that, although the intelligible species received in the possible intellect are individuated inasmuch as they exist in the possible intellect, still the universal, which is conceived by abstraction from individuating principles, is known in these species inasmuch as they are immaterial. For universals with which the sciences are concerned, are what are known (through intelligible species) and not the intelligible species themselves. Moreover, concerning these intelligible species, not all sciences study them, but only physics [32] and metaphysics. For an intelligible species is *that by which* the intellect knows, but not *that which* it knows—except by reflection inasmuch as it knows that by which it knows in order to know itself.

6. The intellect gives universality to the forms known inas-

---

[31] VII, 14 (1039a 23 ff.).
[32] That is, the philosophy of nature, the science of the first principles of natural bodies, animate and inanimate.

much as it abstracts them from material individuating conditions. Consequently it is not necessary that the intellect be universal, but that it be immaterial.

7. The species of an operation is a natural effect of the species of the form which is the principle of that operation, whereas the ineffectiveness of an operation is a natural effect of the form inasmuch as it inheres in a subject. For a thing heats because it is hot, but it heats more or less effectively according as heat perfects it to a greater or lesser degree. Now to understand universals pertains to the species of intellectual operation. Hence this activity is the natural effect of an intellectual species as its proper operation; but so far as this activity is exercised more or less perfectly by the one understanding, it follows that the one understanding does so in a more or less perfect way.

8. The resemblance which the Philosopher observes between geometrical figures and the parts of the soul is to be regarded in this way: that just as a quadrilateral contains the elements of a triangle and additional characteristics; and a pentagon, the elements of a quadrilateral; so also does the sentient soul possess the characteristics of the nutritive, and the intellective possesses the characteristics of the sentient and others as well. Therefore it is not shown in this way that the nutritive and sentient parts of the soul differ essentially from the intellective, but rather that one of these [parts] contains another.

9. Just as animal and man are not conceived simultaneously, so neither are animal and horse, as the Philosopher points out in the same place. Therefore this statement [of the Philosopher] is not based on the argument that the sentient soul, existing substantially in man, is a principle by which he is an animal, and the intellective soul another principle by which he is a man. For it cannot be said that there are many different principles in a horse, one making it an animal, another, a horse. But this statement [of the Philosopher] is made for this

reason, that in the concept of animal the imperfect operations appear first, and then the more perfect; just as every generation is a transition from the imperfect to the perfect.

10. A form does not belong to a genus, as has been shown (Art. I). Consequently, since the intellective soul is the form of man, it does not belong to a different genus from that of the body. But each belongs to the genus animal and the species man, by reduction.

11. One being does not result from the union of two actually existing substances complete in their species and nature.[33] Now the soul and the body are not substances of this sort, because they are parts of human nature. Therefore nothing prevents them from being united to form one being [substantially].

12. Although the human soul is a form united to a body, it totally transcends the capacity of the whole of corporeal matter, and therefore cannot derive actual existence from the potentiality of matter as a result of any motion or change, as do other forms which are immersed in matter.

13. The soul, through that part of it whereby it exceeds every capacity of the body, has an operation in which the body does not share. However this does not prevent the soul from being united to the body in some way.

14. This objection agrees with the position of Origen,[34] who maintained that in the beginning souls were created without bodies together with the spiritual substances [i.e., the angels] and afterwards were united to bodies as though shut up in prisons. However, he did not say souls suffered that innocently, but because of a preceding sin. Hence Origen, in accordance with the position of Plato, held that the human soul was a complete species in itself, and that the body was joined to it

[33] Two complete substances cannot unite to form one substance and still retain their own proper existences as distinct substances.

[34] Origen (185–254), one of the early Christian Fathers of the Alexandrian school. The position of Origen which St. Thomas cites, is found in the *Peri Archon*, I, 7 (*PG*, XI, 171).

accidentally. But since this is false, as we have shown above (Art. I), it is not detrimental to the soul to be united to a body; on the contrary this union makes for the perfection of its nature. However, that the body is the prison of the soul and taints the soul, is merited by the first sin.

15. It is natural to the human soul to apprehend intelligible truth in a manner inferior to that proper to superior spiritual substances, namely, by abstraction from sensible things. But in this also the soul suffers an impediment through the corruption of the body which results from the sin of the first parent.

16. The fact that the flesh desires things that are opposed to the spirit, shows the affinity of the soul for the body. For "spirit" signifies the superior part of the soul whereby man surpasses other animals, as Augustine says [35] in the *Super Genesi contra Manichaeos*. But the flesh is said to desire because the parts of the soul joined to the flesh desire those things which delight the flesh, and now and again these concupiscences fight against the spirit.

17. The possible intellect does not possess any intelligible form actually, but only potentially, just as prime matter does not have any sensible form actually. Therefore it is not necessary, nor does the argument prove, that the possible intellect is one and the same for all men. It only shows that their intellect is one with respect to all intelligible forms, just as prime matter is one with respect to all sensible forms.

18. If the possible intellect had a bodily organ, that organ would have to be a principle [of understanding] together with the possible intellect which is the cause of intellection; just as the pupil of the eye together with the power of vision is the principle of vision; and thus the principle by which we understand would have a determinate sensible nature. This is evidently false in view of Aristotle's demonstration which was

[35] St. Augustine of Hippo (354–430). The text cited is *De Genesi ad Manichaeos*, II, 8 (*PL*, XXXIV, 202).

given above. However, this does not follow from the fact that the soul is the form of the body, because the possible intellect is a power of the soul so far as it transcends the capacity of the body.

19. Although the soul is united to the body in accordance with the body's mode of existing, still the soul has an intellectual nature in virtue of that part whereby it transcends the capacity of the body; and thus the forms received in the soul are intelligible and not material.

Whence the solution to the twentieth objection is evident.

ARTICLE III

## WHETHER THERE IS ONE POSSIBLE INTELLECT, OR INTELLECTIVE SOUL, FOR ALL MEN

In the third article we examine this question: Whether there is one possible intellect, or intellective soul, for all men.[1]

Objections. 1. It seems that there is. For a perfection is proportioned to what is perfectible. But truth is the perfection of the intellect, for truth is the good of the intellect, as the Philosopher says in the *Ethics*.[2] Therefore, since truth, which all men understand, is one, it seems that there is one possible intellect for all men.

2. Further, Augustine says, in the book *De quantitate animae:* [3] "I know what I will say to you about the number of souls. . . . For if I say there is one soul, you will be disturbed, because it is happy in one and sad in another, and one and the same thing cannot be happy and sad. If I say one and many at the same time, you will laugh; nor is it easy for me to know how to suppress your laughter. For if I say there are many only, I will laugh at myself, and I will maintain that I am less displeasing to myself than to you." Therefore the existence of many souls, one for each man, seems to be ridiculous.

3. Further, things that differ from each other, differ because of the determinate nature which each possesses. But the possi-

---

[1] See also *Summa theol.*, Ia, q.76, a.2; *Contra Gentes*, II, 59, 73, 75; *Sent.*, Bk. I, dist., 8, q.5, a.2, ad 6um; Bk. II, dist., 17, q.2, a.1; *De spir. creat.*, a.9; *op.* XVI, *De unit. intell.; op.* II, *Compend. theol.*, 58.
[2] VI, 2 (1139b 11).
[3] XXXII (*PL*, XXXII, 1073).

ble intellect is in potency to all forms, having none actually. Consequently the possible intellect [in one man] cannot differ [from that in another], and thus there cannot be many possible intellects, one for each man.

4. Further, the possible intellect totally lacks everything that it knows, because, prior to actual intellection, it possesses none of the things that it is cognizant of, as is said in the *De anima.*[4] But, as is said in the same book, it completely lacks any nature of its own; [5] and thus it cannot have a multiple existence among different individuals.

5. Further, there must be something in common in all things that are distinct and multiple, for man is common to many men, and animal to many animals. But the possible intellect does not have anything in common with other things, as is said in the *De anima.*[6] Therefore the possible intellect in one man cannot differ from that in another, and thus there cannot be many possible intellects, one for each man.

6. Further, as Rabbi Moses [7] points out, there is multiplicity with respect to cause and thing caused only in things existing in separation from matter. But the intellect or soul of one man is not the cause of the intellect or soul of another. Therefore, since the possible intellect is separate, as is said in the *De anima,*[8] there will not be many possible intellects, one for each man.

7. Further, the Philosopher says, in the *De anima,*[9] that the intellect and what is understood are one and the same. But what is understood is one and the same for all men. Therefore there is one possible intellect for all men.

8. Further, that which is understood is a universal, which is

[4] III, 4 (429a 18 ff.).

[5] In the text cited, Aristotle points out that "mind must be pure from all admixture," and "can have no nature of its own, other than that of a certain capacity"; also that "mind is, before it thinks, not actually any real thing."

[6] III, 4 (429a 23).

[7] Moses Maimonides (1134–1204), author of the work *Guide for the Doubting.*

[8] III, 5 (429a 24 ff.).

[9] III, 7, 8 (431a 1; 431b 21).

a one-in-many (*unum in multis*). But the form understood does not derive this unity from the thing [of which it is the form], for the form man is present in men themselves only as individuated and multiplied among diverse men. Therefore the form derives this unity from the intellect. Consequently there is one [possible] intellect for all men.

9. Further, the Philosopher says in the *De anima*,[10] that the soul is the place (*locus*) of species. But place is common to different things in place. Therefore there are not many souls, one for each man.

10. But it must be said that the soul is the place of species because it contains species. On the other hand, just as the intellect contains intelligible species, so does sense contain sensible species. Therefore, if the intellect is the place of species because it contains them, sense, for a similar reason, will also be the place of species. This is contrary to what the Philosopher says, in the *De anima*,[11] that not every soul is the place of species, but only the intellective soul.

11. Further, a thing operates only in the place in which it is located. But the possible intellect operates everywhere, for it understands things existing in heaven, those existing on earth, and everywhere. Therefore the possible intellect is everywhere, and thus is one for all men.

12. Further, whatever is limited (*definitum*) to some one particular thing, has a determinate matter, because the principle of individuation is matter. But the possible intellect does not have a determinate matter, as is proved in the *De anima*.[12] Therefore it is not found to exist in each particular man, and thus is one for all men.

13. But it must be said that the possible intellect has matter in the thing in which it exists, namely, in the human body in which it is confined. On the other hand, the principle of indi-

---

[10] III, 4 (429a 26).
[11] *Ibid.*
[12] III, 8 (431b 30).

viduation should belong to the individuated essence. But the body is not an essential part of the possible intellect. Therefore the possible intellect cannot be individuated by the body, and consequently cannot have a multiple existence.

14. Further, the Philosopher says in the *De caelo*,[13] that if there were many worlds, there would be many first heavens. But if there were many first heavens, there would be many first movers; and thus these first movers would be material. Therefore, for a similar reason, if there were many possible intellects, one for each man, the possible intellect would be material; which is impossible.

15. Further, if there are many possible intellects, one for each man, they must remain many when their bodies have corrupted. But then, since they can differ only as regards form, they will have to differ specifically. Therefore, since possible intellects do not become specifically different when their bodies have corrupted (because nothing is changed from one species into another unless it is corrupted), possible intellects were specifically different before their bodies corrupted. But man acquires his species from the intellective soul. Therefore diverse men do not possess the same species; which is clearly false.

16. Further, whatever exists in separation from a body cannot be given a multiple existence by bodies. But the possible intellect is separate from the body, as the Philosopher proves in the *De anima*.[14] Therefore the possible intellect cannot be multiplied nor be individuated by bodies. Consequently there are not many possible intellects, one for each man.

17. Further, if a possible intellect exists in each man, intelligible species must exist in each man; and thus it follows that intelligible species are individuated forms. But individuated forms are only potentially intellected, for the universal, which is the proper object of intellection, must be abstracted from

[13] I, 9 (279a 8).
[14] III, 5 (430a 17).

such forms. Therefore the forms which are in the possible
intellect will only be potentially intelligible, and thus the possible intellect will be unable to be actually understood; which
is incongruous.

18. Further, an agent and patient, mover and thing moved,
have something in common. Now a phantasm is related to the
possible intellect, existing in us, as an agent to a patient, and
as a mover to something moved. Therefore the intellect existing in us has something in common with phantasms. But the
possible intellect has nothing in common with the latter, as
is pointed out in the *De anima*.[15] Therefore the [supposedly
separate] possible intellect differs from the intellect which is
present in us, and so is not multiplied among diverse men.

19. Further, a thing, inasmuch as it exists, is one.[16] Therefore neither its act of existing nor its unity depends on another.
But the possible intellect's act of existing does not depend on
the body, otherwise it would be corrupted when the body corrupts. Consequently the unity of the possible intellect does not
depend on the body; and so neither does its multiplicity.
Therefore the possible intellect is not multiplied among different bodies [in such a way that each man possesses his own].

20. Further, the Philosopher says, in the *Metaphysics*,[17] that
in those things which are forms alone [i.e., not composed of
matter and form], the thing and its quiddity (*quod quid erat
esse*), that is, the nature of its species, are one and the same. But
the possible intellect, or intellective soul, is a form alone, for,
if it were composed of matter and form, it would not be the
form of anything else. Hence the intellective soul is the nature
itself of its species. So, if the nature of the species is one and
the same in every intellective soul, the intellective soul is incapable of having a multiple existence among diverse individuals [in such a way that each possesses his own].

---

15 III, 4 (429b 22).
16 That is, being and unity are convertible. See St. Thomas, *De veritate*, q. 1,
a. 1.
17 VII, 2 (1043b 1).

21. Further, the soul has a multiple existence among different bodies only by being united thereto. But the possible intellect belongs to that part of the soul which transcends bodily union. Hence the possible intellect does not have a multiple existence among diverse men [in such a way that each possesses his own intellect].

22. Further, if many human souls exist because of the multiplicity of bodies, and many possible intellects because of the multiplicity of souls, and since it is certain that there must be many intelligible species if there are many possible intellects, it follows that the first principle of multiplicity must be corporeal matter. But whatever is made multiple by matter is individual, and is not actually intelligible. Therefore the species which are in the possible intellect will not be actually intelligible objects; which is incongruous. Hence there will not be many human souls and possible intellects, one in each man.

On the contrary, man understands by the possible intellect. For it is said in the *De anima*,[18] that the possible intellect is that by which the soul understands. Consequently, if there is one possible intellect for all men, it follows that one man understands what another does; which is clearly false.

Further, the intellective soul is related to the body as a form to matter, and as a mover to an instrument. But every form requires a determinate matter, and every mover a determinate instrument. It is impossible, therefore, that there be one intellective soul for all men.

I answer: This question depends in a certain way on the preceding one. For if the possible intellect is a substance having existence separate from the body, it must be unique; because those things which have existence apart from a body can in no way have a multiple existence as a result of a multiplicity of bodies. However, the unicity of the intellect must be given

18 III, 5 (430a 15).

special consideration because it involves a peculiar difficulty. For it is at once apparent that there cannot be one [possible] intellect for all men. It is, indeed, clear that the possible intellect is related to the perfections, which sciences [19] are, as a primary perfection to a secondary one, and that we have scientific knowledge potentially because of a possible intellect. This fact compels us to maintain that a possible intellect exists. Moreover, it is obvious that not all men possess the same scientific knowledge, because some know sciences which others do not. Now it is evidently incongruous and impossible for one and the same primary subject to be in act and in potency with regard to the same form. For example, [it is impossible that] a surface be at the same time potentially and actually white.

Now those maintaining that there is one possible intellect for all men try to avoid the absurdity of this position by pointing to the fact that the intelligible species, on which the perfection of science is based, have a twofold subject, as was shown above (Art. II), namely, the phantasms themselves, and the possible intellect. And they argue that intelligible species are not the same in all men, because phantasms are not the same in all. In fact, as existing in the possible intellect, intelligible species are not multiple. So it is that one man possesses a science which another lacks, because he has different phantasms. But this is evidently foolish in view of what has previously been said. For species are actually intelligible only by being abstracted from phantasms and by existing in the possible intellect. Therefore diversity of phantasms cannot be the cause of the unity or multiplicity of a perfection having the character of scientific knowledge. Nor do scientific habits exist in some part of the sentient soul as their subject, as these men claim.

But an even greater difficulty faces those who maintain that

[19] A science is a "habitus," a quality perfecting a power for operation. Hence it is a secondary perfection in relation to the power which it perfects, which power is a perfection of man.

there is one possible intellect for all men. For it is evident that the act of intellection has its origin in the possible intellect as the first principle whereby we understand, just as the operation of sensing has its origin in a sentient power. Also, while it was shown above (Art. II) that if the possible intellect exists apart from man, the act of understanding, which belongs to the possible intellect, cannot be the operation of this or that man; nevertheless, from the hypothesis of one possible intellect for all men, it follows that this or that man understands by the possible intellect's own act of understanding. Yet an operation can be multiplied in only two ways: either on the side of the objects [known], or on that of the principle operating. A third way [of multiplying operation] can also be envisaged from the point of view of time, as, for instance, when an operation involves temporal changes. Hence the act of understanding, which is the operation of the intellect, can be multiplied with respect to objects known, so that it is one thing to know a man, another thing to know a horse. The act of understanding can also be multiplied with respect to time, so that to understand what happened yesterday is one act, and to understand what happens today, another, if, of course, the operation is not continuous. However, the act of understanding cannot be multiplied respecting the principle operating, if there is only one possible intellect. Therefore, if the possible intellect's own act of understanding is this or that man's act of understanding, this man's act of understanding, and that man's, could be different if they were understanding different things. A reason for this can be found in the diversity of phantasms. The act of understanding by different men understanding the same thing, according to the one possible intellect theory, could be multiplied similarly, so that one understands today and another tomorrow. This can also be attributed to the different use of phantasms. But in the case of two men who understand the same thing at the same time, their act of understanding would have to be numerically one and the same; which is clearly impossible. Therefore it is impossible for the possible intellect, by which we understand formally,[20] to be one and the same for all men.

However, it would be more reasonable to hold that we understand by the possible intellect as an active principle existing in us, and causing in us actual understanding. For one mover puts different things into operation; but that different things should act through some one thing formally, is absolutely impossible.

Moreover, the forms and species of natural things are known through their proper operations; but the proper operation of man, as man, is understanding and reasoning. Hence the principle of this operation, whereby man is made to be specifically what he is, must be the intellect. It cannot be the sensory soul, nor any other power of man. Therefore, if the possible intellect, existing as a separate substance, is one for all men, then all men are made to be specifically what they are by one substance existing apart from them. This position is reminiscent of the doctrine of Ideas,[21] and labors under the same difficulty.

Consequently it must be said absolutely that there is not one possible intellect for all men, but that there are many intellects, one for each man. And since the intellect is a certain power or capacity of the human soul, it is multiplied according as the substance of the soul itself is multiplied; which multiplication can be considered in the following way. For if a thing having a certain common character is multiplied materially, it must be multiplied numerically while remaining specifically the same. For instance, flesh and bones belong to the very notion of animal. Hence the distinction between animals, which is based on individual bodily differences, makes them numerically, but not specifically, diverse. Moreover, it is clear from what was said above (Arts. I and II),[22] that the human soul

---

[20] I.e., as a formal principle.
[21] An allusion to the Platonic theory of Ideas.
[22] See also the *De spiritualibus creaturis,* Art. III.

by its very nature is capable of union with the human body, because the human soul is not a complete species in itself, but acquires the completion of its species [23] in the composite [24] itself. Hence the fact that the soul is capable of being united to this or to that body, multiplies the soul numerically, not specifically; just as this whiteness differs numerically from that, because it belongs to this or that subject. But the human soul differs from other forms in this way, that its act of existing does not depend on the body. Nor does this individuated act of existing which it has, depend on the body; for inasmuch as a thing is one, it is undivided in itself and distinct from other things.

Answers to objections. 1. Truth is the conformity of the intellect with the thing [known]. Therefore there is one truth which different men understand, inasmuch as their conceptions conform to the same known object.

2. Augustine acknowledges that his position is ridiculous, not if he says many souls, but if he says many without qualification, so that souls would be many both numerically and specifically.

3. The possible intellect is not multiplied among different individuals because of any formal diversity, but because the substance of the soul, of which the intellect is a power, has a multiple existence.

4. It is not necessary for the intellect as such (*commune*) to completely lack what it understands, but only the intellect in potency; just as every recipient lacks the nature received. Hence, if there exists an intellect which is Act alone (as the divine intellect is), it understands itself through itself. But the possible intellect is said to be intelligible, just as other intelligible things are, because it understands itself through the intelligible species of other intelligible things. For it knows its

---

[23] The human soul united to the body constitutes the complete man.
[24] That is, the composite of matter and form.

operation with respect to an object, and acquires knowledge of itself through this operation.

5. The possible intellect must be understood to have nothing in common with any of the sensible natures from which it derives its intelligible species. However, one possible intellect is specifically the same as another.

6. Those things which exist apart from matter can differ from one another only specifically. Moreover, things which are specifically diverse belong to different grades [of being]. Hence they resemble numbers which differ specifically from one another as a result of the addition and subtraction of a unit. Consequently it follows, from the position of those who maintain that inferior beings are caused by superior ones, that in the case of beings existing in separation from matter there is multiplicity so far as cause and thing caused are concerned. But this position may not be held according to faith.[25] Therefore the possible intellect is not a substance existing apart from matter. Hence the reason given does not support the argument.

7. The intelligible species through which the intellect understands formally, is present in the possible intellect of this and of that particular man, and for this reason it follows that there are many possible intellects. Nevertheless the quiddity (*quod*) known through such a species is one, if we consider this quiddity in relation to the thing known; because the universal which is understood by both of these men is the same in all the things [of which it is the universal representation]. Moreover, the fact that what is one-in-all [i.e., the universal] can be understood through species multiplied among diverse individuals, is made possible by the immateriality of these species. For species represent a thing without the

[25] According to the Gnostics not all beings were created directly by God, but inferior beings were created through the intermediary of superior ones. This position is contrary to faith, because it denies that God alone can create.

material individuating conditions which give the simple specific nature a multiple existence among diverse things.

8. According to the Platonists the reason why something is understood as a one-in-many [i.e., universally], is not to be attributed to the intellect, but to the thing. They argue that, because our intellect knows a thing as a one-in-many, it would apparently be empty of any real content unless there were one real nature shared by many individuals. For in that case the intellect would have in itself nothing corresponding to this one-in-many in reality. Hence the Platonists felt obliged to posit Ideas, by participation in which both natural things are given their specific nature, and our intellects made cognizant of universals. But according to Aristotle, the fact that the intellect understands a one-in-many in abstraction from individuating principles, is to be attributed to the intellect itself. And though nothing abstract exists in reality, the intellect is not void of any real content, nor is it misrepresentative of things as they are; because, of those things which necessarily exist together, one can be truly understood or named without another being understood or named. But it cannot be truly understood or said of things existing in this way, that one exists without the other. Thus whatever exists in an individual which pertains to the nature of its species, and in respect of which it is like other things, can be known and spoken of truly without taking into consideration its individuating principles, which distinguish it from all other individuals [of the same species]. Consequently, by its abstractive power the intellect makes this universal unity itself, not as though it were a unity existing in things themselves, but as an immaterial representation of them.

9. The intellect is the place of species because it contains them. Hence it does not follow that there is one possible intellect for all men, but that it is one and common to the whole species.

10. Sense does not receive species without an organ, and therefore sense is not said to be the place of species in the same manner as the intellect is.

11. The possible intellect can be said to operate everywhere, not because it actually does so, but because its intellectual operation comprehends things which exist everywhere.

12. Although the possible intellect has no determinate matter, the substance of the soul, of which the intellect is a power, has a determinate matter. However it does not have matter as a constituent part, but as something in which it exists.

13. The individuating principles of all forms are not of the very essence of these forms. This is true only in the case of things composed of matter and form.

14. The Prime Mover of the heavens exists in complete separation from matter. Therefore He canot be multiplied numerically in any way whatever. However, the same thing is not true of the human soul.

15. Souls existing apart from bodies do not differ specifically, but numerically, because they are capable of being united to this or to that particular body.

16. Although the possible intellect is separated from the body so far as its operation is concerned, nevertheless it is a power of the soul which is the act of the body.

17. Something is potentially known, not because it is individual, but because it is material. Hence the intelligible species that are received in the intellect immaterially are actually known, even though they are individuated. Furthermore, the same [incongruity set forth in this objection] follows logically from the position of those who maintain that there is one possible intellect for all men. For if there is one possible intellect existing as a separate substance, it must be an individual thing. This is the argument that Aristotle employs against Plato's Ideas. The intelligible species in the intellect would be individuated for the same reason, and would differ in diverse sepa-

rate intellects as well, because every intelligence is filled with intelligible forms.

18. A phantasm moves the intellect so far as the possible intellect is made actually cognizant by the power of the agent intellect to which the possible intellect is related as potency is to act. This is the way in which the intellect has something in common with a phantasm.

19. Although the soul's act of existing does not depend on the body, nevertheless it is related by its very nature to the body for the completion of its species.

20. Although the human soul does not contain matter as an intrinsic part of itself, it is still the form of the body. Therefore its nature involves relationship with the body.

21. Although the possible intellect transcends the body, it does not transcend the entire substance of the soul, which has a multiple existence because it inhabits diverse bodies.

22. This argument would be true if the body were united to the soul in such a way as to embrace the whole essence and power of the soul, for then whatever exists in the soul would necessarily be material. But this is not the case as was shown above, and therefore this argument is not legitimate.

# ARTICLE IV

## WHETHER IT IS NECESSARY TO ADMIT THAT AN AGENT INTELLECT EXISTS

In the fourth article we examine this question: Whether it is necessary to admit that an agent intellect exists.[1]

Objections. 1. It seems unnecessary to admit that an agent intellect exists. For whatever can be accomplished in nature by one thing is not done by many. Now a man can understand quite well by means of one intellect, namely, the possible intellect. Therefore it is unnecessary to admit that an agent intellect exists. The minor proposition is proved thus: powers that are rooted in one and the same essence of the soul influence one another. It is for this reason that an impression is made on the imagination as a result of a change in the [external] sense powers, for the imagination is moved [i.e., actuated or informed] when the external senses are actuated, as is said in the *De anima*.[2] Therefore, if the possible intellect belongs to our soul, and is not a separate substance, as we have explained above (Art. II), it must belong to the same essence of the soul as the imagination does. Hence a change in the imagination flows into the possible intellect, and thus it is unnecessary to admit that an agent intellect exists which makes phantasms intelligible by abstracting [species] from the phantasms themselves.

2. Further, touch and sight are different powers. Now in the case of one who is [born] blind, it happens that the imagination

---

[1] This problem is also discussed in the *Summa theol.*, Ia, q.79, a.3; q.54, a.4; *Contra Gentes*, II, 77; *De spir. creat.*, a.9; *op.* II, *Compend. theol.*, chap. 83; *Comm. in De anima*, Bk. III, lect. 10.

[2] III, 3 (429a 1).

is moved to imagine something that belongs to the sense of sight from a change produced in the imagination by the sense of touch, and this occurs because sight and touch are rooted in one and the same essence of the soul. Therefore, if the possible intellect is a certain power of the soul, then, for a similar reason, an impression will be produced in the possible intellect from a change in the imagination. Thus it is unnecessary to admit that an agent intellect exists.

3. Further, an agent intellect is held to exist in order that the potentially intelligible may be made actually intelligible. Moreover, some things are made actually intelligible by being abstracted from matter and from material conditions. Thus an agent intellect is held to exist in order that intelligible species may be abstracted from matter. However, this can be accomplished without an agent intellect, for, since the possible intellect is immaterial, it must receive things in an immaterial way, because whatever is received is in the recipient according to the mode of the recipient. Therefore it is unnecessary to admit that an agent intellect exists.

4. Further, in the *De anima*,[3] Aristotle compares the agent intellect to light. But light is necessary for sight only inasmuch as it makes the medium (*diaphanus*) [4] to be actually luminous; for color is visible in virtue of its own nature, and moves the medium which is actually luminous,[5] as is explained in the *De anima*.[6] However, the agent intellect is not required in order to prepare the possible intellect for the reception of species, because the possible intellect is in potency to intelli-

---

[3] III, 5 (430a 15).

[4] "The diaphane," literally means, "to show through," and is used to designate what is transparent, or has the property of transmitting rays of light so that bodies can be distinctly seen through it; it is the medium through which visible species are transmitted. In discussing the same problem in the *Summa theologica*, St. Thomas simply uses the term, "medium" (*medium*).

[5] According to Aristotle, in the *De anima*, color is visible of itself and light merely removes the opacity of the intervening medium, making it to be actually luminous or transparent. When this occurs, color can move the actually luminous medium and transmit visible species to the eye.

[6] II, 7 (418a 26 ff.; 418b 27 ff.).

gible species by its very nature. Therefore it is unnecessary to maintain that an agent intellect exists.

5. Further, just as our intellect is related to intelligible things, so are our senses related to sensible things. Now sensible things require no agent [sense] in order that they may move the senses, yet sensible things are present with an immaterial mode of existence, both in the senses, which are receptive of sensible things without matter, as is said in the *De anima*,[7] as well as in the medium [e.g., the air], which receives the species of sensible things in an immaterial way. This is evident from the very fact that the species of contrary qualities, such as white and black, are received in the same part of the medium. Therefore neither do intelligible things require an agent intellect.

6. Further, in order for something in potency to be made actual in the case of natural things, something actual belonging to the same genus is sufficient; for example, in the case of matter, whatever is ablaze potentially is set ablaze actually by fire, which is in act. Therefore, for our intellect, which is in potency, to be actuated, nothing more is required than the intellect in act, either of the knower himself, as when we proceed from a knowledge of principles to a knowledge of conclusions, or of someone else, as when someone learns from a teacher. Consequently it seems unnecessary to maintain that an agent intellect exists.

7. Further, an agent intellect is held to exist in order that it may illuminate our phantasms, just as the light of the sun illuminates colors. But the divine light, "which illuminates every man coming into this world" (John 1:9), suffices for our illumination. Consequently it is unnecessary to maintain that an agent intellect exists.

8. Further, intellection is the activity of an intellect. Therefore, if there are two intellects, that is, an agent and a possible intellect, the intellection of one and the same man will be twofold. This is incongruous.

---

[7] III, 8 (431b 25 ff.).

9. Further, it is seen that an intelligible species perfects our intellect. Therefore, if there are two intellects, namely, a possible and an agent intellect, there are two distinct acts of intellection. This seems unnecessary.

On the contrary, in the *De anima*,[8] Aristotle concludes that, since in every nature there is something active and something potential, these two things must be found within the soul itself, and one of these is the agent intellect, the other the possible intellect.

I answer: We must admit that an agent intellect exists. To make this evident we must observe that, since the possible intellect is in potency to intelligibles, the intelligibles themselves must move [i.e., actuate] the possible intellect. But that which is non-existent cannot move anything. Moreover, the intelligible as such, that which the possible intellect understands, does not exist in reality;[9] for our possible intellect understands something as though it were a one-in-many and common to many [i.e., universal]. However, such an entity is not found subsisting in reality, as Aristotle proves in the *Metaphysics*.[10] Therefore, if the possible intellect has to be moved by an intelligible, this intelligible must be produced by an intellective power. And since it is impossible for anything in potency, in a certain respect, to actuate itself,[11] we

---

8 III, 5 (430a 10 ff.).

9 The universal as such does not exist in reality. Only individuals have real existence. The intentional existence in the intellect of the thing known gives that thing its universality.

10 VII, 13 (1039a 15 ff.).

11 This is a fundamental principle of Thomistic metaphysics and is commonly stated thus: "Nothing is brought from potency to act except by a being already in act"; or "Whatever is being moved is being moved by another." See *Summa theol.*, Ia, q. 2, a. 3. To deny this is to deny the principle of contradiction. A thing cannot give a perfection which it does not possess. Hence in order for something potential to actuate itself, it would have to have the perfection actually, and then it would be in act and in potency simultaneously as regards the same perfection; which is absurd. Consequently, if the possible intellect is in potency to intelligibles, it cannot actuate itself as regards such intelligibles, but an agent intellect is required to do this.

must admit that an agent intellect exists, in addition to the possible intellect, and that this agent intellect causes the actual intelligibles which actuate the possible intellect. Moreover, it produces these intelligibles by abstracting them from matter and from material conditions which are the principles of individuation. And since the nature as such of the species does not possess these principles by which the nature is given a multiple existence among different things, because individuating principles of this sort are distinct from the nature itself, the intellect will be able to receive this nature apart from all material conditions, and consequently will receive it as a unity [i.e., as a one-in-many]. For the same reason the intellect receives the nature of a genus by abstracting from specific differences, so that it is a one-in-many and common to many species.

However, if universals subsisted in reality in virtue of themselves, as the Platonists [12] maintained, it would not be necessary to admit than an agent intellect exists; because things which are intelligible in virtue of their own nature move the possible intellect. Therefore it appears that Aristotle was led by this necessity to posit an agent intellect, because he did not agree with the opinion of Plato on the question of Ideas. Nevertheless there are some subsistent things in the real order which are actual intelligibles in virtue of themselves; the immaterial substances, for instance, are of this nature (see Art. VII). However, the possible intellect cannot attain a knowledge of these immediately, but acquires its knowledge of them through what it abstracts from material and sensible things (see Art. XVI).

[12] Nominalists maintain that universals are merely terms that we invent for convenience, but that they are without any basis in reality. Plato taught that universals have an existence independent of our mental consideration. Thomism, between these two extremes, holds that universals are the result of intellectual abstraction from data furnished by really existing things.

St. Thomas is here referring to the "exaggerated" or "extreme" realism of Plato and the Platonic tradition. For a complete analysis of this position, see St. Thomas' discussion in Article XV (Answer).

Answers to objections. 1. Our act of intellection cannot be accomplished by the possible intellect alone, for the possible intellect can understand only when it is moved by an intelligible, and this intelligible, since it does not already exist in the real order, must be produced by the agent intellect. Moreover, it is true that two powers, which are rooted in one and the same substance of the soul, do influence each other; but this influence can be understood to occur in two ways: first, inasmuch as one power is hindered or totally prevented from performing its operation when another power operates intensely; however, this has no bearing on the problem; [13] secondly, inasmuch as one power is moved by another, as the imagination is moved by the [external] senses. Now this is possible because the forms in the imagination and those in the external senses are generically the same, for all are individual forms. Therefore the forms which are in the external senses can impress those forms which exist in the imagination by moving the imagination, because they are similar to these forms. However, the forms in the imagination, since they represent things as individuals, cannot cause intelligible forms, because these are universal.

2. The species received in the imagination from the sense of touch are not enough to cause the imagination to produce forms belonging to the sense of sight, unless forms previously received by the sense of sight are stored up in the repertory of memory or imagination. For one who is born blind cannot imagine color by any other kind of sensible species whatever.

3. The condition of the recipient cannot cause a species which has been received, to be transferred from one genus to another; however, it can alter a received species of the same genus according to some mode of being. Hence, since a universal species and a particular species differ generically, it follows that the cognitive activity of the possible intellect alone

---

[13] That is, the first way in which one power can influence another by hindering it in its operation, does not explain human intellection.

is not enough to give the particular species in the imagination the universality which they possess in the intellect, but that an agent intellect is required to do this.

4. There are two opinions concerning light, as the Commentator [14] points out in the *De anima*.[15] For some said that light is necessary for sight inasmuch as it gives to colors the power of moving the sense of sight, as if color were not visible of itself, but only through light. But this seems to contradict Aristotle, since he points out in the *De anima*,[16] that color is visible in virtue of itself, and this would not be the case if it were made visible by light alone. For this reason others offer a different and more acceptable explanation, namely, that light is necessary for sight inasmuch as it perfects the medium, making it to be actually luminous. Wherefore the Philosopher says in the *De anima*,[17] that color has the power of moving what is actually luminous. Nor is this position rendered untenable by the fact that someone in the dark sees things which are in the light, but not vice versa. For this occurs because the medium, which surrounds a visible thing, must be illuminated in order that the medium may receive the visible species; and this remains visible as long as the act of light continues to illuminate the medium, although it illuminates it more perfectly the nearer it is, and more weakly the farther it is away. Consequently the comparison between light and the agent intellect does not hold in all respects, because the agent intellect is necessary for this reason, that it may make the potentially intelligible to be actually intelligible. Aristotle pointed this out in the *De anima*,[18] when he said that the agent intellect is like light in some respects.

5. Since a sensible is something particular, it does not impress a species of a higher genus, either on the sense or on the

---

14 The "Commentator" is the name given to Averroes. See Art. II, note 28.
15 II, 67 (VI, 140r).
16 II, 7 (418a 29 ff.).
17 II, 7 (418a 33).
18 III, 5 (430a 15).

medium, because the species existing in the medium and in the sense is a particular and nothing more. The possible intellect, however, receives species of a higher genus than those present in the imagination; because the possible intellect receives universal species, whereas the imagination contains only particular species. Therefore we require an agent intellect in the case of intelligible things, but need no additional agent power in the case of sensible things. Indeed, all the sentient powers are passive powers.[19]

6. The possible intellect in act is not sufficient to cause knowledge in us unless an agent intellect is presupposed. For if we speak of the intellect in act of one who is learning, it so happens that his possible intellect is in potency with respect to some things, and in act with respect to others; and his intellect can be put into act, so far as the things to which it is in potency are concerned, by the things that are already actually known; just as one is made to be actually knowing conclusions, which were previously known only potentially, by actually knowing principles. However, the possible intellect can be actually knowing principles only through the activity of the agent intellect; for our knowledge of principles is received from sensible things, as is stated at the end of the *Posterior Analytics*.[20] Moreover, intelligibles can be derived from sensible things only by the abstractive activity of the agent intellect. Thus it is evident that the intellect in act with respect to principles, does not suffice to move the possible intellect from potentiality to act without the agent intellect. Indeed, in this actuating of the possible intellect, the agent intellect acts like an artisan and the principles of demonstration like tools. However, if we speak of the intellect in act of the teacher, it is evident that when the teacher causes knowledge in one who is learning, he does not act as an interior agent, but as an external administra-

---

[19] In the *Summa theol.*, Ia, q. 79, a. 3, ad 1 um, St. Thomas points out that all the vegetative powers are active powers, all sentient powers are passive powers, and the intellective powers either active or passive.
[20] II, 19 (100a 10).

tor, just as in the production of health a physician acts as an external administrator, whereas the nature of the patient acts as an interior agent.

7. Just as real things of any kind require proper active principles, even though God is the first and universal agent, so too does man require a proper intellective light, even though God is the First Light illuminating all men in common.

8. There is a proper activity for each one of the two intellects, that is, the possible intellect and the agent intellect. For the activity of the possible intellect consists in receiving intelligibles, whereas that of the agent intellect consists in abstracting them. Nor does it follow that there are two distinct acts of understanding in a man, because it is necessary that the activities of both intellects concur to produce one act of understanding.

9. The same intelligible species is related to the agent intellect and to the possible intellect. However, it is related to the possible intellect as a recipient, and to the agent intellect as the one producing species of this sort by abstraction.

## ARTICLE V

## WHETHER THERE IS ONE SEPARATELY EXISTING AGENT INTELLECT FOR ALL MEN

In the fifth article we examine this question: Whether there is one separately existing agent intellect for all men.[1]

Objections. 1. It seems that there is. Because the Philosopher says, in the *De anima*,[2] that the agent intellect is not at one time knowing and at another not. But nothing of this nature exists in us. Hence the agent intellect exists apart from men, and therefore is one and the same for all men.

2. Further, nothing can be in potency and in act with respect to the same thing simultaneously. Now the possible intellect is in potency with respect to every intelligible species. However, the agent intellect is in act with respect to them, because it is the act [3] [producing] them. Therefore it seems that the possible and agent intellect cannot be rooted in the same substance of the soul. Hence, since the possible intellect is rooted in the essence of the soul, as is evident from the preceding articles (Arts. I, II, and III), the agent intellect will exist apart from the soul.

3. But it might be said that the possible intellect is in potency to intelligible species, and the agent intellect in act with respect to them according to different modes of existence.

---

[1] This argument is directed against the Averroists. See also *Summa theol.*, Ia, q.79, a.4, 5; *Contra Gentes*, II, 76, 78; *Sent.*, Bk. II, dist. 17, q.2, a.1; *De spir. creat.*, a.10; *Comm. in De anima*, Bk. III, lect. 10; *op.* II, *Compend. theol.*, chap. 86.

[2] III, 5 (430a 22).

[3] A reference to the principle: "Nothing is brought from potentiality to actuality except by a being that is already in act."

On the other hand, the possible intellect is not in potency to intelligible species when it possesses them, because then it is actuated by them. Hence it is in potency to intelligible species as existing in phantasms. But the agent intellect is related to such species as the act [which produces them], because it makes them actually intelligible by abstraction. Hence the possible intellect is in potency to intelligible species with respect to that mode of existence according to which the agent intellect is related to them as the one producing them.

4. Further, in the *De anima*,[4] the Philosopher attributed to the agent intellect certain properties which seem to belong only to separate substances. For he says that "this [i.e., the intellect] alone is perpetual, incorruptible, and separate." Therefore its seems that the agent intellect is a separate substance.

5. Further, the intellect does not depend on any bodily disposition, because it is not united to a bodily organ. But our faculty of understanding is affected by different physical dispositions.[5] Consequently this [intellective] faculty of ours is not identical with this intellect which is present in us; so it seems that the agent intellect has a separate existence.

6. Further, in order to have activity, an agent and a patient alone are necessary. Therefore, if the possible intellect, which is the patient in cognition, is a part of our substantial principle, as was previously shown (Art. III), and the agent intellect is also a part of our soul, it seems that we possess within ourselves everything necessary in order that we may be able to understand. Hence we require nothing more in order to be able to do so. But this is clearly false. For we need the senses through which we acquire the experience necessary for cognition. This is the reason why a man deprived of a sense, for in-

---

[4] III, 5 (430a 17).

[5] The sensory powers function through the body, so that the condition of the body (for example, poor health) has considerable bearing on the acuteness of our sensory cognition. Now the intellect depends on the senses for its knowledge of things, hence anything that affects the body affects the intellect, even though the intellect itself does not function through the body.

stance, sight, lacks a knowledge of colors. In order to learn we also require instruction, which is given by a teacher. And above all we stand in need of the illumination given by God, for it is said: "It was the true Light that enlightens every man who comes into this world" (John 1:9).

7. Further, the agent intellect is related to intelligible objects as light is to visible objects, as is evident in the *De anima*.[6] But one light existing apart from things, that is, the sun, suffices to make all things actually visible. Consequently one [intellectual] light existing apart from men, suffices to make everything actually intelligible. Hence it is unnecessary to maintain that an agent intellect exists in each one of us.

8. Further, the agent intellect is similar to an art, as is clear in the *De anima*.[7] But an art is a principle separate from the objects produced by it. Therefore the agent intellect is also a separate principle.

9. The perfection of a nature consists in being like its agent, for a thing generated is perfect when it resembles the thing producing it. A thing produced by art is also perfect when it resembles the form in the mind of the artisan. Therefore, if the agent intellect belongs to our soul, the ultimate perfection and happiness of our soul will be found in some part of the soul itself; which is evidently false. For in that case the ultimate happiness of the soul would be the enjoyment of itself. Consequently the agent intellect is not something that exists within ourselves.

10. Further, an agent is nobler than a patient, as is pointed out in the *De anima*.[8] Therefore, if the possible intellect is separated in some measure from the body, the agent intellect will be separated to an even greater degree; and we see that this can be so, only if the agent intellect is held to be completely separated from the substance of the soul.

---

[6] III, 5 (430a 14).
[7] *Ibid.* (430a 15).
[8] *Ibid.* (430a 17 ff.).

On the contrary, there is this statement in the *De anima:* [9] that since there is something in every nature like matter [i.e., potential] and something which is productive [i.e., active], these two distinct elements must likewise be found within the soul. The possible intellect corresponds to one of these, the agent intellect to the other. Therefore both the possible and agent intellect belong to the soul.

Further, the operation of the agent intellect is to abstract intelligible species from phantasms. Now it is certain that this operation is not continually taking place in us. However, there would be no reason why such abstraction should sometimes occur and sometimes not, as is seen to be the case if the agent intellect were a separate substance. Consequently the agent intellect is not a separate substance.

I answer: It is obviously more reasonable to maintain that the agent intellect is unique and separate, than to hold that this is true of the possible intellect. For the possible intellect, in virtue of which we are capable of understanding, is sometimes in potency and sometimes in act. The agent intellect, on the other hand, is that which makes us actually understanding. Now an agent exists in separation from the things which it brings into actuality, but obviously whatever makes a thing potential is wholly within that thing.

For this reason many maintained that the agent intellect is a separate substance, and that the possible intellect is a part of our soul. Furthermore they held that this agent intellect is a specific kind of separate substance, which they call an intelligence. They held that it is related to our souls, and to the entire sphere of active and passive qualities,[10] as superior separate substances (which they also call intelligences) are related to the souls of the celestial bodies (for they considered these to be animated), and to the celestial bodies themselves. Hence they

[9] *Ibid.* (430a 10).
[10] The terrestrial sphere, the lowest of the spheres in classical astronomy.

maintained that, as superior bodies receive their motion from these separate substances, and the souls of the heavenly bodies their intelligible perfections, so also do all the bodies of this inferior sphere receive their forms and movements from the separate agent intellect, while our soul receives its intelligible perfections from it. But because the Catholic faith maintains that God is the agent operating in our souls, and not some separate substance in nature, some Catholics asserted that the agent intellect is God himself, who is "the true Light that enlightens every man who comes into this world" (John 1:9).

But this position, if anyone examines it carefully, is seen to be implausible, because the superior substances are related to our souls as celestial bodies are to inferior bodies. For, as the powers of superior bodies are certain universal active principles in relation to inferior bodies, so also are the divine power and the powers of different secondary substances (if the latter do influence us in any way) related to our souls as universal active principles.

However, we see that there must exist in addition to the universal active principles of the celestial bodies, certain particular active principles which are powers of inferior bodies, limited to the proper operation of each and every one of them. This is particularly necessary in the case of perfect animals, because certain imperfect animals are found, for whose production the power of a celestial body suffices, as is evident in the case of animals generated from decomposed matter.[11] However, in the generation of perfect animals a special power is also required in addition to the celestial power, and this power is present in the seed. Therefore, since intellectual operation is the most perfect thing existing in the entire order of inferior bodies, we need in addition to universal active principles

---

11 Allusion to the traditional theory of generation in the case of certain lower forms of animal life (imperfect animals). The appearance of life in decomposed matter was attributed to the power of celestial bodies, since inert matter itself is obviously incapable of producing life. For St. Thomas, "perfect animals" are those possessing the totality of sense powers, external and internal.

(namely, the power of God enlightening us, or the powers of any other separate substance) an active principle existing within us by which we are enabled to understand actually. This power is the agent intellect.

We must also consider this, that, if the agent intellect is held to exist as a separate substance along with God, a consequence repugnant to our faith will follow: namely, that our ultimate perfection and happiness consists not in a certain union of our soul with God, as the Gospel teaches, saying "This is life eternal, that you may know the true God" (John 17:3), but with some other separate substance. For it is evident that man's ultimate beatitude or happiness depends upon his noblest operation, intellection, which operation, in order to be fully completed, requires the union of our [possible] intellect with its active principle. For, indeed, anything passive in any way whatever is perfected [i.e., fully actuated] only when joined with the proper active principle which is the cause of its perfection. Therefore those maintaining that the agent intellect is a substance existing apart from matter, say that man's ultimate happiness consists in being able to know the agent intellect.

Moreover, if we give the matter further careful consideration, we will find that the agent intellect cannot be a separate substance for the same reason that the possible intellect cannot be, as was shown above (Arts. I, II, and III). For, as the operation of the possible intellect consists in receiving intelligible [species], so also does the proper operation of the agent intellect consist in abstracting them, for it makes them actually intelligible in this way. Now we experience both of these operations in ourselves, because we receive our intelligible species, and abstract them as well. However, in anything that operates there must be some formal principle whereby it operates formally, because a thing cannot operate formally through something that possesses existence distinct from itself. But, although the motive principle of an activity [i.e., an efficient cause] is separate from the thing which it causes, nevertheless there must be some intrinsic principle whereby a thing operates formally, whether it be a form or some sort of impression.[12] Therefore there must exist within us a formal principle through which we receive intelligible species, and one whereby we abstract them. These principles are called the possible and the agent intellect respectively. Consequently each exists within us. Moreover, [the formal intrinsic existence in us of the agent intellect] is not accounted for simply by the fact that the action of the agent intellect, namely, the abstracting of intelligible species, is carried out through phantasms illumined in us by its action. For every object produced by art is the effect of the action of an artificer, the agent intellect being related to the phantasms illumined by it as an artificer is to the things made by his art.

Now it is not difficult to see how both of these can be present in one and the same substance of the soul: that is, the possible intellect, which is in potency to all intelligible objects, and the agent intellect which makes them actually intelligible; because it is not impossible for a thing to be in potency and in act with respect to one and the same thing in different ways. Therefore, if we consider the phantasms themselves in relation to the human soul, in one respect they are found to be in potency, inasmuch as they are not abstracted from individuating conditions, although capable of being abstracted. In another respect they are found to be in act in relation to the soul, namely, inasmuch as they are [sensible] likenesses of determinate things. Therefore potentiality with respect to phantasms must be found within our soul so far as these phantasms are representative of determinate things. This belongs to the possible intellect which is, by its very nature, in potency to all intelligible objects, but is actuated by this or that object through species abstracted from phantasms. Our soul must also possess some active immaterial power which abstracts the phantasms them-

[12] A received accidental form of a transitory nature, in opposition to a natural and permanent form.

selves from material individuating conditions. This belongs to the agent intellect, so that it is, as it were, a power participated from the superior substance, God. Hence the Philosopher says,[13] that the agent intellect is like a certain habit and light. In the Psalms it is also said: "The light of Thy countenance is signed upon us, O Lord" (Ps. 4:7). Something resembling this in a certain degree is apparent in animals who see by night. The pupils of their eyes are in potency to every color inasmuch as they have no one determinate color actually, but make colors actually visible in some way by means of a certain innate light.

Indeed, some men thought that the agent intellect does not differ from our *habitus* of indemonstrable principles. But this cannot be the case, because we certainly know indemonstrable principles by abstracting them from singulars, as the Philosopher teaches in the *Posterior Analytics*.[14] Consequently the agent intellect must exist prior to the *habitus* of first indemonstrable principles in order to be the cause of it. Indeed, the principles themselves are related to the agent intellect as certain of its instruments, because the intellect makes things actually intelligible by means of such principles.

Answers to objections. 1. The Philosopher's statement that "the intellect is not at one time knowing and at another not." [15] is not understood of the agent intellect, but of the intellect-in-act. For after Aristotle had determined the role of the possible and agent intellect, he had to determine the role of the intellect-in-act.[16] He first distinguishes it in relation to the possible intellect, because the possible intellect and the thing known are not one and the same. However, the intellect or science-

---

[13] *De anima,* III, 5 (430a 14).

[14] II, 19 (100b 4).

[15] *De anima,* III, 5 (430a 22).

[16] The "intellect-in-act" is not a power distinct from the agent and possible intellect but simply designates the combined activities of the agent and possible intellects in the act of intellection.

in-act is the same as the thing actually known. Aristotle had said the same thing about sense, namely, that sense and what is potentially sensible differ from each other, but that sense and what is actually sensed are one and the same. Secondly, he shows how the possible intellect is related to the intellect-in-act, because in one and the same individual, intellect in potency precedes intellect-in-act. However, it does not precede it absolutely, for he very often uses this manner of speaking concerning things that pass from potentiality to actuality. Then he makes the statement quoted above,[17] in which he shows the difference between the possible intellect and the intellect-in-act, because the possible intellect sometimes understands and sometimes does not, which cannot be said of the intellect-in-act. He points out a similar difference, in the *Physics*,[18] between causes in potency and causes in act.

2. The substance of the soul is in potency and in act with respect to the same phantasms, but not in the same way, as was shown above.

3. The possible intellect is in potency with respect to intelligible species, and the agent intellect in act with respect to them, in relation to the existence which such species have in phantasms; but for different reasons, as was shown.

4. Those words of the Philosopher, "This alone is separate, immortal, and perpetual," cannot be understood to apply to the agent intellect. For Aristotle had also previously stated that the possible intellect is separate. However, they must be understood to apply to the intellect-in-act in view of the context in which they occur, as was shown above (Ans. obj. 1). For intellect-in-act embraces both the possible intellect and the agent intellect. And only that part of the soul which contains the agent and possible intellects is separate, perpetual, and immortal. For the other parts of the soul have no existence without the body.

[17] Aristotle, *De anima*, III, 5 (430a 22 ff.).
[18] III, 1 (201a 20 ff.).

5. Diversity of dispositions causes the intellective faculty to understand more or less perfectly by reason of the powers which aid the intellect in abstracting. These are the powers employing corporeal organs, such as imagination, memory, and the like.

6. Although our soul possesses an agent and a possible intellect, nevertheless something extrinsic is required so that we may be able to understand. First of all, indeed, we need phantasms, derived from sensible things, by means of which the likenesses of particular things are presented to the intellect. For the agent intellect is not an act in which the determinate species of all things can be received in order to be known, any more than light can cause sight to apprehend particular kinds of colors, unless those particular kinds of colors are present to sight. Moreover, since we maintained above that the agent intellect is a certain power in which our souls share, as a kind of light, we must maintain that some exterior cause exists from whom such light is participated, and we call this exterior cause, God, who teaches within us inasmuch as He infuses light of this kind into our soul. Because of His munificence He bestows upon us, in addition to this natural light, a richer one in order that we may be able to know those things which the natural light of reason cannot attain. Such, for instance, is the light of faith and of prophecy.

7. The colors moving the sense of sight are outside the soul. However, the phantasms which move the possible intellect are within us. Therefore, although the exterior light of the sun is adequate for making colors actually visible, nevertheless in order that phantasms may be made actually intelligible, an interior light is required, and this is the light of the agent intellect. Furthermore, the intellective part of the soul is more perfect than the sensory. Hence it is even more necessary that adequate principles be present to the intellect for the performance of its proper operation. Also, for this reason: it is a matter of experience that by the intellective part of our soul we both

receive intelligible species and abstract them, which indicates that there exists in us intellectually not only a passive but also an active power. This is not true in the case of the senses.

8. Although there is a certain likeness between the agent intellect and an art, the likeness need not hold in all respects.

9. The agent intellect is not sufficient of itself to actuate completely the possible intellect, because the determinate natures of all things do not exist in it, as has been explained. Therefore, to acquire complete perfection, the possible intellect needs to be united in a certain way to that Agent in whom the exemplars of all things exist, namely, God.

10. The agent intellect is nobler than the possible intellect, because an active power is nobler than a passive power. It is also more independent of matter than the possible intellect, inasmuch as it is further removed from any participation in matter. But its independence is not that of a separate substance.

# WHETHER THE SOUL IS COMPOSED OF MATTER AND FORM

In the sixth article we examine this question: Whether the soul is composed of matter and form.[1]

Objections. 1. It seems that the soul is composed of matter and form. For Boethius [2] says in his book, the *De Trinitate:* [3] "A simple [4] form cannot be a subject." But the soul is the subject of sciences and virtues. Therefore the soul is not a form in its entirety (*simplex*) and, consequently, is composed of matter and form.

2. Further, Boethius says in the *De hebdomadibus.*[5] "Whatever exists, can participate in something else; but the act of existing (*esse*) itself cannot participate in anything." For a similar reason, subjects participate in something but forms do not; for example, a white thing can participate in something besides whiteness, but whiteness itself cannot participate in anything. Now the soul participates in something, namely, in those things by which it is informed. Therefore the soul is not a form alone, but is composed of matter and form.

---

[1] See also *Summa theol.*, Ia, q.75, a.5; *Contra Gentes*, II, 50; *Sent.*, Bk. I dist. 8, q.5, a.2; Bk. II, dist. 17, a.1, a.2; *Quodl.*, III, q.8, a.1; IX, q.4, a.1; *De spir. creat.*, a.1; a.9, ad 9um; *op.* XV, *De subst. separatis*, chap. 7.

[2] Boethius (c. 480–525), a Roman consul under Theoderic, king of the Ostrogoths. Boethius is one of the famous "transmitters" of classical culture to the Middle Ages. He is noted for his celebrated *Consolation of Philosophy* and for his translations of Aristotle's *Categories* and *De interpretatione;* also for a number of theological writings, among which is the *De Trinitate.*

[3] II, (*PL*, LXIV, 1250).

[4] "Simple" (*simplex*), that is, whatever is a form only, or a form in its entirety.

[5] *PL*, LXIV, 1311.

3. Further, if the soul is a form in its entirety and is in potency to something, it seems that its act of existing (*esse*) above all is its act, for the soul is not its own act of existing.[6] But act will be the simplest thing belonging to a simple potency. Therefore the soul could not be the subject of anything else than its own act of existing. However, it is evident that it is the subject of other things. Therefore the soul is not a simple substance, but is composed of matter and form.

4. Further, accidents proceeding from the form belong to the entire species; however, those coming from matter belong to this or to that individual; for the form is the principle of the species, whereas matter is the principle of individuation. Therefore, if the soul is a form alone, all of its accidents will belong to the entire species. This appears to be false, however, because music and grammar and things of this sort do not belong to the entire species. Therefore the soul is not a form alone, but is composed of matter and form.

5. Further, a form is a principle of action, and matter, the principle of passion [i.e., being-acted-upon]. Therefore anything in which there is action and passion is composed of matter and form. But action and passion are found in the soul itself, because the operation of the possible intellect consists in being-acted-upon (*patiendo*), and for this reason the Philosopher says [7] that to understand is to undergo something. The operation of the agent intellect, on the other hand, consists in acting, for it makes the potentially intelligible, actually intelligible, as is said in the *De anima*.[8] Consequently the soul is composed of form and matter.

6. Further, matter must enter into the composition of anything in which the properties of matter are found to exist. But the properties of matter are present in the soul, namely, to be in potency, to receive, to be a subject, and other things of

---

[6] In finite beings, essence and act of existing (*esse*) are really distinct from each other. See Art. 17, notes 11 and 12.

[7] *De anima*, III, 4 (429b 32).

[8] III, 5 (430a 14 ff.).

this kind. Therefore the soul is composed of matter and form.

7. Further, agents and patients must have a common matter,[9] as is shown in the *De generatione et corruptione*.[10] Hence anything that can be acted upon by something material possesses matter. But the soul can be acted upon by something material, namely, by the fire of hell, which is corporeal fire, as Augustine proves in the *De civitate Dei*.[11] Therefore the soul possesses matter.

8. Further, the action of an agent does not terminate in a form, but in a composite of matter and form, as is shown in the *Metaphysics*.[12] But the action of one agent, namely, God, terminates in the soul. Therefore the soul is composed of matter and form.

9. Further, whatever is a form in its entirety, is at once a being and a unity, and does not require anything to make it a being and a unity, as the Philosopher points out in the *Metaphysics*.[13] The soul, however, requires something which makes it a being and a unity, namely, God, who creates it. Therefore the soul is not a form in its entirety.

10. Further, an agent is necessary in order that something may be reduced from potentiality to actuality. But to be brought from potentiality to actuality belongs only to those things in which there is matter and form. Therefore, if the soul is not composed of matter and form, it does not require an efficient cause; which is clearly false.

11. Further, Alexander [14] says, in the book *De intellectu,* that the soul has a hyleic intellect. Now "hyle" means prime

---

[9] One being cannot act upon another unless there is some common matter between them acting as a common bond. Without it there can be no connection between agent and patient.

[10] I, 7 (324a 34).

[11] XXI, 10 (*PL*, XLI, 725).

[12] VII, 8 (1033b 16).

[13] VIII, 6 (1045b 5).

[14] Alexander of Aphrodisias (c. A.D. 200), one of the famous commentators of Aristotle.

matter. Therefore the soul contains prime matter as a constituent part.

12. Further, whatever exists, is either pure act, pure potency, or is composed of potency and act. However, the soul is not pure act, because this is characteristic of God alone; nor is the soul pure potentiality, for in that case it would not differ from prime matter. Hence the soul is composed of potency and act, and consequently is not a form in its entirety, because a form is an act.

13. Further, whatever is individuated, is individuated by matter. But the soul is not individuated by the matter in which it exists, that is, by the body, because when the body corrupted the individuation of the soul would cease. Therefore the soul is individuated by matter which enters into its constitution, and thus contains matter as an integral part.

14. Further, an agent and a patient must have something in common, as is shown in the *De generatione et corruptione*.[15] But the soul is acted upon by sensible things which are material; nor can it be said that the substance of the sentient soul differs from that of the intellective. Consequently the soul has something in common with material things; and thus it seems that it contains matter.

15. Further, since the soul is not simpler than an angel, it must belong to a genus as a species of that genus, for this is proper to an angel. But whatever belongs to a genus, as one of its species, seems to be composed of matter and form, for a genus has the character of matter, and a specific difference has the character of form.[16] Therefore the soul is composed of matter and form.

16. Further, a form common to [several individuals] is multiplied among these individuals as a result of material division.

[15] I, 7 (324a 34).

[16] That is, a genus is something potential and undetermined like matter, and a specific difference is a determinant like a form. Hence a specific difference determines a genus, just as a form determines a matter.

But intellectuality is a form which is common not only to the souls of men, but to the angels as well. Therefore there must be some matter in the angels and in human souls, through whose division a form of this kind is multiplied among many individuals.

17. Further, whatever is moved contains matter. But the soul is moved, for Augustine shows,[17] in this way, that the nature of the soul is not divine, because it is subject to change. Therefore the soul is composed of matter and form.

On the contrary, everything composed of matter and form, has a form. Therefore, if the soul is composed of matter and form, the soul itself has a form. But the soul is a form. Therefore a form has a form; but this is evidently impossible, because it would result in an infinite regression.

I answer: There are different opinions about this question. Some say that the soul and, indeed, every substance, with the exception of God, is composed of matter and form. The first to maintain this position is Avicebron,[18] the author of the *Fons vitae*. The reason for this position, which is also mentioned in one of the objections (Obj. 6), is this: that matter is found wherever the properties of matter exist. Wherefore, since the properties of matter are found in the soul, namely, to receive, to be in potency, and other things of this kind, Avicebron is of the opinion that there must be matter in the soul. But this argument is silly, and the position itself is impossible.

Now the weakness of this argument becomes apparent if we consider that to receive, to be a subject, and other things of

17 *De spir. et an.*, XL (*PL*, XL, 809). This work was not written by St. Augustine, as St. Thomas points out in Art. XII, ans. obj. 1.

18 Avicebron (1020–70), also called Avicebrol; a Jewish religious poet and philosopher. He is the author of the *Fons vitae*. His most celebrated doctrine is that all created things, even the highest angels, are composed of matter and form. God, however, is pure act.

this sort, are not found in the soul and in prime matter in the same specific way. For prime matter is actuated by means of change and motion, and since every change and motion may be reduced to local motion, as the primary and most universal type of motion, as is proved in the *Physics*,[19] it follows that matter is present only in those things in which there is potency to place (*ab ubi*). Moreover, things of this kind, which are circumscribed by place alone, are corporeal. Hence, in accordance with the way in which the philosophers have spoken about matter, matter is present only in corporeal things; unless, of course, someone wishes to employ matter in an equivocal sense. The soul, however, does not receive something by means of motion and change, but, on the contrary, by being separated from motion and from movable things. Accordingly, it is said in the *Physics*,[20] that the soul becomes cognitive and possesses prudence when at rest. Wherefore the Philosopher also states, in the *De anima*,[21] that intellection is referred to as a passion, but is a passion of a different nature from that present in corporeal things. Therefore, if anyone wishes to conclude that the soul is composed of matter because it is receptive or is acted upon, he is clearly deceived by an equivocation. Consequently it is evident that the aforesaid argument is foolish.

Moreover, it can be shown in several ways that this position is impossible. First, for this reason, that when a form accrues to matter, it constitutes a species. Therefore, if the soul is composed of matter and form, a certain species will be established in the natural order, as a result of the union itself of the form and matter of the soul. However, a thing which possesses a specific nature in its own right, is not united to some other thing in order to constitute a species, unless each is corrupted

---

[19] VIII, 7 (260b 6 ff.); 9 (265b 16 ff.).
[20] VII, 3 (247b 10 ff.).
[21] III, 4 (429a 30 ff.).

in some manner: just as, for example, the elements are united in order to constitute the species of the mixed bodies.[22] The soul, therefore, is not united to the body in order to constitute the human species, but the complete human species is comprised of the soul alone. This is clearly false, for if the body does not belong to the human species, it is joined to the soul in an accidental way.

Moreover, it cannot be said, according to this, that the hand is not composed of matter and form because it does not have a complete species of its own, but is a part of a species; for it is evident that the matter of the hand is not perfected separately by its own form, but that there is one form which perfects at the same time the matter of the whole body and that of all its parts. This could not be said of the soul if it were composed of matter and form. For in that case the matter of the soul would first have to be perfected in the order of nature by its own form, and the body in turn perfected by the soul; unless, perhaps, someone might care to say that the soul's matter is some part of corporeal matter, which is utterly absurd.

The position of Avicebron is also shown to be impossible for this reason, that in everything composed of matter and form, matter occupies the position of that which receives existence, and not that by which something exists; for this is peculiar to the form alone. Therefore, if the soul is composed of matter and form, it is impossible for the entire soul to be the formal principle which gives to the body its act of existing. The whole soul, therefore, will not be the form of the body, but only a part of the soul will be so. The soul, however, is certainly that entity which is the form of the body. Therefore the soul is not that thing which was considered to be a composite of matter and form, but the form of it alone.

This position [of Avicebron] is seen to be impossible also

<hr/>

[22] The "mixed bodies" are bodies which result from some admixture of the elements, and in which the elements remain in a virtual way only. The mixed bodies correspond to what are now called chemical compounds.

for another reason. For if the soul is composed of matter and form, and the body as well, each of them will have its unity in virtue of itself, and then it will be necessary to admit that some third entity exists which unites the soul to the body. Indeed, some of the adherents of the aforesaid position do maintain this. For they say that a soul is united to its body by the instrumentality of light; the vegetal soul by the mediating light of the sidereal heaven, the sentient soul by the mediating light of the crystalline heaven, and the rational soul by the mediating light of the empyrean heaven. These explanations are entirely fictitious, because the soul must be united to the body without any intermediary, just as act is to potency, as is shown in the *Metaphysics*.[23]

It becomes evident, then, that the soul cannot be composed of matter and form. However, act and potency are not excluded from the soul, for potency and act are found not only in immovable things, but in movable things as well; and they are more common here, as the Philosopher points out in the *Metaphysics*,[24] because matter itself may not exist in immovable things. Now the manner in which act and potency are found in the soul must be discovered by proceeding from material things to immaterial ones. For we observe three things in substances composed of matter and form: namely, matter, form, and the act of existing itself, the principle of which is the form; for matter receives an act of existing because it receives a form. Therefore a thing's act of existing is the natural effect of the form itself of that thing. However, the form is not identical with its own act of existing, because the form is the principle of that act of existing. And although matter receives its act of existing only through some form, yet a form as such does not stand in need of matter in order to exist, because the act of existing is the natural effect of the form itself. However, a form requires matter in order to exist when it is a form of that

23 VIII, 6 (1045b 16 ff.).
24 VIII, 5 (1044b 26).

specific type which does not subsist of itself. Consequently a form having its act of existing in itself is not prevented in any way from existing apart from matter, and the act of existing is found in a form of this kind. For the very essence of a form is related to its act of existing as a potency is to its proper act.

It is in this way, then, that both potency and act are found in forms which subsist of themselves, inasmuch as the act of existing itself is the act of a subsisting form which is not its own act of existing. Moreover, if there is a thing which is its own act of existing, and this is proper to God alone, it does not contain potency and act, but is pure act. It is for this reason that Boethius says, in his *De hebdomadibus*,[25] that in the beings which are beneath God in perfection, the act of existing (*esse*) and quiddity (*quod est*) are really distinct; or as some say, *that which is* (*quod est*) and *that by which it is* (*quo est*) differ from each other.[26] For the act of existing itself of a thing is that by which a thing exists; just as running is that by which someone runs. Consequently, since the soul is a certain form which subsists of itself, it can be composed of act and potency, that is, of an act of existing and an essence, but not of form and matter.

Answers to objections. 1. Boethius is speaking here of that form which is absolutely simple, namely, of the divine essence itself, which cannot be a subject in any way whatever because it contains no potency, but is pure act. However, other simple forms such as the angels and the human soul, even though they are subsisting beings, can, nevertheless, be subjects inasmuch as they possess some degree of potentiality which enables them to receive new perfection.

2. The act of existing itself is the highest act in which all things are capable of participating, but the act of existing itself does not participate in anything. Therefore, if there is

---

25 *PL,* LXIV, 1311.
26 That is, *quod est* is the essence, and *quo est* is the act of existing of a thing.

a being which is itself a subsisting act of existing (*ipsum esse subsistens*), just as we speak of God, we say that it does not participate in anything. However, this is not true of other subsisting forms which necessarily participate in the act of existing itself, and which are related to it as potency is to act; and thus, since these forms are in potentiality in some measure, they can participate in something else.

3. Not only is a form related to its act of existing as potency is to act, but, indeed, nothing prevents one from being related to another as potency is to act; just as the transparent medium is related to light, and light in turn to color. Hence, if transparency were a separate form subsisting in virtue of its own nature, it would be receptive not only of an act of existing, but of light as well. Similarly, nothing prevents subsisting forms like the angels and the soul from receiving not only the act of existing itself, but other perfections as well. However, the more perfect subsisting forms of this kind are, the less do they participate in their perfection, seeing that they have more of that perfection in the very principles of their nature.

4. Although human souls are forms in their entirety, nevertheless they are forms individuated in bodies, and are multiplied numerically because of the multiplication of bodies. Consequently, nothing prevents certain accidents which do not belong to the entire species from belonging to these forms inasmuch as they are individuated.

5. The sort of passion which is in the soul, and which is attributed to the possible intellect, does not belong to the same genus as the passions attributed to matter; for in these two cases matter is spoken of equivocally, as is evident from what the Philosopher says in the *De anima;* [27] because the passion of the possible intellect consists in a reception inasmuch as it receives something immaterially. In like manner, the action of the agent intellect is not of the same mode as the action of natural forms, for the action of the agent intellect consists in

[27] III, 4 (430a 3).

abstracting forms from matter, whereas the action of natural agents consists in impressing forms on matter. Consequently it does not follow, from the kind of action and passion present in the soul, that the soul is composed of matter and form.

6. To receive, to be a subject, and other things of this kind, are proper to the soul in a different way from the way they are to prime matter. Therefore it does not follow that the properties of matter are found in the soul.

7. Although the fire of hell, by which the soul is acted upon, is material and corporeal, nevertheless the soul is not acted upon by it in a material way, as material bodies themselves are, but undergoes a spiritual affliction by means of it, inasmuch as it is the instrument of the judgment of divine justice.

8. The action of a generator terminates in something composed of matter and form, because a natural generator only produces something from matter; creative activity, however, does not depend upon matter. Consequently, creative activity does not necessarily have to terminate in a composite of matter and form.

9. Those things which are subsisting forms, in that each is a unity and a being, do not require a formal cause, because they themselves are forms. However, they do require an external cause which gives them existence.

10. An agent, by its motion, brings something from potentiality to act. However, an agent that acts without any motion does not bring something from potentiality to actuality, but gives actual existence to what by nature is potentially existing. Creating is action of this kind.

11. The hyleic intellect, that is, the material intellect, is the name which some men give to the possible intellect, not because it is a material form, but because it bears some likeness to matter inasmuch as it is in potency to intelligible forms, as matter is to sensible forms.

12. Although the soul is neither pure act nor pure potency,

yet it does not follow that it is composed of matter and form, as was shown above (in the Answer to this Art.).

13. The soul is not individuated by any matter of which it is composed, but by reason of its relationship to the matter in which it exists. How this is possible was shown in the preceding questions.[28]

14. The sensitive soul is not acted upon by sensible things, but the soul conjointly with the body; for sensing, which is to undergo something, does not belong to the soul alone, but to the animated organ.

15. The soul does not belong properly to a genus as a species thereof, but as a part of the human species. Therefore it does not follow that it is composed of matter and form.

16. Intelligibility does not belong to many beings, as though it were one specific form divided among many because of a division of matter, for it is a spiritual and immaterial form; rather is it diversified because of a diversity of forms, whether the forms be specifically different, like the soul of a man and an angel, or numerically different only, like the souls of different men.

17. The soul and an angel are called changeable spirits inasmuch as they can be changed by choice; which change, indeed, is from one operation to another. Matter is not required for this kind of change, but only for natural changes, which are changes from one form to another, or from one place to another.

[28] See the *De spiritualibus creaturis,* Arts. II and VIII.

# ARTICLE VII

## WHETHER THE ANGEL AND THE SOUL ARE OF DIFFERENT SPECIES

In the seventh article we examine this question: Whether the angel and the soul are of different species.[1]

Objections. 1. It seems that they are not. For things which possess the same proper and natural operation have the same species, because the nature of a thing is known by its operations. Now the same proper and natural operation of intellection belongs to the soul and to the angel. Consequently the soul and the angel are of the same species.

2. But it will be said that the soul's act of understanding is discursive,[2] whereas the angel's is not.[3] Thus the [proper] operation of the soul and that of the angel are not specifically the same. On the other hand, operations which are specifically diverse are not operations of the same power. But by one and

---

[1] See also *Summa theol.*, Ia, q.75, a.7; *Contra Gentes*, II, 94; *Sent.*, Bk. II, dist. 3, q.1, a.6.

[2] Discourse is "reasoning." St. Thomas defines this term in the following objection, where he points out that "Discourse is a certain movement of the intellect from one thing to another." In the *Summa theol.*, Ia. q.85, a.5, he says: "The human intellect does not acquire perfect knowledge of a thing by its first apprehension, but first apprehends something of the thing, such as its quiddity; . . . and then it understands the properties, accidents, and various dispositions affecting the essence. Thus it necessarily relates one thing to another by composition and division, and from one composition and division it necessarily proceeds to another, and this is reasoning."

[3] In the *Summa theol.*, Ia, q.58, a.3, the Angelic Doctor draws the distinction between human and angelic intellection, pointing out that, whereas human knowledge acquires its full perfection through discourse, angelic knowledge is already perfect and non-discursive. For the angels "in the truths which they know naturally, at once behold all things whatsoever that can be known in them."

the same power, that is, the possible intellect, we understand certain things without discourse, namely, first principles, and understand certain other things discursively, namely, conclusions. Hence understanding discursively and understanding without discourse do not diversify species.

3. Further, to understand discursively and to do so without discourse, are seen to differ as being-in-motion differs from being-at-rest, for discourse is a certain movement of the intellect from one thing to another. But to be in motion and to be at rest do not differ specifically, because a motion belongs to that genus wherein the termination of the motion is found, as the Commentator says in the *Physics*.[4] Hence the Philosopher also says, in the same work,[5] that "there are as many species of motion as there are species of being," that is, terminations of motion. Consequently, to understand discursively and to do so without discourse do not differ specifically from each other.

4. Further, as the angels understand things in the Word, so also do the souls of the blessed. But the knowledge contained in the Word is not discursive. Hence Augustine says, in the *De Trinitate*,[6] that there will be no discursive knowledge in heaven. Therefore the soul does not differ from an angel because the former understands discursively, the latter without discourse.

5. Further, all angels are not specifically the same [7] as many maintain. But every angel understands without discourse. Therefore to understand discursively and to do so without discourse do not cause specific diversity in the case of intellectual substances.

6. But it must be said too that some angels understand more perfectly than others. On the other hand, more and less do not diversify species. But to understand more perfectly and to do so less perfectly, differ only in terms of more and less. There-

---

[4] Averroes, *Comm. in Phys.*, III, 1 (Venice ed., 1560, IV, 71).
[5] *Phys.*, III, 1 (201a 8).
[6] XV, 16 (*PL*, XLII, 1079).
[7] Each angel is a complete species in itself. See *Summa theol.*, Ia, q.50, a.4.

fore angels do not differ in species because some understand more perfectly, others less perfectly.

7. Further, all human souls are of the same species. However, all do not understand equally well. Therefore intellectual substances do not differ specifically from one another because the act of understanding of one is more perfect than that of another.

8. Further, the human soul is said to understand discursively, in view of the fact that it understands a cause through its effect, and vice versa. But this also occurs in angels, for it is said in the book *De causis*,[8] that an intelligence is cognizant of the being that is above it, because it is caused by that being. It also knows the being beneath it because it is the cause of this being. Hence the angel does not differ specifically from the soul because the latter understands discursively and the former without discourse.

9. Further, things perfected by the same perfections evidently belong to the same species, for a particular actuality perfects a particular potency. But the angel and the soul are perfected by the same perfections, namely, grace, glory, and charity. Therefore they are specifically the same.

10. Further, things having the same end are seen to be specifically the same, for a thing is directed to its end by its form, which is the principle of its species. But the end of the angel and that of the soul is the same, namely, eternal beatitude, as is clear from the statement that the children of the resurrection shall be as the angels in heaven (Matt. 22:30). Gregory [9] also says that souls are elevated to the ranks of the angels.[10] Therefore the angel and the soul are specifically the same.

11. Further, if the angel and the soul differ specifically, the angel must be superior to the soul in the order of nature, and

---

[8] *De causis*, VIII. This work, originally attributed to Aristotle, is an Arabian adaptation of Proclus' *Elements of Theology*.

[9] Pope Gregory I, surnamed "the Great" (540–604). He is the author of many works, among which are *Homilies on the Gospels, Dialogues,* and *Morals*.

[10] *In Evang.*, II, 34 (*PL*, LXXVI, 1252).

so will be midway between the soul and God. But there is nothing midway between our soul and God, as Augustine says.[11] Consequently the angel and the soul are not specifically diverse.

12. Further, impressions of the same image in different individuals are not thereby made specifically diverse, for the image of Hercules in gold and that in silver are specifically the same. Now the image of God is present in the soul and in the angel as well. Therefore the angel and the soul do not differ specifically.

13. Further, things having the same definition are specifically the same. But the definition of the angel is the same as that of the soul, for Damascene says [12] that an angel is "an incorporeal substance always moved by free choice, ministering to God by grace, not by nature, and remaining unchanged." Now this is proper to every human soul. Consequently the soul and the angel are specifically the same.

14. Further, things agreeing in an ultimate difference are specifically the same, because an ultimate difference determines the species. But the angel and the soul share a common ultimate difference, namely, the possession of intellectual being. This must be an ultimate difference, because there is nothing nobler [13] than this in the nature of the soul or in that of the angel, for an ultimate difference is always most complete. Therefore the angel and the soul do not differ specifically.

15. Further, things not found in a species, cannot differ specifically. Now the soul is not found in a species, rather is it part of a species. Hence it cannot differ specifically from an angel.

16. Further, the definition coincides expressly with the species. Consequently things not definable apparently do not exist in a species. But the angel and the soul are not definable, be-

---

[11] *De Trin.,* XV, 1 (*PL,* XLII, 1057).

[12] St. John Damascene, author of the *Expositio accurata fidei orthodoxae.* Text cited is *De fide orth.,* II, 3 (*PG,* XCIV, 865).

[13] A specific difference determines a genus, just as an act determines a potency. Hence it is the noblest principle in a thing's nature.

cause they are not composed of matter and form, as has been shown above (Art. II).[14] For in every definition there is something like matter and something like form, as is evident from what the Philosopher says in the *Metaphysics*,[15] where he himself points out that, if the species of things were devoid of matter, as Plato held, they would not be definable. Therefore the angel and the soul cannot properly be said to differ in species.

17. Further, every species is comprised of a genus and a [specific] difference. Now genus and difference have their foundation in different things. For instance, the genus of man, which is "animal," has its foundation in his sensory nature, and his difference, which is "rational," is rooted in his intellective nature. However, in the angel and the soul there are no diversities on which genus and difference can be based, because their essence is constituted of form alone. Furthermore, their act of existing can be neither a genus nor a difference,[16] for the Philosopher proves in the *Metaphysics*,[17] that the act of existing is neither a genus nor a species. Consequently the angel and the soul have neither a genus nor a specific difference, and so cannot differ specifically.

18. Further, things differing specifically, differ through contrary differences. But there is no contrariety in immaterial substances, for contrariety is the principle of corruption. Hence the angel and the soul do not differ specifically.

19. Further, the angel and the soul are seen to differ above all because the angel is not united to a body, whereas the soul is. But this cannot make the soul differ specifically from the angel, since the body is related to the soul as matter, and matter does not give species to form, but rather the reverse. Therefore the angel and the soul do not differ specifically in any way whatever.

[14] See also *De spir. creat.*, Art. I.
[15] VII, 6 (1031b 4).
[16] The act of existing (*esse*) is analogous, whereas genus and species are univocal. Therefore it can be neither a genus nor a difference.
[17] III, 3 (998b 20 ff.).

On the contrary, things differing not specifically, but numerically, differ only because of matter. But the angel and the soul do not have matter, as is clear from the preceding question.[18] Therefore, if the angel and the soul do not differ specifically, neither do they differ numerically; which is evidently false. Therefore it follows that they differ specifically.

I answer: Some say that the human soul and the angels are of the same species, and this seems to have been maintained first by Origen. Wishing to avoid the errors of the ancient heretics,[19] who attributed the diversity of things to different principles by introducing a duality of good and evil, Origen held that the diversity of all things had proceeded from free choice.[20] For he said that God made all rational creatures equally perfect in the beginning: certain of these adhering to God, acquired greater perfection in proportion to the measure of their adherence; others, falling away from God through an act of free choice, descended to positions of lesser importance in proportion to the extent of their fall. Accordingly some were incorporated into the celestial bodies, others were perverted to the point of demonic maliciousness, though all were equally perfect in the beginning. So far as Origen's position [21] is concerned, it can be seen that he regarded the good of singular creatures and neglected to consider the good of the whole. Now a wise artificer arranging the parts [of his work], takes into consideration not only the good of the individual parts, but the good of the whole even more. For this reason a builder does not make all parts of a house equally valuable, but gives them greater or lesser importance inasmuch as this is required for the good disposition of the house. Likewise, in an animal's body, not all parts have the transparency of the eye, because

18 *De spir. creat.*, Art. I.
19 The Gnostics.
20 That is, free choice was the cause not only of evil but of the diversity of things.
21 *Peri Archon,* I, 7 (*PG*, XI, 171).

the animal would then be imperfect, but in an animal's parts there is diversity in order than the animal may be perfect. In the same way, God, in His wisdom, did not make all things in the universe of equal worth, because if He had, the universe, lacking many grades of being, would be imperfect. Consequently to inquire why God, by His activity, made one creature better than another, is the same as asking why an artificer introduced a diversity of parts into his work.

Hence this view of Origen having been shown to be false, there are some who adopt a similar position, claiming that all intellectual substances are specifically the same for the reasons mentioned in the objections. However, this position is seen to be impossible. For if angels and the soul are not composed of matter and form, but are forms alone, as was explained in the preceding question,[22] every difference whereby angels are distinguished from one another, or from the soul as well, must be a formal one; unless perhaps it might be maintained that angels, like souls, were also united to bodies in order that there might be a material difference in them resulting from this relationship with bodies, as we explained above [23] is true of souls. But this view is not commonly held,[24] and even if it were it would not lend any weight to this position, because it is evident that the bodies [which angels would have] would differ specifically from human bodies to which souls are united. Moreover, there must be different specific perfections for bodies that are specifically diverse. Therefore, this position that angels are forms of bodies having been shown to be false, since they are not composed of matter and form, it follows that angels differ from one another, or from the soul, only by reason of a formal difference. But a formal difference diversifies species, for the form gives a thing its mode of existing. Hence it

---

[22] *De spir. creat.*, Art. I.
[23] *Ibid.*, Arts. II, III, IV.
[24] The view that angels have bodies differing from human bodies.

follows that angels not only differ specifically from the soul, but also from each other.

However, even if someone claims that angels and souls are composed of matter and form, this position [that souls and angels are specifically the same] cannot be upheld. For if there were one matter [25] common to angels and souls alike (just as there is one matter for inferior bodies, diversified only by form), the division of that one common matter would have to be the principle whereby angels are made distinct from one another, and from the soul. Now since it is of the very nature of matter in itself to be void of all form, the division of matter could not be understood to exist before it received a form (which form is given a multiple existence as a result of the division of matter), unless matter itself were divided by quantitative dimensions. Hence the Philosopher says in the *Physics*,[26] that substance remains indivisible when quantity is removed. However, things which are composed of matter determined by dimensions are themselves bodies, not merely things united to a body. According to this argument, therefore, the angel and the soul are bodies. Now no one of sound mind maintained this, particularly because it has been proved that intellection cannot be the act of a body. Certainly, if the matter of the angels and that of the soul is not one and common (just as it is maintained that there is not one common matter for celestial and earthly bodies), but belongs to diverse orders, this can only be because it is ordered to different forms and thus material diversity of this sort causes specific diversity.

For this reason it is clearly impossible for the angels and the soul to be specifically the same. However, the way they differ remains to be investigated. We must acquire our knowledge of intellectual substances by considering material sub-

[25] The matter referred to here is "prime matter," which is analogously common to all physical bodies.
[26] I, 2 (185b 3).

stances. Now in material substances different grades of natural perfection constitute different species. Indeed this becomes quite obvious if we reflect upon the genera of material substances. For it is evident that mixed bodies surpass the elements in the order of perfection; plants surpass minerals; animals surpass plants; and in singular genera a diversity of species is found in accordance with the order of natural perfection. For among the elements, earth is lowest, and fire most noble.[27] Likewise in the case of minerals [i.e., mixed bodies], nature is found to ascend by degrees through diverse species up to the species of gold. In plants also, nature ascends progressively up to the species of perfect trees; and in animals up to the species of man. Moreover, certain animals are more like plants, that is the immobile ones which have touch only. Similarly, certain plants are more like inanimate bodies, as is clear from what the Philosopher says in the book *De plantis*.[28]

For this reason the Philosopher, in the *Metaphysics*,[29] says that the species of natural things are like the species of numbers, wherein the addition or subtraction of a unit changes the species. Consequently in immaterial substances also a different grade of natural perfection causes difference in species. But a grade of perfection is in some respect different in the case of immaterial substances from what it is in the case of material substances. For wherever diversity of grades exists, the grades must be considered through their order to some one principle. Therefore in material substances diverse grades are observed to diversify species in relation to the first principle, matter. For this reason first species [i.e., those nearest to matter] are most imperfect, whereas species farther removed [from matter] are more perfect, and related to the first by the addition [of higher perfections]. For instance, mixed bodies have a more perfect species than the elements have, because

[27] The four elements of classical physics were classed in the following order of ascendancy: earth, water, air, and fire.
[28] I, 1 (815b 35 ff.).
[29] VIII, 3 (1043b 33 ff.).

they possess in themselves the perfections of the elements and higher perfections as well. Hence the relation of plants to mineral bodies, and that of animals to plants, is similar.

In the case of immaterial substances the order of diverse grades of species is certainly not considered in relationship to matter, which they do not have, but in relationship to the First Agent [i.e., God], who must be most perfect. Consequently in the case of immaterial substances the first species [i.e., the one nearest to God] is more perfect than the second, inasmuch as the former bears greater likeness to the First Agent. The second species has less perfection than the first, and so on successively down to the last of them. Now the entire perfection of the First Agent consists in this, that He has in one simple nature [30] all His goodness and perfection. Therefore the nearer an immaterial substance is to the First Agent, the more does it have its perfection and goodness in one simple nature, and the less does it require inhering forms for its perfection. This continues progressively down to the human soul which occupies the lowest place [among immaterial substances], just as prime matter holds the lowest place in the genus of sensible things. Hence the soul does not have intelligible forms in its very nature, but is in potency to them, just as matter is to sensible forms. Therefore in order to perform its proper operation, the soul requires to be actuated by intelligible forms by acquiring them from external realities through its sensory powers. And since the operation of a sense is performed through a bodily organ, it is proper to the soul, according to the very condition of its nature, to be united to the body, and to be part of the human species, not having a complete species in itself.

Answers to objections. 1. The act of understanding of the angel and that of the soul are not specifically the same. For it

[30] A reference to the absolute simplicity of the divine nature. See *Summa theol.*, Ia, q.3, a.7.

is evident that if forms, which are principles of operation, differ in species, their operations must differ in species as well. For instance, the act of heating and that of cooling differ from each other because heat and cold differ. Now the intelligible species, through which the soul understands, are abstracted from phantasms, and thus are not of the same nature as the intelligible species through which angels understand, because these are innate in the angels. Accordingly it is said in the book *De causis*,[31] that every intelligence is filled with forms. Therefore the act of understanding of a man and that of an angel are not specifically the same. In view of this difference it follows that the angel understands without any discourse, whereas the human soul understands discursively. It does this of necessity in order to know the powers of causes from their sensible effects, and to understand the essences of things, not perceived by the senses, from their sensible accidents.

2. Therefore the act of understanding discursively and that of understanding without discourse do not differ specifically from each other.

3. A motion is reduced to the genus and species of that particular order in which the motion is terminated, inasmuch as it is the same form that is in potency only before the motion begins, midway between act and potency during the motion itself, in complete act at the termination of the motion. However, an angel's act of understanding, which takes place without any discourse, is not specifically the same as that of the soul so far as the form is concerned. Consequently it is not necessary that these two ways of understanding be specifically one and the same.

4. A thing's species is declared to be such in virtue of the operation that belongs to it by its own nature, and not in virtue of one that belongs to it because it participates in a higher nature. The species of iron, for instance, is not judged to be such because it is combustible, which belongs to it inasmuch

[31] *De causis*, X.

as it is set on fire, for then the species of iron and that of wood, which also may be set on fire, would be considered to be the same. Moreover, I say that the act of intellection in the Word is an operation surpassing the nature of the soul and that of an angel, yet proper to each according as they participate in a superior nature, namely, the divine nature, through the light of glory. Consequently it cannot be concluded that an angel and the soul are specifically the same.

5. Intelligible species are not of the same nature in different angels; for the more superior an intellectual substance is, and the nearer to God (whom all understand through one thing, His essence), the more elevated are the intelligible forms within that substance, and thus more capable of knowing many things. Wherefore it is said in the book *De causis*,[32] that superior intelligences understand through more universal forms. Dionysius also says [33] that superior angels have greater universal knowledge. Therefore the act of understanding of different angels is not specifically the same, although each takes place without discourse, because they understand through innate species and not through species received in some other way.

6. More and less are found in things in two ways. First, according as matter participates in different ways in the same form, as wood participates in whiteness. In this way more and less do not cause things to differ in species. Secondly, according as more and less are found in the different grades of perfection of forms. This causes difference in species. For colors differ in species by being related more or less closely to light. This is the way in which more and less are found in different angels.

7. Although all souls do not understand equally well, nevertheless all understand through species of the same nature, namely, those derived from phantasms. Hence the fact that men do not understand equally well is a result of the dif-

[32] *Ibid.*
[33] *De cael. hier.*, XII, 2 (*PG*, III, 292).

ference in their sensory powers through which species are abstracted. This results in turn from the different disposition of their bodies. Consequently it is evident, according to this, that more and less do not cause difference in species, since they are a consequence of material diversity.

8. To be cognizant of one thing through another occurs in two ways. First, when something known is understood through the knowledge of some other thing in such a way that there is a distinct knowledge of each, as a man knows conclusions from principles by considering both [the principles and the conclusions] separately. Secondly, when something known is understood through the species whereby it is understood, as when we see a stone through the species of the stone, which [species] exists in the eye. Now it is in this way that angels know a cause through an effect and an effect through a cause, inasmuch as the essence itself of the angel bears some likeness to its cause, while the angel in turn causes its effect to be like itself.

9. The perfections of grace befit the soul and the angel by a participation in the divine nature. Hence it is said: "By whom He hath given us most great and precious promises: that by these you may be made partakers of the divine nature: flying the corruption of that concupiscence which is the world" (II Pet. 1:4). Therefore it cannot be concluded that the angel and the soul are specifically the same because they have these perfections in common.

10. Things having one and the same proximate and natural end are one and the same specifically. However, eternal beatitude is an ultimate and supernatural end. Therefore the conclusion stated in the objection does not follow.

11. Augustine understands that there is nothing midway between our mind and God so far as the grades of dignity and of nature are concerned, not because one nature is not nobler than another, but because our mind is immediately justified by God and beatified in Him; just as if it might be said, for example, that a simple soldier is immediately under the king,

not because there are no others superior to him under the king, but because no one has dominion over him except the king.

12. Neither the soul nor an angel is a perfect image of God, but the Son alone. Consequently it is not necessary that the angel and the soul possess the same species.

13. The aforesaid definition is not applicable to the soul in the same way as it is to an angel, for an angel is an incorporeal substance, because it is not a body nor is it united to a body. This cannot be said of the soul.

14. To maintain that the soul and the angel are specifically the same makes them, for this reason, equal in power. But this does not necessarily follow, for the ultimate difference should be nobler, not only with respect to nobility of nature, but also with respect to the way in which the nature is determined; because the ultimate difference is like an act in relation to all preceding differences. Consequently the angel is nobler than the soul not because it is intellectual, but because it is intellectual in some particular way. This is evident in sensible things, otherwise all brute animals would be of the same species.

15. The soul is a part of a species, and is also a principle conferring species. The species of the soul is investigated in this way.

16. Although a species alone may be properly defined, yet it is not necessary that every species be definable. For the species of immaterial things are known neither by definition nor by demonstration, as something is known in the speculative sciences, but some of them are known by a simple intuition. Consequently an angel cannot properly be defined, for we do not know what its essence is; but it can be known by certain negations or distinguishing characteristics. Again, the soul is defined inasmuch as it is the form of the body.

17. Genus and difference can be regarded in two ways. First, from an existential point of view, so far as they are considered

by metaphysics and by natural philosophy. Here it is manifest that genus and difference are based on different natures. Thus nothing prevents us from saying that there is no genus and difference in spiritual substances, but that they are forms in their entirety, and simple species. Genus and difference can also be regarded from the logical point of view. In this case it is not necessary that genus and difference be founded on different natures, but on one and the same nature in which something proper and something common may be distinguished. In this way nothing prevents us from distinguishing genus and difference in spiritual substances.

18. Speaking of genus and difference from the point of view of the real order, differences must be contraries. For matter, on which the nature of genus is based, is receptive of contrary forms. However, from the point of view of logic, any opposition whatever in differences is sufficient, as is clear in the differences between numbers in which there is no contrariety. It is similar in the case of spiritual substances.

19. Although matter is not the basis of species, nevertheless the nature of a form is considered according to the relationship of matter to form.

# ARTICLE VIII

## WHETHER THE RATIONAL SOUL SHOULD BE UNITED TO A BODY SUCH AS MAN POSSESSES

In the eighth article we examine this question: Whether the rational soul should be united to a body such as man possesses.[1]

Objections. 1. It seems that it should not. For the rational soul is the subtlest of all forms united to a body. Now earth is the lowest of all [elemental] bodies. Therefore the soul is not fittingly united to an earthly body.

2. But in view of the fact that an earthly body is reduced to a harmonious combination [of the elements], it must be said that such a body is similar to a celestial body, which is without contraries altogether, and thus is ennobled in order that a rational soul may be fittingly united to it. On the other hand, if the nobility of the human body consists in its likeness to a celestial body, it follows that a celestial body is nobler. But the rational soul is nobler than all other forms, because it transcends all bodies by its intellectual capacity. Therefore the rational soul should be united rather to a celestial body.

3. But it must be said that a celestial body is perfected by a nobler perfection than the rational soul. On the other hand, if the perfection of a celestial body is nobler than that of a rational soul, it must be intelligent, because any intelligent being is nobler than any non-intelligent being whatever. Therefore, if a celestial body is perfected by an intellectual

---

[1] See also *Summa theol.,* Ia, q.76, a.5; *Contra Gentes,* II, 90; *Sent.,* Bk. II, dist. 1, q.2, a.5; *De malo,* q.5, a.5.

substance, this substance will be either the mover only of such a body, or will be its form. If it is only a mover, it follows that the human body is perfected in a nobler way than a celestial body is, for a form gives species to the thing of which it is the form, whereas a mover does not. Again, nothing prevents certain things ignoble by nature from being instruments of the noblest agent. However, if an intellectual substance is the form of a celestial body, such a substance has either an intellect alone, or senses and other powers together with an intellect. If it has senses and other powers, it follows that a celestial body is an organic body, because powers of this sort must be the acts of organs, which are required for the operations of such powers. This is opposed to the simplicity, uniformity, and unity of a celestial body. If, indeed, such a substance has an intellect alone and receives nothing from sense, then it does not need to be united to a body, because the operation of an intellect is not performed through a bodily organ. Therefore, since the body is united to the soul not for the sake of the body but for that of the soul (because any matter exists for the sake of form, and not vice versa), it follows that an intellectual substance is not united as a form to a celestial body.

4. Further, every created intellectual substance is capable of sinning by reason of its nature, because it can turn away from the Highest Good, which is God. Therefore, if intellectual substances were united [substantially] as forms to celestial bodies, it would follow that they could commit sin. But the punishment for sin is death, that is, the separation of the soul from the body, and the punishment of the sinners in hell. Consequently it could happen that celestial bodies would corrupt by having their souls separated from them, and that these souls would be cast into hell.

5. Further, every intellectual substance is capable of attaining beatitude. Therefore, if celestial bodies are animated by intellectual souls, such souls are capable of beatitude; and

thus not only angels and men, but also certain intermediate natures [2] enjoy eternal beatitude. However, when the holy doctors consider this matter, they say that the society of the blessed is composed of men and angels.

6. Further, the body of Adam was proportioned to a rational soul. But our body is unlike his, for his body was immortal and unchangeable before he sinned. Our bodies do not have these characteristics. Therefore bodies such as we possess are not proportioned to a rational soul.

7. Further, the best disposed instruments, and those which cooperate in operation, belong to the noblest mover. Now the rational soul is nobler than all other inferior movers.[3] Hence the rational soul should have a body that cooperates with it to the fullest extent in carrying out its operations. However, a body such as ours is not of this sort, because the flesh lusts against the spirit (Gal. 5:17), and the soul is drawn here and there as a result of the struggle between concupiscences. Consequently the rational soul should not be united to a body such as we possess.

8. Further, an abundance of spirits [4] falls to the lot of a rational soul in a perfectible body. Hence in contrast to other animals, the heart of man is the hottest so far as the power of generating spirits is concerned. The human body's erectness, resulting from the power of heat and spirits, is a sign of this. Therefore it would be most fitting for the rational soul to be united entirely to a spiritual body.

9. Further, the soul is an incorruptible substance. However, our bodies are corruptible. Consequently rational souls are not fittingly united to bodies such as we possess.

10. Further, the rational soul is united to the body in order

---

[2] If a celestial body possessed a soul, its nature would be midway between that of the human soul and that of an angel.

[3] That is, movers in the lowest sphere, the earth.

[4] Allusion to the ancient belief that the heart by its natural heat produced certain "animal spirits" which passed through the body and accounted for most of its vital operations.

to constitute the human species. Now the human species would be better preserved if the body to which the rational soul is united, were incorruptible, because then it would not be necessary for the human species to be preserved by generation, for it would be preserved numerically in the same individuals. Hence the human soul should be united to an incorruptible body.

11. Further, the human body, being the noblest of inferior bodies, should resemble most a celestial body, which is the noblest of bodies. However, a celestial body lacks contrariety altogether. Therefore the human body ought to have the least contrariety. But our bodies do not have the least contrariety, because other bodies, such as stones and trees, are more enduring, and contrariety is the principle of disintegration. Consequently the rational soul should not be united to bodies such as we have.

12. Further, the soul is a simple form. Now a simple matter befits a simple form. Hence the rational soul should be united to some simple body such as fire or gold or something of this kind.

13. Further, the human soul seems to have something in common with principles. Hence the ancient philosophers maintained that the soul is composed of principles, as is clear in the *De anima*.[5] Now the principles of bodies are the elements. Therefore, if the soul is not an element, nor composed of elements, it should at least be united to some elementary body such as fire or gold, or something of this sort.

14. Further, bodies composed of similar parts come closer to being simple than bodies composed of dissimilar parts. Consequently the soul should be united to a body composed of similar parts rather than to one composed of dissimilar parts, because the soul is a form in its entirety (*simplex*).

15. Further, the soul is united both as a form and as a mover to the body. Therefore the rational soul, which is the noblest

[5] I, 2 (404b 7 ff.).

of forms, should be united to a body best adapted for movement. But we see that the contrary of this is true, for the bodies of birds and those of many other animals as well, are better adapted for movement than the human body is.

16. Further, Plato says [6] that forms are conferred by the giver of forms according to the merits of matter, which are called material dispositions. But apparently the human body does not have a disposition in keeping with the nobility of its form, for the body is "gross" and corruptible. Therefore the soul should not be united to such a body.

17. Further, the intelligible forms existing in the human soul, in contrast to those in superior intellectual substances, are in the highest degree representative of particulars. But such forms befit the operation of a celestial body, which is the cause of the generation and corruption of these particulars. Consequently the human soul should be united to a celestial body.

18. Further, nothing is moved naturally so long as it occupies its [proper place], but only when it is outside its proper place.[7] However, a heaven is moved while it exists in its [proper] place. Therefore it is not moved naturally. Consequently it is moved with respect to place by a soul, and thus has a soul united to it.

19. Further, "to proclaim" is an act of an intellectual substance. But "the heavens proclaim the glory of God," as is said in the Psalms (Ps. 18:5). Hence the heavens are intelligent, and therefore possess an intellective soul.

20. Further, the soul is the most perfect of forms. Therefore it should be united to a most perfect body. However, the human body seems to be most imperfect, for it neither has arms

---

[6] *Laws*, XXXIV.

[7] According to Aristotle, the four simple bodies (i.e., the four elements) fall into two pairs, each pair having its proper place or region. "Earth and water" move toward the "center" of the universe, which constitutes their proper place; "air and fire" tend upward toward the "limit" (outer boundary of the universe), which is their proper place. See *De gen. et corr.*, II, 3 (330b 30 ff.).

to defend itself and to fight, nor covering nor anything of this sort which nature has bestowed on the bodies of other animals. Therefore a soul of this kind should not be united to a body such as ours.

On the contrary, it is said: "God created man of the earth and made him after His image" (Eccles. 17:1). But the works of God are fitting works, for it is said: "God saw what He had made and that His works were good" (Gen. 1:4). Therefore the rational soul, in which the image of God exists, is fittingly united to an earthly body.

I answer: Since matter exists for the sake of form and not vice versa, we must discover, on the side of the soul, the reason why the body should be united to it. Hence it is said, in the *De anima*,[8] that the soul is not only the form and mover of the body but also its end. Moreover, it is evident, from the preceding Disputed Questions,[9] that it is natural for the human soul to be united to the body. For, although the soul is lowest in the order of intellectual substances (as primary matter is lowest in the order of sensible things), it does not have intelligible species naturally impressed on it, as superior intellectual substances have, whereby it can perform its proper operation of intellection; but is in potency to them because it is like a wax tablet on which nothing is written, as is said in the *De anima*.[10] For this reason it must receive its intelligible species from external things through its sensory powers, which cannot perform their proper operations without bodily organs. Consequently it is necessary for the human soul to be united to a body.

Therefore, if the human soul is capable of being united to a body, because it needs to receive intelligible species from

[8] II, 4 (415b 10).
[9] *De spiritualibus creaturis*, Art. III.
[10] III, 4 (429b 32).

things through the intermediary of the senses, then the body, to which the rational soul is united, must be one which can most adequately present to the intellect those sensible species from which are derived the intelligible species existing in the intellect. Hence the body to which the rational soul is united must be best disposed for sensory operation. But although there are several sensory powers, still there is one which is the basis of the others, namely, touch, in which every sensible nature is principally rooted. For this reason it is also said in the *De anima*,[11] that an animal derives its name from this sense. This is the reason why, when this sense is unmoved, as occurs during sleep, all other senses are unmoved. Again, not only are all the other senses rendered inactive by an excess of their proper sensible [objects],[12] as sight, for instance, is made inoperative by very bright objects, and hearing by too intense sounds, but so also is the sense of touch rendered incapable of performing its proper operation (*solvuntur*) by an excess of its sensible object, for example, excessive warmth or cold. Therefore, since the body to which the rational soul is united must be best disposed for a sentient nature, it must have the most competent organ of touch. And so it is said in the *De anima*,[13] that among all animals we have this sense to a greater degree, and also that one man is more adept than another in intellectual operations as a result of this sense. For we see that those who have tender flesh (those who are of good touch) are well-endowed mentally.

Now since the organ of any sense must not possess actually any of the contraries of which a sense is perceptive, but must be in potency to them in order that it may be able to receive them (because the recipient must be deprived of the thing received), the case must be otherwise for the organ of touch than it is for the organs of the other senses. For the organ of

11 II, 2 (413b 8).
12 See Art. XVI, note 4.
13 II, 9 (421a 20).

sight, that is, the pupil of the eye, is deprived completely of
white and of black, and of every kind of color whatever. It is
similar in the case of hearing and smell. But this cannot occur
in the case of the sense of touch, for touch is capable of experiencing those qualities which the animal body must be composed of, namely, hot and cold, wet and dry.[14] For this reason
it is impossible for the organ of touch to be deprived completely of its sensible objects; rather must it be reduced to a
mean, because in this way it is in potency to contraries. Therefore, since the body to which the rational soul is united must
be best disposed for the sense of touch, it must be brought in
the fullest measure to an intermediate state by the harmonious
combination [of its constituent elements and their qualities].

In this way it is evident that the total operation of an inferior
nature reaches its highest peak in man as a most perfect being.
For we see that the operation of nature ascends progressively
from the simple elements, by blending them, until it reaches
the most perfect mode of combination, which is the human
body. Consequently this disposition of the human body, to
which the rational soul is united, must exist in order that the
body may possess the most tempered combination.

Moreover, if anyone also wishes to examine the particular
dispositions of the human body, he will find them ordered to
this end, that man may have the best sense. Therefore man, in
proportion to his size, has a larger brain than any other animal,
because a good disposition of the brain is necessary for the
good condition of the internal sentient powers, namely, the
imagination, the memory, and the cogitative power.[15] And
in order that his operation may be freer, he has his head placed

14 Each of these is a proper quality of one of the four elementary bodies. Terrestrial things, being composed of various proportions of the four elements,
manifest the qualities of these elements.

15 The internal senses are four in number, namely, common sense (sensus
communis), imagination, memory, cogitative power or particular reason (estimative power in the brute).

on high. For man is the only erect animal, the others, indeed, are bent over. Furthermore, in order to have this erectness and to preserve it, there must exist in the heart an abundance of heat (by which many spirits are generated) so that the body may be maintained erect by this copious amount of heat and spirits. The fact that a man stoops over when he is old is a sign of this, because his natural heat is diminished.

In the light of what is stated above, the nature of a disposition of the human body must be determined in relation to the particular [dispositions] proper to man. However, we must take into consideration that in those things which are constituted of matter, some dispositions exist in the matter itself, and that on account of these a definite matter is chosen for a definite form. There are also some dispositions which proceed from the necessary character of matter, and not from the choice of the agent. For instance, when an artisan chooses hardness in iron to make a saw in order that it may be useful for sawing. But the fact that sharpness can be given to iron, and that it can rust, results from the necessary character of matter. For the artisan would rather choose a matter in which defects are not present, if it could be found. But because it cannot be found, the artisan does not neglect to work with the available matter of this kind simply because of the defects intrinsic to such matter. This also occurs in the human body, for, likewise, whatever is combined and disposed according to parts in order that such a body may be best fitted for sentient operations, is selected in this matter by the Maker of man. But that this body is corruptible, that it may become fatigued, and have defects of this kind, follows from the necessary character of this matter. For the body, as a mixture of contraries, must be subject to such defects. Nor can any objection be raised in view of the fact that God could make it otherwise,[16] because we do not investigate what God could make in the establishment of

16 See Art. XXI, note 7.

nature, but what the nature of things undergoes as made, as Augustine says in the *Super Genesim ad litteram*.[17]

Moreover, it must be recognized that when God remedied these defects in man at his creation, He employed the help of original justice whereby the body was made subject completely to the soul and the soul to God, so that neither death nor passion nor any defect could affect man unless the soul were first separated from God. But when the soul turned away from God through sin, man was deprived of this gift, and is subject to the defects which are intrinsic to the nature of matter.

*Answers to objections.* 1. The soul, being intellectual, is the subtlest of forms, but it is lowest in the order of intellectual forms, and must be united to a body in order to acquire intelligible species through the senses. This union is effected through a combination of the elements. The body, to which the soul is united, had to contain a greater quantity of the heavy elements, namely, of earth and water [than the light elements, fire and air]. For fire is the most active of all the elements. If the lower elements [earth and water] were not present in greater quantity, the aforesaid combination could not be brought about nor above all be reduced to a mean, because fire would consume the other elements. For this reason the Philosopher, in the *De generatione et corruptione*,[18] states that earth and water are more abundant [than air and fire] in mixed bodies.

2. The rational soul is united to this kind of body, not because it is like a celestial body, but because it is composed of a harmonious combination [of the elements]. But it follows that it bears some likeness to a celestial body, in this way, by being relatively independent of contraries. However, according to the opinion of Avicenna,[19] the soul is united to such a

---

17 II, 1 (*PL*, XXXIV, 263).

18 II. 8 (334b 31).

19 Avicenna (980–1037), Arabian philosopher and physician. One of the famous commentators of Aristotle. See Art. XV, note 15.

body particularly because of its likeness to a celestial body. For he desired that inferior things be caused by the superior beings, in order that inferior bodies might be caused by the celestial bodies. And [he maintained] that these inferior bodies possess a form similar to that of a celestial body (which is considered to be animated), since such inferior bodies bear some likeness to celestial bodies because of their harmonious combination.

3. There is a diversity of opinion, both among philosophers and among the doctors of the faith, concerning the animation of the celestial bodies. For among the philosophers, Anaxagoras [20] maintained that the agent intellect was altogether simple (*immixtum*) and existed apart from things, and that the celestial bodies were inanimate. Hence it is said that he was even condemned to death because he claimed that the sun was a fiery stone, as Augustine relates in the work *De civitate Dei*.[21] Other philosophers, indeed, maintained that the celestial bodies are animated. Some of these stated that God is the soul of the heavens, which was idolatrous inasmuch as it attributed divine worship to the heavens and the heavenly bodies. Others, indeed, such as Plato and Aristotle, who, although they claimed that the celestial bodies are animated, nevertheless maintained that God is a supreme being, quite distinct from the soul of the heavens. Among the doctors of the faith as well, Origen [22] and his followers held that such bodies are inanimate, as Damascene did.[23] This is also the more common position among modern theologians. That Augustine remained in doubt [on the question, is shown in] the *Super Genesim ad litteram*,[24] and in the work *Enchiridion*.[25] Therefore, holding this for

---

[20] Anaxagoras (500–428 B.C.), early Greek philosopher. He is noted for his doctrine of the *nous*, or world-governing reason. See Aristotle, *Metaph.*, I, 4 (985a 18).
[21] XVIII, 41 (*PL*, XLI, 601).
[22] *Peri Archon*, II, 7 (*PG*, XI, 172).
[23] *De fide orth.*, II, 6 (*PG*, XCIV, 885).
[24] II, 18 (*PL*, XLIV, 885).
[25] 58 (*PL*, XL, 260).

a fact, that the celestial bodies are moved by an intellect which
is separate, we say (maintaining both positions on account of
the arguments supporting both sides) that an intellectual substance, as a form, is the perfection of the celestial body, and
that it has an intellective power alone but no sensory power, as
can be seen from the words of Aristotle in the *De anima* [26] and
in the *Metaphysics*,[27] even though Avicenna maintains that the
soul of the heavens has an imagination in addition to its intellect. However, if it has an intellect only, it is still united as a
form to the body, not for the sake of intellectual operation,
but for the sake of executing its active power according to
which it can attain a certain likeness to divine causality by
moving the heavens.

4. Although all created intellectual substances by nature
are capable of committing sin, still many are preserved from
so doing by divine choice and predestination through the aid
of grace. One can maintain that the souls of the celestial bodies
are among this number, particularly if the demons who sinned
were of an inferior order, as Damascene held.[28]

5. If the celestial bodies are animated, their souls belong to
the society of the angels. For Augustine says in the *Enchiridion:* [29] "I do not hold for certain that the sun and moon, and
the other stars belong to the same society," namely, that of
the angels, "for although some are luminous bodies, still they
do not appear to be sentient or intellective."

6. The body of Adam was made proportionate to a human
soul, as was explained, not only with respect to what nature
requires, but also with respect to what grace conferred. Now,
we are deprived of this grace, but our nature remains the same.

7. The struggle which occurs in man as a result of contrary
concupiscences, also results from the necessary character of

[26] II, 1 (413a 6).
[27] XI, 2 (1060a 10 ff.).
[28] *De fide orth.*, II, 4 (*PG*, XCIV, 874).
[29] 58 (*PL*, L, 260).

matter. For, given the fact that man has sense, it is necessary that he sense delectable objects, and that he pursue his concupiscence for such objects, which is generally opposed to reason. But in the state of innocence, man was also given a remedy against this through grace so that the inferior powers were not moved in any way contrary to reason. However, man lost this through sin.

8. Although spirits are the vehicles of powers, they still cannot be organs of the senses. Therefore the human body could not be composed of spirits alone.

9. Corruptibility is a result of the defects which belong intrinsically to the human body from the necessary character of matter. This is particularly true after man sinned, because sin removes the assistance of grace.

10. Whatever is better must necessarily exist in those things which exist for an end, but not in those things which are a result of the necessary character of matter. For it would be better if an animal body were incorruptible, and if this were permitted by nature, an animal form would require such a matter.

11. Those things which are most akin in nature to the elements, and possess greater contrariety, such as stones and metals, are more enduring, because in them the elements are less subtly proportioned (*harmonia*), and thus they are not easily disintegrated. For the blending of the elements in those things which are subtly proportioned, is easily destroyed. Notwithstanding, the cause of longevity in animals is attributed to the fact that the moisture which they contain is not easily dried up or made inactive, nor is their heat easily extinguished, because heat and moisture are indispensable for life. Moreover, this is found in man to the extent that it is necessary for a combination [of the elements] reduced to a mean. Hence in men some combinations are more enduring, others less so, and as a result of this some men live longer than others.

12. The human body could not be a simple body,[30] nor could it be a celestial body, because of the determinable character of a sense organ, particularly that of touch. Nor could it be a simple elementary body, because actual contraries exist in an element, whereas the human body must be reduced to a mean.

13. The nature philosophers [31] of antiquity thought that the soul, which knows all things, must actually be like all things. And therefore they maintained that the soul possessed the nature of an element, which they held was the principle from which all things are said to be constituted, so that in this way the soul knew all things inasmuch as it was like all things. However, Aristotle later showed that the soul knows all things inasmuch as it is like all things potentially, not actually. Consequently the body to which it is united must be composed not of extremes but of a mean, so that it may thus be in potency to contraries.

14. Although a soul is simple in essence, yet it has many powers. And the more numerous its powers, the more perfect will it be. For this reason it requires an organic body constituted of dissimilar parts.

15. The soul is not united to the body for the sake of local motion; rather is the local motion of man, like that of other animals, directed to conserving the body which is united to the soul. But the soul is united to the body for the sake of intellection, which is its proper and principal operation. For this reason the body, being united to the rational soul, must be best disposed to serve the soul with respect to the things necessary for intellection. It is also necessary that the body possess agility

---

30 The simple bodies are the four elements (earth, water, air, and fire) and the celestial bodies.

31 The "Ionian physicists": Thales, Anaximander, and Anaximenes. This group tried to explain the constitution of things by one simple material principle. Thales suggested water; Anaximander, the "boundless"; Anaximenes, "air." See Aristotle, *Metaph.*, I, 3 (983b 7 ff.).

and other things of this kind, so far as such a disposition permits this.

16. Plato maintained that the form of things subsisted of themselves, and that the participation of forms by material things is for the sake of material things inasmuch as they are thereby perfected, and not for the sake of the forms themselves, which subsist of themselves. From this it follows that forms are given to material things so far as they merit them. Now according to the view of Aristotle, natural forms do not subsist of themselves. Hence a form is united to matter not for the sake of matter, but for the sake of form. Therefore a certain form is given to matter not because matter is so disposed, but because a certain form requires matter to be so disposed. For this reason it was said above that the human body is disposed in a manner befitting such a form as the human soul.

17. Although a celestial body is the cause of the particular things which are generated and corrupted, nevertheless it causes them as a common agent. For this reason determinate agents of a particular species are required beneath it. Hence it is not necessary for the mover of a celestial body, whether it be a soul or a separate mover, to have particular forms, but only universal ones. Now Avicenna maintained [32] that the soul of a celestial body had to have an imagination through which it could apprehend particulars. For the soul of a heaven, being the cause of its motion, must know the here and the now, and therefore must have some sensory power, because it is the cause of the celestial motion whereby a heaven revolves in this or that [particular] place. But this is not necessary. First, indeed, because celestial motion is always uniform and is not hindered, and therefore a universal conception is sufficient to cause such movement. For a knowledge of the particular is required in the case of animal movements on account of the irregularity of such movement, and because obstacles can

[32] *Metaph.*, X, 1.

hinder such movement. Secondly, because superior intellectual substances can apprehend particulars without a sensory
power, as was shown elsewhere.

18. The movement of a heaven is natural on account of a
passive principle or of movement received, because such movement belongs naturally to such a body. But the active principle
of this movement is a certain intellectual substance. Now the
statement that no body is moved naturally when it is in its
proper place, is understood of a body moved by rectilinear
movement, and this body changes place with respect to the
whole of itself not only from the point of view of reason, but
also from that of the subject itself. But a body which is moved
circularly does not change place with respect to the whole of
itself [from the point of view of the subject] but only from that
of reason. Hence it never is outside its [proper] place.

19. This argument is foolish despite the fact that Rabbi
Moses proposes it. Because, if "to proclaim" is taken in its
proper sense, when it is said that "the heavens proclaim the
glory of God," the heavens would require not only an intellect
but also a tongue. Therefore the heavens are said to proclaim
the glory of God, if taken in a literal sense, inasmuch as
through them the glory of God is made manifest to men. In
this way, also, insensible creatures are said to praise God.

20. Other animals have a natural estimative power directed
to definite activities, and therefore nature could provide them
sufficiently with certain definite aids. But not so in the case of
man who is capable of an unlimited number of conceptions
because of his reason. And therefore, in place of all the aids
which other animals possess by nature, man has an intellect,
which is a mirror of all forms, and hands, which are the organs
of organs, whereby he can provide for himself whatever he
requires.

## WHETHER THE SOUL IS UNITED TO CORPOREAL MATTER THROUGH A MEDIUM

In the ninth article we examine this question: Whether the soul is united to corporeal matter through a medium.[1]

Objections. 1. It seems that the soul is united to the body in this way, because it is stated in the work *De spiritu et anima*,[2] that the soul has powers (*vires*) by which it is united to the body. But the powers of the soul are distinct from the soul's essence. Therefore the soul is united to the body through some medium.

2. But it must be said that the soul is united through the medium of its powers to the body as the mover of the latter and not as its form. On the other hand, the soul is the form of the body inasmuch as it is an act, but is a mover inasmuch as it is a principle of operation. And certainly a thing is a principle of operation inasmuch as it is an act, because a thing acts inasmuch as it is actual. Hence the soul is the form and mover of the body in the same respect. Consequently no distinction is to be drawn between the soul as the mover of the body and as its form.

3. Further, inasmuch as the soul is the mover of the body, it is not united to the body accidentally, because then a being that is substantially one (*unum per se*) would not result from the union of soul and body. Therefore the soul is united to the body substantially. But whatever is united to a thing substanti-

---

[1] See also *Summa theol.*, Ia, q.76, a.6; a.7; *Contra Gentes*, II, 71; *Sent.*, Bk. II, dist. 1, q.2, a.4, ad 3um; *Quodl.*, XII, q.6, a.9; *De spir. creat.*, a.3; *Comm. in Metaph.*, Bk. VIII, lect 5.

[2] X (*PL*, XL, 785).

ally, is united to it without a medium. Consequently the soul is not united as a mover to the body through a medium.

4. Further, the soul is united as a mover to the body inasmuch as it is the body's principle of operation. However, the soul's operations do not belong to the soul alone, but to the composite, as is pointed out in the *De anima*,[3] and thus there is no medium between the soul and the body so far as the soul's operations are concerned. Hence the soul, inasmuch as it is the mover of the body, is not united to the body through a medium.

5. Further, it seems that the soul, as a form, is united to the body through a medium. For a form is not united to any kind of matter but to one befitting it (*propria*). Now the matter of any particular form is prepared to receive that form through proper dispositions which are proper accidents of a thing, just as hot and dry are proper accidents of fire. Therefore, a form is united to its matter through the medium of proper accidents. But the proper accidents of living things are the powers of their soul. Therefore, as a form, the soul is united through the medium of its powers to the body.

6. Further, an animal is a thing that moves itself. But a thing that moves itself is divided into two parts, one of which is a mover, the other a thing moved, as is proved in the *Physics*.[4] Now the part causing movement is a soul; however, the moved part cannot be matter alone, because whatever is in potency only is not moved, as is said in the *Physics*.[5] Hence although heavy and light bodies have movement in themselves, they do not move themselves because they are divided only into matter and into form, which cannot be moved. It follows, then, that an animal is divided into a soul and into some part which is composed of matter and form. Consequently the soul is united to corporeal matter by means of some form.

[3] I, 4 (408b 11).
[4] VIII, 4 (254b 15 ff.).
[5] V, 1 (225a 20 ff.).

7. Further, the proper matter of any form is given in the definition of that form. Now "a physical organic body potentially having life" is given in the definition of the soul inasmuch as it is the form of the body, as is evident in the *De anima*.[6] Consequently the soul is united to such a body as its proper matter. But "a physical organic body potentially having life" can exist as such only because of some form. Therefore the soul is united to its matter through some form which first perfects its matter.

8. Further, it is said: "God made man from the slime of the earth and breathed into his face the breath of life" (Gen. 2:7). Now the breath of life is the soul. Hence some form exists in matter prior to its union with the body, and thus the soul is united to corporeal matter through the medium of some other form.

9. Further, forms are united to matter so far as matter is in potency to them. But matter is first in potency to the forms of the elements rather than to other forms. Consequently the soul and other forms are united to matter only through the intermediary forms of the elements.

10. Further, the body of a man and that of an animal are mixed bodies. But the forms of the elements must remain essentially in a mixed body, otherwise there would be a corruption of the elements and not a mixture. Therefore the soul is united to matter through the medium of other forms.

11. Further, the intellective soul as such is a form. But its act of understanding is accomplished with the aid of its other powers. Therefore the soul, inasmuch as it is a form, is united to the body through the medium of these other powers.

12. Further, the soul is not united to any sort of body, but to one proportioned to it. Therefore there must be a proportion between the soul and the body; and thus the soul is united to the body by means of a proportion.

13. Further, a thing operates in something remote through

[6] II, 1 (412a 28).

that which is closest to itself. But the powers of the soul are diffused throughout the whole body by the heart. Therefore the heart is nearer to the soul than the other parts of the body, and thus the soul is united to the body by means of the heart.

14. Further, a diversity of parts mutually related are present in the body. However, the soul is simple so far as its essence is concerned. Therefore, since a form is proportioned to the matter that is capable of being perfected by it, it seems that the soul is united first to one part of the body, and then to the other parts of the body through the intermediary of this [first] part.

15. Further, the soul is superior to the body. But the inferior powers of the soul are united to the superior parts of the body, for the intellect requires the body only because of the imagination and the external senses from which it receives species. Therefore, conversely, the soul is united to the body through those things which are highest and simplest, as through spirits and humors.

16. Further, that which when taken away destroys the unity among things united to one another, is seen to be a medium between them. But the union of soul and body is dissolved when the spirits have been removed, the natural heat extinguished, and the basic moisture exhausted. Therefore these things are media between the soul and the body.

17. Further, as a soul is naturally united to a body, so is this soul united to this body. But this body is this [particular] body through the fact that it possesses certain terminated dimensions. Therefore the soul is united to the body by the medium of terminated dimensions.

18. Further, things which differ from one another are united only through a medium. But the soul and the human body are seen to differ from each other to the greatest degree, because one of them is incorporeal and simple, the other corporeal and particularly complex. Therefore the soul is united to the body only through a medium.

19. Further, the human soul is similar in intellectual nature to the separate substances which move the celestial bodies. Now these are seen to be related to one another as movers and things capable of being moved. Consequently it seems that the human body, which is moved by the soul, has within itself something of the nature of a celestial body, and that the soul is united to the body by means of this.

On the contrary, the Philosopher says in the *Metaphysics*,[7] that a form is united to its matter directly. Now the soul is united as a form to the body. Therefore it is united to the body directly.

I answer: Among all [principles] the act of existing (*esse*) is that which most immediately and intimately belongs to things, as is pointed out in the book *De causis*.[8] Hence the form which gives matter its act of existing, must be understood to come to matter prior to anything else, and to be present in it more immediately than anything else, because matter receives its act of existing from a form. Moreover, it is proper to a substantial form to give matter its act of existing pure and simple (*esse simpliciter*), because it is through its form that a thing is the very thing that it is. For a thing is not given an act of existing pure and simple through accidental forms, but only a relative one (*esse secundum quid*), such as to be large or colored, and so on. Therefore, if there is a form which does not give to matter its act of existing pure and simple, but comes to matter already possessing an act of existing through some form, such a form will not be a substantial one. From this it is obvious that an intermediary substantial form cannot intervene between a substantial form and matter, as some wished to maintain. For these men held that there exists in matter an order of diverse forms, one of which is arranged under another in ac-

---

7 VIII, 6 (1045b 16 ff.).
8 *De causis*, IV.

cordance with the order of genera; as if one were to say, for instance, that matter is given the act of existing of a substance through one form; the act of existing of a body through another; the act of existing of a living body through still another; and so on.

But if this position is adopted, only the first form which gives a thing its act of existing as a substance, would be a substantial one. The other forms, indeed, would all be accidental ones, because it is a thing's substantial form that makes it be *a* substance (*hoc aliquid*), as we have already shown (Art. I). Therefore it is necessary to say that a thing has substantiality, exists in the ultimate species, under which there are no other species (*specialissima*), and in all intermediate genera, through one and the same form. Now the forms of natural things are like numbers, whose species change when a unit is added or subtracted, as is pointed out in the *Metaphysics*.[9] It follows, therefore, that the diversity of natural forms, in accordance with which matter is constituted in diverse species, is to be understood as resulting from this fact, that one adds a perfection over and above another. For example, one form gives matter corporeal existence only. (This must be below the grade of animal forms, because matter is in potency only to corporeal forms. For those things which are incorporeal are immaterial, as was shown in the preceding question.) A second more perfect form gives matter vital existence in addition to corporeal existence. Another, still higher, form confers on it sensory existence in addition to vital and corporeal existence; and so on successively.

Therefore a more perfect form, constituting with matter a composite being in the perfection of an inferior grade, must be considered as matter with respect to a higher perfection; and so on up the scale. For instance, prime matter, so far as it now exists in a corporeal mode, is matter with respect to the higher perfection of life. (And so body is the genus of living body, and

9 VIII, 3 (1043b 33 ff.).

animated or living is the specific difference. For genus is derived from matter, and difference from form.) Thus, in a certain way, one and the same form actualizing matter in a lower grade of perfection, is midway between matter and that same form actualizing matter in a superior grade. But matter, so far as it is understood to have substantial existence as a perfection of an inferior grade, can, therefore, be regarded as the subject of accidents. For a substance in that inferior grade of perfection must have a proper accident which necessarily inheres in it. Likewise, from the fact that matter has corporeal existence through forms, it immediately follows that there are dimensions in matter whereby it is understood to be divisible into different parts, so that it can receive different forms corresponding to its different parts. Furthermore, from the fact that matter is known to have a certain substantial mode of existing, matter can be understood to receive accidents by which it is disposed to a higher perfection, so far as it is fittingly disposed to receive that higher perfection. Moreover dispositions of this kind are understood to exist in matter prior to the form, inasmuch as they are given existence in matter by an agent, although there are some improper accidents of the form that are caused in the matter only by the form itself. Hence such accidents are not understood to exist as dispositions in matter prior to the form; rather is the form understood to be prior to the proper accidents as a cause is to its effects.

Consequently, since the soul is a substantial form, because it places man in a determinate species of substance, no other substantial form intervenes between the soul and prime matter. But man is perfected in different grades of perfection by the rational soul itself, so that he is a body, a living body, and a rational animal. However, matter (being understood to receive from the rational soul itself, perfections of an inferior grade, for instance, that of being a body, a living body, and an animal) must also be understood to have, at the same time, appropriate dispositions so that it may be a matter befitting a human soul, inasmuch as the soul gives the body its ultimate perfection. So, therefore, the soul inasmuch as it is the form which gives the act of existing absolutely, does not have any intermediary between itself and prime matter. But because the same form which gives matter its act of existing, is also a principle of operation (for a thing acts so far as it is in act), then the soul like any other form must be a principle of operation.

But it must be considered that a gradation of forms in the order of operation corresponds to the gradation of forms in the order of existence, for an operation is an act of an agent in act. Therefore the greater perfection a form possesses with respect to conferring the act of existing, so much the greater is its power of operating. Hence more perfect forms have a greater number of operations and more diverse ones than less perfect forms. And so it is that a diversity of accidents suffices for a diversity of operations in the case of less perfect things. But in the case of more perfect things a diversity of parts is required as well; and the greater the diversity of parts, the more perfect the form will be. For we see that diverse operations are proper to fire because its accidents differ, for example, to rise upward in virtue of its lightness; to heat in virtue of its heat; and so on. However, any one of these operations belongs to any part of fire. But in animate bodies which have nobler forms, different operations are allotted to different parts, for instance, in plants there is one operation performed by the roots, another by the trunk, and still another by the branches. And the more perfect that living bodies are, so much the more diverse must their parts be in view of their greater perfection. Therefore, since the rational soul is the most perfect of natural forms, there is found in man the greatest diversity of parts because of his different operations. Furthermore the one soul performing these operations confers substantial existence in a manner befitting the operations of the parts themselves. An indication of this fact is that, when the soul ceases to animate the body, neither flesh nor eye remains except in an equivocal sense. But since there must be an order of instruments in keeping with the order of operations, and since there is a natural precedence among the different operations which flow from the soul, one part of the body must be moved to perform its operations by another part. Thus a medium intervenes between the whole body and the soul as the mover and principle of its operations. For after a certain primary mediating part of the body has been moved, that part moves the other parts to perform their operations. So it is that the soul, by means of the heart, moves the other members of the body to perform their vital operations. But since the soul gives to the body its act of existing, it immediately gives to all parts of the body their substantial and specific mode of existing. And this is what many assert, namely, that as a form the soul is united to the body without an intermediary, but that as a mover it is united to the body through an intermediary.

Moreover, this view is in keeping with the position of Aristotle, who maintains that the soul is the substantial form of the body. However, some who, following Plato's theory, hold that the soul is united to the body as one substance is to another, had to posit media through which the soul is united to the body. For diverse and disparate substances are unified only if something exists to unite them. For this reason some held that there is a certain spirit and humor existing as a medium between soul and body; other posited light; still others, the powers of the soul, or something else of this sort. But none of these [entities] are necessary if the soul is the form of the body, because anything whatever, inasmuch as it is a being, is one. Hence a form is united to prime matter by virtue of itself and not by any other bond, because a form, by its very nature, gives to matter its act of existing.

Answers to objections. 1. The powers of the soul are the qualities by which it operates. Therefore they serve as inter-

mediaries between the soul and the body inasmuch as the soul
moves the body, but not inasmuch as it gives to the body its act
of existing. Moreover, it must be understood that the work
which is called *De spiritu et anima* [10] is not a work of Augustine, and that its author is of the opinion that the soul is its
powers. Hence the objection fails completely.

2. Although the soul is a form inasmuch as it is an act, and
similarly is a mover inasmuch as it is an act, and thus is a form
and a mover in one and the same respect, nevertheless the effect
which it produces as a form differs from that which it produces
as a mover. The distinction is made for this reason.

3. One being pure and simple (*unum per se*) does not result
from the union of a mover and a thing moved inasmuch as they
are mover and moved, but from [the union of] this mover
which is the soul, inasmuch as the soul is the form of the body,
and this mobile thing which is the body.

4. Nothing intervenes between the soul and any part of the
body with respect to any operation of the soul which is an operation of the composite. However, there is one part of the body
through which the soul first exercises its operation, which
[part] falls midway between the soul, so far as it is the principle
of that operation, and all the other parts of the body which
share in that operation.

5. The accidental dispositions which dispose matter properly for [receiving] some form are not media absolutely between form and matter, but between form inasmuch as it
bestows the highest perfection, and matter inasmuch as it is
already perfected by some perfection of an inferior order. For
matter by its very nature is first with respect to the lowest grade
of perfection, because matter of itself is in potency to substantial corporeal existence. Moreover, it does not require to
be disposed in this way. But matter, having this perfection already in existence, requires dispositions to a higher perfection.
Moreover it must be recognized that the powers of the soul are

10 See Art. XII, note 21.

its proper accidents and do not exist without the soul. Therefore, inasmuch as they are its powers, they do not have the
nature of a disposition in relation to the soul except so far as
the powers of the inferior part of the soul are called dispositions in relation to the powers of the superior part, just as
the powers of the vegetal soul are dispositions in relation to the
sentient soul, as can be seen from the preceding argument.

6. This argument concludes that the soul or the animal is
divided into two parts, one of which is like a mobile thing, the
other like a mover. This, indeed, is true, but we must understand that the soul moves the body through knowledge and appetite. Now knowledge and appetite in man are of two kinds.
First, that which belongs to the soul alone and which does not
depend on a bodily organ. This belongs to the intellective part
of the soul. Secondly, that which belongs to the composite.
This belongs to the sentient part of the soul. Now whatever belongs to the intellective part moves the body only by means of
that which belongs to the sentient part. For when a movement
has to do with some particular thing, the universal apprehension which belongs to the intellect causes movement only by
means of something particular belonging to sense. Hence
when we divide a man or an animal into a part that causes
movement, and one that is moved, we do not divide them into
a soul and a body exclusively, but into a soul and an animated
body. For that part of the animated body whose operation it is
to apprehend and to desire, moves the whole body. But if it be
supposed that the intellective part moves [the body] directly,
so that the part causing movement in man is the soul alone,
then the answer will be in accordance with the preceding explanation (i.e., the one given in the Answer). For the human
soul will be a mover in virtue of what is supreme in itself,
namely, its intellective part. Moreover, the moved part will
not be prime matter alone, but prime matter inasmuch as it
is given a corporeal and vital act of existing (*esse*). Nor will it
be moved by any other form than the soul. Hence it will not be

necessary to maintain that a substantial form acts as an intermediary between the soul and prime matter. However, there is a certain movement in the animal which is not the result of apprehension and desire, that is, the movement of the heart, the movement also of growth and decay, and the movement of nutrition which is diffused throughout the whole body, and which the animal has in common with plants. Now with respect to this kind of movement, we must maintain that, as inferior forms are the principles of movement in natural bodies, so also is the soul the principle of movement in animal bodies. For the animal soul not only bestows what is proper to its nature as such, but also gives those perfections which belong to a lower order of forms, as is evident from what has been said. Hence the Philosopher says, in the *De anima*,[11] that the soul is the nature [12] of this specific type of body. For this reason the operations of the soul are divided into animal operations and natural operations. That is to say, those operations which proceed from the soul in keeping with its proper nature, are called animal operations, whereas those which come from the soul inasmuch as it produces the effect of inferior natural forms, are called natural operations. According to this, therefore, it must be said that, as fire through its natural form has a natural movement whereby it tends upwards, so also does any part of an animated body in which there is found movement not resulting from apprehension, have this movement naturally through its soul. For as fire tends upward by nature, so also is the blood moved naturally to its proper and determinate place. Similarly, the heart is moved naturally by its proper movement, although the dissolution of spirits, made from the blood, by which the heart is expanded and contracted, cooperates in this activity, as Aristotle points out in the place where he treats of exhalation and inhalation. Consequently the first part of the body in which such movement is found is not a self-mover,

11 II, 2 (414a 18).
12 I.e., the principle of activity.

but is moved naturally, just as fire is. However, this part moves another part, and thus the whole animal is a self-mover, because one part of it is a mover, and another is moved.

7. A physical organic body is related to the soul as matter to form, not that it is such a body as a result of some other form, but because it has this nature through the soul, as was shown above.

8. The eighth argument must be answered similarly. For the statement in Genesis: "God formed man out of the slime of the earth," is not prior in time to the following: "And breathed into his face the breath of life"; but is prior in the order of nature only.

9. Matter is in potency to forms with respect to a certain order, not that it receives different substantial forms in a certain order, but because it receives whatever is proper to a superior form only through the medium of what is proper to an inferior form, as was shown. In this way matter is understood to receive other forms by way of the forms of the elements.

10. The forms of the elements do not exist according to their very essence in a mixed body, although Avicenna maintained this, for they cannot exist in one and the same part of matter. However, if they were to exist in different parts of matter, there would not be a mixture with respect to the whole, as is the case in a true mixture,[13] but there would be a mixture of the most insignificant kind, that is to say, one which appears to be a mixture to the senses. Again, to say that the forms of the elements may receive more and less, as Averroes does, is ridiculous, because there are substantial forms which cannot receive more and less. Nor is there a medium between a substance and an accident as he imagined. Moreover it must be said that the forms of the elements are not corrupted completely, but that they remain virtually, as Aristotle says. And they are virtually

[13] A "mixed body" is a body compounded of different proportions of the four elements in such a way that the elements themselves are present only virtually.

present inasmuch as the proper accidents of the elements, in which the power of the elements is found, remain in some measure.

11. The intellective soul is the form of the body according to its very essence, but not according to its intellectual operation.

12. The proportion that exists between the soul and the body is in the things proportioned. Consequently it does not necessarily have to be an intermediary between soul and body.

13. The heart is the first instrument through which the soul moves the other parts of the body. Therefore, as a mover, the soul is united to the other parts of the body through the medium of the heart. However, as a form, the soul is united to every part of the body essentially and directly.

14. Although the soul is a form in its entirety so far as its essence is concerned, yet it is many by its powers inasmuch as it is the principle of different operations. Furthermore, because a form perfects a matter not only with respect to its act of existing, but also with respect to its operation, it is necessary that the parts of the body be perfected in different ways by the soul, even though it is a form in its entirety, and that each part be perfected in a way befitting its operation. For this reason there must be an order among the parts of the body in accordance with the order among operations, as was explained. However, this order exists inasmuch as the operation of the body belongs to the soul as the mover of the body.

15. The inferior powers of the soul, so far as their operations are concerned, can be understood to unite the superior powers to the body inasmuch as the superior powers stand in need of the operations of the inferior powers which are exercised through the body. Similarly the body, so far as operation and movement are concerned, is joined through its superior parts to the soul.

16. A form accrues to matter only when matter is properly disposed by fitting dispositions, and thus a form cannot remain

in matter when the proper dispositions cease to exist. In this way, when the heat, natural humidity, and the like, are removed from the body, the union of soul and body is destroyed, because the body is disposed to receive the soul by means of these things. Hence things of this kind intervene as dispositions between the soul and the body. The explanation of this was given above.

17. Dimensions can be considered to exist in matter only so far as matter is given substantial corporeal existence through a substantial form. In man this kind of existence is not bestowed by any other form than the soul, as has been explained. Consequently these dimensions are not understood actually to precede the existence of the soul in matter absolutely, but relative to the highest grades of perfection, as was explained above.

18. The soul and the body do not differ from each other as things of different genera and species do, because neither of them exists in a genus or a species, but only the composite of which they are parts, as we have shown in the preceding questions. However, the soul by its very essence is the form of the body giving it its act of existing. Hence it is united to the body essentially and directly.

19. The human body has something in common with a celestial body; not inasmuch as something characteristic of a celestial body, such as light, intervenes as a medium between the soul and the body, but inasmuch as the human body is given a certain tempered combination lacking contrariety, as was shown in preceding questions.[14]

14 See *op*. LIX, *De pluralitate formarum.*

## ARTICLE X

## WHETHER THE SOUL EXISTS IN THE WHOLE BODY AND IN EACH OF ITS PARTS

In the tenth article we examine this question: Whether the soul exists in the whole body and in each of its parts.[1]

Objections. 1. It seems that the soul does not. For the soul exists in the body as a perfection in something perfectible. But the thing capable of being perfected by the soul is an organic body, because the soul is "the actuality of a physical organic body having life potentially," as is stated in the *De anima*.[2] Therefore the soul exists only in an organic body. But each part of the body is not an organic body. Therefore the soul does not exist in each part of the body.

2. Further, a form is proportioned to a matter. But the soul as the form of the body is a certain simple essence. Therefore a complex matter is not proportioned to the soul. But the diverse parts of the body, either of a man or of an animal, are certainly complex matter, because these parts differ greatly from one another. Therefore the soul is not the form of each part of the body, and so does not exist in each part of the body.

3. Further, no part of a whole exists in separation from the whole. Therefore, if the whole soul exists in one part of the body, no part of the soul can exist outside that part of the body. Therefore it is impossible for the soul to exist in each part of the body.

4. Further, the Philosopher says in the work *De causa motus*

[1] See also *Summa theol.*, Ia, q.76, a.8; *Contra Gentes*, II, 72; *Sent.*, Bk. I, dist., 8, q.5, a.3; *De spir. creat.*, a.4.
[2] II, 1 (412a 28).

*animalium:* [3] "The animal must be considered as similar to a
state which is well governed by laws. For when order is once
established in it, there is no further need of a separate monarch
to preside over each particular work. But each individual performs the task to which he is directed by the authority of the
ruler, and these things are done continually in a customary
manner. In animals, however, the same order results from their
nature, and each part performs the proper work for which it
has been constituted by nature. Hence there is not a soul for
each part, but one single principle of the body exists, and the
different parts of the body live because they are connected to
one another. Moreover, they perform the proper operation
allotted to them by nature." Therefore the soul does not exist
in each part of the body, but only in one part.

5. Further, the Philosopher says, in the *Physics,*[4] that the
mover of the heavens must occupy either the center or some
sign of the circumference,[5] since these two things are the
principles of circular motion. Now he proves that it cannot
occupy the center but must exist at the circumference, for the
nearer things are to the circumference and the farther away
from the center, the swifter is their motion. Therefore, similarly the movement of the soul must exist in that part of the
animal in which movement is most apparent. Now this part is
the heart. Therefore the soul exists only in the heart.

6. Further, the Philosopher says in the book *De juventute
et senectute,*[6] that plants have a nutritive principle midway
between their upper and lower parts. But upper and lower are
found not only in plants, but in animals as well, and these also
have a right and left side, a front and a back. Therefore the
principle of life, namely, the soul, exists in an animal in the
midst of its particular parts. But this [position is occupied by]
the heart. Therefore the soul exists only in the heart.

[3] X (703a 30 ff.).
[4] VIII, 10 (267b 6 ff.).
[5] I.e., a sign of the zodiac.
[6] II (468a 20 ff.).

7. Further, every form existing in a whole and in each of its parts, is predicated of the whole and of each of its parts, as is evident in the case of fire, for each part of fire is fire. However, each part of an animal is not an animal. Therefore the soul does not exist in each part of the body.

8. Further, the act of intellection belongs to a part of the soul. But this act is not present in any part of the body. Therefore the whole soul does not exist in each part of the body.

9. Further, the Philosopher says in the *De anima*,[7] that as the soul is related to the body, so also is a part of the soul related to a part of the body. Therefore, if the soul exists in the whole body, the whole soul will not exist in each part of the body, but a part of the soul only will exist in a part of the body.

10. But it has been said that the Philosopher is speaking of the soul and of its parts inasmuch as it is a mover and not a form. On the other hand, the Philosopher says in another place, that if the eye were an animal, sight would be its soul. But the soul is the form of an animal. Hence, in the body, part of the soul has the character of a form, so that the soul is not merely a mover.

11. Further, the soul is the principle of life in an animal. Therefore, if the soul were in each part of the body, each part would receive life directly from the soul. Then one part would not depend on another for life, which is clearly false, for the other parts of the body depend on the heart for life.

12. Further, the soul is moved accidentally by the movement of the body in which it exists. Similarly it is at rest accidentally when the body in which it exists is at rest. However, it happens that when one part of a body is at rest, another is moved. Therefore, if the soul exists in each part of the body, the soul must be moved and at rest simultaneously; which is evidently impossible.

13. Further, all powers of the soul are rooted in the essence of the soul. Therefore, if the essence of the soul exists in each

[7] II, 1 (412b 25 ff.).

part of the body, each power of the soul must exist in each part of the body. This is obviously false, for the sense of hearing does not exist in the eye but in the ear alone; and similarly for the other powers.

14. Further, whatever exists in another exists there according to the mode of the thing in which it exists. Therefore, if the soul exists in the body, it must exist there in a manner proper to the body. But it is proper to a body that no part of it may exist where another part exists. Therefore, where one part of the soul exists, another does not exist; and thus the whole soul does not exist in each part of the body.

15. Further, certain imperfect animals, called ring-worms, continue to live after they have been dissected, because a soul exists in each part of the body after its dissection. But man and the other perfect animals do not live after they have been dissected. Consequently in them the soul does not exist in each part of the body.

16. Further, as a man and an animal are certain wholes composed of different parts, so also is a house. But the form of a house does not exist in each of its parts but in the whole [house]. Therefore the whole soul, which is the form of the animal, does not exist in each part of the animal but in the whole [animal].

17. Further, the soul as a form gives to the body its act of existing (*esse*). However, the soul is the form of the body through its essence, which is simple. Therefore the simple essence of the soul gives to the body its act of existing. But only one thing comes naturally from something that is one. Therefore, if the soul as a form were in each part of the body, it would follow that it would give existence uniformly to each part of the body.

18. Further, a form is united to matter more intimately than a thing in place is united to its place. But a thing existing in one place cannot exist in different places simultaneously, especially if it is a spiritual substance. For the teachers [of the-

ology] do not admit that an angel exists in different places simultaneously. Therefore the soul cannot exist in different parts of the body.

On the contrary, Augustine says in the *De Trinitate*,[8] that the whole soul exists in the whole body and in each of its parts.

Further, the soul gives to the body its act of existing, only by being united to the body. But the soul confers the act of existing on the whole body and on each of its parts. Therefore the whole soul exists in the whole body and in each of its parts.

Further, the soul operates only where it exists. But the operations of the soul are seen to exist in each part of the body. Therefore the soul exists in each part of the body.

I answer: The true solution to this question depends on the preceding one. For it was shown that the soul as the form of the body is not united to the whole body through the medium of any of its parts, but is united directly to the whole body, because it is the form of the body as a whole and of each of its parts. And this must be maintained, for, since the body of a man or that of any other animal is a certain natural whole, it will be said to be one because it has one form whereby it is perfected, and not simply because it is an aggregate or a composition, as occurs in the case of a house and other things of this kind. Hence each part of a man and that of an animal must receive its act of existing and species from the soul as its proper form. Therefore the Philosopher says [9] that when the soul leaves the body, neither the eye nor the flesh nor any part remains except in an equivocal sense. Moreover, it is impossible for a thing to receive its act of existing and species, as it does from a form, from a principle existing in separation from it; because this would be similar to the position of the Platonists, who maintained that such sensible things receive their

---

8 VI, 5 (*PL*, XLII, 929).
9 *De anima*, II, 1 (412b 20 ff.).

act of existing and species by participating in forms which exist apart from things themselves. But a form must be an intrinsic principle of the thing whose act of existing it is responsible for, because form and matter are the intrinsic principles constituting the essence of a [corporeal] thing.

Hence, according to the teaching of Aristotle, if the soul as a form gives to each part of the body its act of existing and species, it must be present as a form in each part of the body. And for this reason the soul is said to exist in the whole body because it is the form of the whole. Therefore, if it is the form of each part [of the body], it must exist in each part and not in the whole alone, nor in one part alone. Moreover, this definition of the soul is an appropriate one, for the soul is the act of an organic body.[10] However, an organic body is composed of different organs. Hence, if the soul as a form existed in one part of the body only, it would not be the act of an organic body, but that of one organ alone, for instance, the heart or some other part; and the remaining parts would be perfected by different forms. And thus the whole would not be one thing by nature but merely by composition. Hence it follows that the soul exists in the whole body and in each of its parts.

But since it is also asked whether the whole soul exists in the whole body and in each of its parts, we must consider how this is to be explained. For totality can be attributed to a form in a threefold manner, according to the three ways in which it is proper for a thing to have parts. For a thing has parts, in one way, resulting from quantitative division, that is, according as a number or a magnitude is divided. However, totality of number or that of magnitude does not apply to a form, except perhaps in an accidental way; for instance, in the case of forms which are divided accidentally by the division of a continuum, as whiteness is divided as a result of dividing a surface. A thing is said to be a totality in another way in relation to the

10 *Ibid.* (412a 28).

essential parts of its species, as matter and form are said to be parts of a composite, and genus and difference, in a certain respect, parts of a species. This kind of totality is also attributed to simple essences by reason of their perfection, in this way, that as composites have a perfect species from the union of their essential principles, so also do substances and simple forms which have a perfect species in virtue of themselves. A thing is said to be a totality in a third way in relation to its active and passive powers, inasmuch as these are considered to be parts of it which are distinguished from one another because their operations differ.

Therefore, if we take a form which is divided as a result of dividing a continuum, and inquire whether the whole form is in each part of the body (for example, whether whiteness exists in its entirety in a part of the surface), and if the form is considered in relation to quantitative parts (which totality, indeed, pertains to whiteness accidentally), then the whole form does not exist in each part [of the body], but the whole form exists in the whole [body], and a part of the form in a part of the whole. However, if it is a question of totality so far as the species is concerned, then the whole [form] exists in each part [of the body]; for whiteness is as equally intense in any part [of the surface] as it is in the whole. But so far as its power is concerned, it is true that the whole form does not exist in each part [of the body], for the whiteness existing in a part of the surface cannot disperse as much light as the whiteness existing in the whole surface; just as the heat in a small fire alone, cannot cause warmth like the heat in a large fire.

Now if we suppose, for the present, that there is only one soul in the human body (we will explain this later), we must maintain that it is not divided by dividing that species of quantity which is numerical in nature.[11] It is also obvious that the soul is not divided by dividing a continuum. This is particu-

---

[11] There are two kinds of quantity: (a) extension or continuous quantity, and (b) number, which is discontinuous or discrete quantity. (See St. Thomas, *Comm. in Metaph.*, Bk. V, lect. 15, *Cathala*, no. 978.)

larly true of the souls of perfect animals which do not live when dissected. However, it would perhaps be different in the case of the souls of ring-worms, in which there is one soul actually and many potentially, as the Philosopher teaches.[12] Therefore, in the case of the soul of man and that of any perfect animal, it follows that totality can be considered only so far as the soul's species and its passive or active power are concerned. Hence we say that the soul by its very essence is the form of the body, and that it exists as such in each part of the body, as has been shown, because the perfection of the species comes from the soul in virtue of its very essence. Consequently the whole soul exists in each part of the body according to the whole of its specific perfection.

However, if totality is taken so far as the soul's active and passive powers are concerned, then the whole soul does not exist in each part of the body. Nor, if we speak of the soul of man, does the whole soul [according to the totality of its powers] exist in the whole body. For it was shown in the preceding articles (Arts. I, II, and V) that the human soul possesses the power of performing certain operations without communicating in any way with the body, that is, the acts of understanding and willing, as it exceeds the capacity of the body. Hence the intellect and the will are not the acts of any bodily organ. However, with respect to those operations which the soul exercises through bodily organs, the soul's active and passive powers as a whole exist in the whole body, although not in each part of the body, because different parts of the body are proportioned to different operations of the soul. Consequently, with respect to any one power, the soul exists only in that part of the body which takes care of the operations exercised by that particular part.

Answers to objections. 1. Since matter exists for the sake of form, and since a form is directed to a proper operation, the matter to which a form is united must be one that is suitable

---

[12] *De anima*, II, 2 (413b 13).

for the proper operations of that form, just as the matter of a saw must be iron, which is suitable for sawing due to its hardness. Hence, since the soul can exercise different operations because of the perfect power which it has, its matter must be a body composed of different parts (which parts are called organs) suitable for the different operations of the soul. And for this reason the whole body, to which the soul is related principally as a form, is the organ of the soul. However, parts exist for the sake of the whole. Hence it is only by being intrinsically related to the body as a whole, that a part of the body is related to the soul as that which is properly and principally capable of being perfected by the soul. Consequently it is not necessary for each part of an animal to be an organic body, even though the soul is the form of each of the animal's parts.

2. Since matter exists for the sake of form, form gives an act of existing and species to matter inasmuch as matter is disposed for the operations of the form. And therefore the soul, even though it is one and simple in its essence, perfects the parts of the body in different ways, because the body, which is capable of being perfected by the soul, requires diversity in its parts in order that it may be disposed for the different operations of the soul.

3. Since the soul exists in a part of the body in the manner just described, no part of the soul is found outside the soul which is in this part of the body. However, it does not follow that no part of the soul exists outside this part of the body, but rather than no part of the soul exists outside the whole body which the soul perfects as a principle.

4. In this passage the Philosopher is speaking about the motive power of the soul. For the body's principle of motion exists in one part, namely, in the heart, and moves the whole body through this part. This is clear from the example which he gives of the ruler.

5. The mover of the heavens, so far as its substance is concerned, is not confined to some particular place [as bodies are].

Rather does the Philosopher intend to show where the mover of the heavens exists as the principle of motion. It is in this way that the soul, as the principle of motion, exists in the heart.

6. The soul in plants, inasmuch as it is the principle of certain operations, is also said to exist in the midst of their upper and lower parts. The soul exists in animals in the same way.

7. Therefore each part of an animal is not an animal as each part of fire is fire, because every operation of fire is found in each part of fire. However, all the operations of an animal are not found in each of its parts. This is particularly true of perfect animals.

8. The conclusion of this argument is that the whole soul, so far as its power is concerned, does not exist in each part of the body. This was shown to be true.

9. The Philosopher does not distinguish parts in the soul with respect to its essence, but with respect to its powers. Hence he says that, as the soul exists in the whole body, so also does a part of the soul exist in a part of the body. For as the whole organic body is so constituted that it may serve the operations of the soul which are exercised through it, so also is one organ disposed to one particular operation.

10. A power of the soul is rooted in its essence. Therefore, wherever a power of the soul exists, there also does the essence of the soul exist. Hence the Philosopher's statement that, if the eye of an animal were itself an animal, sight would be its soul, is not to be understood of a power of the soul without its essence; just as the sentient soul is said to be the form of the whole body through its essence, not through its sensory power.

11. Since the soul operates in different parts of the body through one particular power (moreover the body is disposed in this way that it is proportioned to the soul's act of existing through the action of the soul itself which is the efficient cause of the body, as Aristotle says in the *De anima*,[13]) it is necessary that the disposition of the different parts of the body, inasmuch

[13] II, 4 (415b 9).

as they are capable of being perfected by the soul, depend on one first part of the body, namely, on the heart. For this reason the life of the other parts depends upon the heart, because, after the necessary dispositions cease to exist, the soul is not united as a form to the body. However, this does not prevent the soul from being the form of each part of the body directly.

12. The soul is moved or at rest only in an accidental way when the body is moved or at rest. Moreover, it is not incongruous for a thing to be moved and at rest accidentally at one and the same time, just as it is not implausible for a thing to be moved accidentally by contrary movements, as for instance, when someone on a ship walks in the direction opposite to that of the course of the ship.

13. Although all powers of the soul are rooted in its essence, yet each part of the body is informed by the soul in the manner befitting each. Therefore different powers of the soul exist in different parts of the body. But it is not necessary that all of the soul's powers exist in each part of the body.

14. When it is said that one thing exists in another in accordance with the mode of the thing in which it exists, this is understood of the mode of its capacity, not of its nature. For it is not necessary that whatever exists in something else have the nature and properties of that thing in which it exists, but that it be received in that thing according to the thing's capacity; because it is obvious that water does not have the nature of the vessel [in which it exists]. Hence it is not necessary for the soul to possess this characteristic of a body, namely, that wherever one part exists, another may not exist.

15. Ring-worms continue to live after they have been dissected, not only because their soul exists in each part of the body, but because their soul, being imperfect and performing a minimum of operations, requires the least diversity of parts. This is also found in any part segregated from a living thing of this sort. Hence a soul remains in each part because each part retains that disposition whereby the whole body is made

capable of being perfected by a soul. However, the soul exists differently in perfect animals.

16. The form of a house, like other artificial forms, is an accidental one. Hence it does not give to the whole house and to each of its parts their act of existing and species. Indeed, a whole [of this sort] is not a substantial unity, but is a one by aggregation. However, the soul is the substantial form of the body, giving to the whole body and to each of its parts their act of existing and species. Furthermore, the whole constituted of these parts is a substantial unity. Hence there is no similarity.

17. Although the soul is one and simple in essence, yet it is capable of performing different operations. And because the soul by nature gives to its perfectible its act of existing and species, inasmuch as it is the form of the body by its very essence (moreover, those things existing naturally, exist for an end), the soul must establish a diversity of parts in the body inasmuch as this is required for its different operations. It is also true in the light of such diversity (which is to be attributed to the end, and not to the form alone) that it is more apparent that nature acts for an end in the constitution of living things than it is in the case of other natural things in which one form perfects, in a uniform way, the thing capable of being perfected by it.

18. The simplicity of the soul and that of an angel must not be thought of in terms of the simplicity of the point, which has a definite position in a continuum, and, therefore, because it is simple,[14] cannot exist in different parts of the continuum at one and the same time. But the angel and the soul are said to be simple because they lack quantity altogether, and thus are related to a continuum only by contact of power. Hence that whole, which it contacted by an angel's power, is present to the angel (which is not united to it as a form) as a single place; and it is present to the soul (which is united to it as a

14 I.e., simple in a geometric sense.

form) as a single perfectible thing. And just as the whole angel exists in each part of the place it is present in [by contact of power], so also does the whole soul exist in each part of the thing perfectible by it.

## ARTICLE XI

## WHETHER THE RATIONAL, SENTIENT, AND VEGETAL SOULS IN MAN ARE SUBSTANTIALLY ONE AND THE SAME

In the eleventh article we examine this question: Whether the rational, sentient, and vegetal souls in man are substantially one and the same.[1]

Objections. 1. It seems that they are not substantially one and the same. For wherever an act of a soul exists, there also does a soul exist. Now in the embryo the act of a vegetal soul precedes that of a sentient soul, and the act of a sentient soul precedes that of a rational soul. Therefore in pregnancy the vegetal soul is prior to the sentient, and the sentient is prior to the rational. Consequently they are not substantially one and the same.

2. But it has been said that the act of a vegetal soul and that of a sentient soul which are present in the embryo, do not belong to a soul existing in the embryo, but to a power of the parent's soul existing therein. On the other hand, a finite agent acts by its power only with respect to a limited distance, as is evident in the motion of throwing. For a thrower casts an object to a definite place according to the power which he possesses. But the movements and operations of a soul appear in the embryo no matter how distant the [male] parent may be, although his power is finite. Therefore the operations of a soul do not exist in the embryo as a result of a power of the parent's soul.

---

[1] See also *Summa theol.*, Ia, q.76, a.3; *Contra Gentes*, II, 58; *De potentia*, q.3, a.9, ad 9um; *Quodl.* XI, q.5, a.1; *De spir. creat.*, a.3; *op.* II, *Compend. theol.*, chaps. 90, 91, 92.

3. Further, the Philosopher states, in the work *De generatione animalium,*[2] that the embryo is an animal before it is
a man. But an animal is such because of its sentient soul, and
a man is a man because of his rational soul. Therefore a sentient soul, and not merely a power of such a soul, exists in the
embryo prior to a rational soul.

4. Further, living and sensing are operations which can issue
only from an intrinsic principle, because they are acts of a soul.
Hence, since the embryo lives and senses before it has a rational
soul, the acts of living and sensing in the embryo will not come
from the soul of the external parent, but from a soul existing
within the embryo itself.

5. Further, the philosopher says in the *De anima,*[3] that the
soul is not only the formal cause of the body, but its efficient
and final cause as well. But it would not be the efficient cause of
the body unless it were present to the body when it is formed.
However, the body is formed before the rational soul is infused. Therefore there is a soul and not merely a power of a
soul in the embryo preceding the infusion of the rational soul.

6. But it has been said that the formation of the body is
brought about, not by a soul existing in the embryo, but by
the soul of the parent. On the other hand, living bodies move
themselves by their own movements. But the generation of a
living body is a certain movement of its own, because the
generative power is one of its principles. Therefore with respect to this activity, a living thing moves itself. But a thing
that moves itself is composed of a part that causes movement
and one that is moved, as is proved in the *Physics.*[4] Hence the
principle of generation, which forms the living body, is a soul
existing in the embryo.

7. Further, it is obvious that the embryo increases in size.
Now increase is a species of local motion, as is stated in the

[2] II, 3 (736a 35).
[3] II, 4 (415b 9).
[4] VIII, 4 (254b 30).

*Physics.*[5] Therefore, since the animal moves itself locally, it will also move itself augmentatively. Hence this movement must come from a principle existing in the embryo and not from an extrinsic soul.

8. Further, the Philosopher says, in the book *De generatione animalium,*[6] that it cannot be said that no soul exists in the embryo, but that first a vegetative soul exists there and then a sentient soul.

9. But it has been argued that the Philosopher does not mean that a soul exists in the embryo actually, but only potentially. On the other hand, a thing acts only so far as it is in act. But there are activities of a soul in the embryo. Therefore a soul actually exists there, and thus it follows that [the souls in the embryo] are not substantially one and the same.

10. Further, it is impossible for one and the same thing to be caused both by an intrinsic principle and by an extrinsic one. But the rational soul in man is caused by an extrinsic principle. The vegetal and sentient souls, however, are caused by an intrinsic principle contained in the semen, as is clear from what the Philosopher says in the book *De generatione animalium.*[7] Therefore in man the vegetal, sentient, and rational souls are not substantially one and the same.

11. Further, it is impossible for a substantial principle of one thing to be an accident of another. Consequently the Philosopher says in the *Metaphysics,*[8] that heat is not the substantial form of fire, because heat is an accident of other things. But the sentient soul is a substantial principle in brute animals. Therefore it is not merely a power in man, because powers are certain properties and accidents of a soul.

12. Further, man is a nobler animal than the brute. Now

[5] IV, 6 (213b 19).
[6] II, 3 (736a 35 ff.).
[7] II, 3 (736b 21 ff.).
[8] XI, 12 (1068a 11). Aristotle does not make the statement which St. Thomas attributes to him here. St. Thomas himself makes this statement in his commentary. See *Comm. in Metaph.,* Bk. XI, lect. 12 (Cathala, no. 2380).

an animal is said to be such because it possesses a sentient soul. Therefore the sentient soul in man is nobler than that in brute animals. But it is a certain substantial entity in brute animals, and not merely a power of their soul. Consequently in man the sentient soul is a substance in virtue of its very nature to an even greater degree.

13. Further, it is impossible for the substance of one and the same being to be both corruptible and incorruptible. Now the rational soul is incorruptible. Sentient and vegetal souls, however, are corruptible. Therefore it is impossible for the rational, sentient, and vegetal souls to be substantially one and the same.

14. But it has been said that the sentient soul in man is incorruptible. On the other hand, the corruptible and the incorruptible differ generically, as the Philosopher states in the *Metaphysics*.[9] Now the sentient soul in brutes is corruptible. Therefore, if the sentient soul in man is incorruptible, the sentient soul in man and that in a horse will not be generically the same. Hence, since an animal is said to be such because of its sentient soul, a man and a horse would not exist in one and the same genus; which is obviously false.

15. Further, it is impossible for the substance of the same being to be both rational and irrational, because a contradiction is not true of one and the same being. But sentient and vegetal souls are irrational. Therefore they cannot be substantially the same as the rational soul.

16. Further, the body is proportioned to the soul. But in a body there are diverse principles of operation of the soul which are called principal members. Therefore in man there is not one soul alone but many souls.

17. Further, the powers of a soul flow naturally from its essence. However, only one thing proceeds naturally from one thing. Therefore, if there were only one soul in man, there

9 X, 10 (1058b 26).

would not come from this soul certain powers that operate through organs, and others that do not.

18. Further, genus is taken from matter, difference from form. But the genus of man is "animal," his difference, "rational." Therefore, since an animal is said to be such because of its sentient soul, it appears that not only the body but also the sentient soul is related as matter to the rational soul. Therefore the rational and sentient souls are not substantially one and the same.

19. Further, a man and a horse share animality in common. Moreover, an animal is said to be such because of its sentient soul. Therefore their sentient souls are the same. But the sentient soul in a horse is not rational. Therefore it is not rational in man.

20. Further, if in man the rational, sentient, and vegetal souls are substantially one and the same, then in every part of the body in which one of them exists, another must exist. But this is false. For the vegetal soul is in the bones, because they are nourished and increased in size. However, the sentient soul does not exist there, because the bones lack sense. Therefore these souls are not substantially one and the same.

On the contrary, it is pointed out in the work *De ecclesiae dogmatibus:* [10] "We do not say that there are two souls in man as Jacobus [11] and other Syrians write: an animal soul by which the body is animated . . . and a rational soul which exercises reasoning; but in man we speak of one and the same soul which gives life to the body by being united to it, and which disposes itself by its reason."

I answer: There are different opinions about this question, not only among the moderns, but also among the ancients.

[10] *De eccles. dogma.*, XV (*PL*, LVIII, 984): The work of Gennadius of Marseilles (fifth century).

[11] James of Edessa (6th cent. A.D.).

For Plato maintained [12] that there are different souls in the body and, indeed, this followed from his principles; because he maintained that the soul is united as a mover and not as a form to the body, saying that the soul exists in the body as a sailor in a ship. Moreover he maintained that it is necessary to posit different movers wherever there are generically different operations. For instance, in a ship there is one who steers, and another who rows. [Hence Plato argued in this way]: the fact that these movers hold different positions does not destroy the unity existing in the ship, because just as the actions of these movers are subordinated to one another, so also are the movers themselves. In like manner it does not seem to be inconsistent with the unity of a man or that of an animal, if in one body there exist many souls subordinated to one another as movers in accordance with the subordination of operations.

However, according to this position, neither a man nor an animal would have its unity absolutely and in virtue of its very nature, because a being that has unity absolutely and in its own right, does not result from the conjunction of a mover and something movable. Nor, on Plato's hypothesis, would generation and corruption strictly speaking exist when a body receives a soul or loses it. Consequently it must be said that the soul is united to the body not only as a mover but as a form. This is also evident from the preceding arguments (Arts. VIII and IX).

But even if this position is adopted, it still follows from Plato's principles that there are several souls in man and in the animal. For the Platonists maintained that universals are separate forms [i.e., existing apart from things] which are predicated of sensible things inasmuch as sensible things participate in them. For example, Socrates is called an animal inasmuch as he participates in the Idea, "animal," and a man inasmuch as he participates in the Idea, "man." The consequence of this is that there is one form essentially in virtue

12 *Timaeus*, XXXII; *Phaedrus*, XXXIV.

of which Socrates is said to be an animal, and another in virtue of which he is said to be a man. Whence it follows in turn that the sentient and rational soul differ substantially. But this cannot be maintained, for a being having unity in its own right cannot be constituted of diverse things having actual existence [in their own right]; because if terms are predicated of some subject by reason of diverse forms having existence of themselves, one is predicated of another accidentally. For instance, it is said of Socrates that he is white according to whiteness, and musical according to music. Therefore musical is predicated of white accidentally. Hence, if Socrates is said to be a man and an animal according to different forms, it would follow that this predication, *man is an animal,* is an accidental one, and that man is not really what an animal is. However, it happens that an essential predication is made through different forms when they are intrinsically related to one another, as when it is said that a thing having surface is colored. For color exists in a substance through the medium of its surface. But this mode of essential predication occurs, not because the thing predicated is placed in the definition of the subject, but rather the reverse. For surface is placed in the definition of color just as number is placed in the definition of the equal. Therefore, if animal were predicated of man through this mode of essential predication, when the sentient soul is related as matter to the rational soul, assuming they are diverse, it would follow that animal is not predicated essentially of man but rather the reverse.

An additional difficulty follows. For a being having unity absolutely cannot be constituted of diverse things having actual existence [in their own right], unless there is something uniting them and binding them to one another in some manner. Therefore, if Socrates were an animal and rational according to different forms, these two forms would need a unitary principle to make them substantially one. Therefore, since, on Plato's hypothesis, no such unitary principle is to be found, it

will follow that the unity of a man will be a unity of aggregation alone, like that of a heap of things which is relatively one
and absolutely many. So neither will man be a being absolutely, because so far as a thing is a being to that extent it is
one.

Still another incongruity follows. For the form in accordance with which an individual substance receives a generic
predication, must be a substantial one, because a genus is a
substantial predicate. And thus the sentient soul in virtue of
which Socrates is said to be an animal, must be his substantial
form, and so must give to the body its act of existing in the
absolute sense (*per se*), and make it to be this particular thing
(*hoc aliquid*). Therefore, if the rational soul differs substantially from the sentient, it does not make the body to be this
particular thing, nor does it give to the body an act of existing
in the absolute sense, but only relatively. For in that case a
rational form will accrue to a thing already actually subsisting.
Consequently it will not be a substantial form but an accidental one, and thus will not make Socrates to be specifically
what he is, for a species also is a substantial predicate.

It follows, therefore, that a man's soul, which is rational,
sentient, and vegetal, is substantially one only. This is a consequence of the argument given in a preceding article (Art.
IX),[13] concerning the order of substantial forms, namely, that
no substantial form is united to matter through the medium
of another, but that a more perfect form gives to matter whatever an inferior form does, and something over and above.
Hence the rational soul gives to the human body everything
that the sentient soul gives to the brute and the vegetal soul
gives to the plant, and something over and above. For this
reason the soul in man is both vegetal, sentient, and rational.

The following example also attests to this, namely, that
when the operation of one power is intense, that of another is
impeded; and contrariwise, there is an overflowing of one

[13] See also the *De spir. creat.*, Art. III.

power into another, which would occur only if all the powers were rooted in one and the same essence of the soul.

Answers to objections. 1. Having premised that the soul existing in the human body is substantially one only, this argument is answered in different ways by diverse men. For some claim that no soul exists in the embryo prior to the rational soul, but a certain power deriving from the soul of the parent. They maintain that the operations perceived in the embryo are caused by this power, which is called a formative one. But this is not altogether true, because there appears in the embryo not only the forming of the body (which can be attributed to the aforesaid power) but other operations as well; and these cannot be attributed to anything but a soul, such as growth, sensation, and the like. Nevertheless this position could be held if the aforesaid active principle in the embryo were called a power of a soul temporarily, and not a soul, because it is not yet a perfect one, just as the embryo is not a perfect animal. But then the same difficulty will remain. For some say that the vegetal soul exists in the embryo before the sentient soul, and the sentient before the rational, but not concomitantly. Indeed, they maintain that the semen gives rise to an actual vegetal soul as a result of an active principle existing in the semen. This soul in the course of time is brought to a higher degree of perfection by the process of generation and itself becomes a sentient soul, which in turn is brought to a still higher degree of perfection by an extrinsic principle, and becomes the rational soul. Now according to this position it follows that the substance itself of the rational soul comes from an active principle existing in the semen, but that an additional perfection accrues to it finally from an extrinsic principle. And thus it would follow that the very substance of the rational soul is corruptible. For that cannot be incorruptible which is caused by a power existing in the semen. Therefore our explanation must be different, namely, that the generation of an animal is not one simple generation alone, but that many generations and corruptions follow one another. For it is said that first the animal has the form of semen, then the form of blood, and so on successively until generation is completed. And therefore since corruption and generation do not take place without the loss of one form and the acquisition of another, the imperfect form which first exists within the embryo must be discarded and a more perfect one assumed. This continues until the thing conceived has acquired its perfect form. Consequently it is said that the vegetal soul first exists in the semen, but that it is lost in the process of generation, and that another soul succeeds it which is not only vegetal, but also sentient. Then another soul is added to this which is at once vegetal, sentient, and rational.

2. The power existing in the semen which is derived from the father is a permanent intrinsic power, not one coming from an extrinsic principle, just as the power of the mover which exists in the thing thrown is intrinsic. Hence the power which is in the semen operates no matter how far away the father may be. For the active power which is in the semen cannot be caused by the mother (although some indeed maintain this), because the woman is not an active principle but a passive one. Nevertheless there is some similarity here, because, just as the thrower's power, which is finite, moves an object to a definite place some distance away by local motion, so does the power of one generating move a thing to a determinate form by the movement of generation.

3. That power has the nature of a soul as has been explained. Therefore the embryo can be called an animal because of it.

The fourth, fifth, sixth, seventh and eighth objections are answered in the same way.

9. Inasmuch as the soul exists actually, but imperfectly, in the embryo, to that extent does it perform imperfect operations.

10. Although the sentient soul in the brute comes from an intrinsic principle, nevertheless in man the substance of the soul, which is at once vegetal, sentient, and rational, comes from an extrinsic principle, as has just been shown.

11. The sentient soul does not exist in man accidentally, but substantially, because it is substantially the same as the rational soul. However, a sentient power is an accident in man just as it is in other animals.

12. The sentient soul in man is nobler than that in other animals, because in man it is not only sentient but also rational.

13. As regards its very substance the sentient soul in man is incorruptible, because its substance is the substance of the rational soul, although perhaps the sentient powers, which are acts of the body, do not remain in existence after the body has corrupted, as some maintain.

14. If the sentient soul existing in brutes and that existing in man could of themselves be placed in a genus and a species, they would belong to one genus only logically speaking, according to some common intention. But the thing that exists expressly in a genus and a species is the composite of body and soul, and this composite is corrupted both in the case of man and in that of the animal.

15. The sentient soul in man is not a non-rational soul but is at once a sentient and rational soul. However, it is true that the soul's sentient powers as such are, indeed, non-rational, but participate in reason inasmuch as they obey reason. Moreover, the powers of the vegetal soul are wholly non-rational, because they do not obey reason, as is clear from what the Philosopher says in the *Ethics*.[14]

16. Although in the body there are several principal members in which the principles of certain operations of a soul are manifested, nevertheless all depend upon the heart as the first bodily principle.

17. Powers operating through organs spring from the hu-

[14] I, 13 (1102b 30).

man soul inasmuch as it is united to the body. But powers not operating through organs spring from the soul inasmuch as it exceeds by its power the capacity of the body.

18. As is clear from the preceding questions, matter receives different grades of perfection from one and the same form. And so far as matter is perfected by an inferior grade of perfection, the material disposition for a higher grade of perfection still remains. Thus so far as the body is perfected in sensible being by the human soul, the body retains to that extent the nature of matter with respect to a higher perfection. And according to this, "animal," which is a genus, is derived from matter, and "rational," which is a difference, is derived from form.

19. As an animal as such is neither rational nor non-rational (but rational animal is man, and non-rational animal is brute animal), so is the sentient soul as such neither rational nor non-rational, but is rational in man and non-rational in the brute.

20. Although the sentient and vegetal soul is one soul, still it is not necessary that the operation of one appear wherever the operation of the other appears, because of the diverse dispositions of parts. For this reason it also happens that all of the sentient soul's operations are not exercised through one part; but sight is exercised through the eye, hearing through the ear, and so on for the rest.

# ARTICLE XII

## WHETHER THE SOUL IS ITS POWERS

In the twelfth article we examine this question: Whether the soul is its powers.[1]

Objections. 1. It seems that the soul is its powers. For it is said in the work *De spiritu et anima:* "The soul has its own natural powers, and is all of these, for its active and passive powers are the same as itself. It has accidents, and these are not its powers, nor are its virtues itself; for it is not its own prudence, temperance, justice, and fortitude."[2] According to this it seems to be clearly maintained that the soul is its powers.

2. Further, it is stated in the same work: "The soul is designated by different names in accordance with the way in which it operates. For it is called soul when it vegetates, sense when it senses, spirit when it knows, mind when it understands, reason when it discerns, memory when it remembers, and will when it wills. However, these do not differ substantially but only in name, because all of these are the soul itself."[3] According to this the same thing would be maintained as is stated above.

3. Further, Bernard says: "I distinguish three powers in the soul: memory, understanding, and will; and these three are the soul itself."[4] But the same thing is also true of the other powers of the soul. Hence the soul is its powers.

---

[1] See also *Summa theol.*, Ia, q.77, a.1; q.54, a.3; *Sent.*, Bk. I, dist. 3, q.4, a.2; *Quodl.* X, q.3, a.1; *De spir. creat.*, a.11.

[2] XIII (*PL*, XL, 789).

[3] *Ibid.* (*PL*, XL, 788).

[4] *Liber meditationum*, I (*PL*, CLXXXIV, 485). This work was not written by St. Bernard of Clairvaux. Its author is probably Hugh of St. Victor.

4. Further, Augustine says in the *De Trinitate*,[5] that memory, understanding, and will, are one life, one essence. Now the essence of the soul is nothing if not one. Therefore the powers of the soul are the same as its essence.

5. Further, no accident goes beyond its subject. Now memory, understanding, and will, go beyond the soul; for the soul not only remembers itself, and understands and wills itself, but other things as well. Therefore these three powers are not accidents of the soul. Hence they are the same as its essence, and so also are its other powers for the same reason.

6. Further, an image of the Trinity is found in the soul with respect to these three powers. But an image of the Trinity is present in the soul so far as the soul itself is concerned, and not merely so far as its accidents are concerned. Therefore the aforementioned powers are not accidents of the soul and, consequently, belong to its essence.

7. Further, an accident is something that can be present or absent without its subject being corrupted. But the powers of the soul cannot be withdrawn from the soul. Therefore they are not accidents of it. Thus the conclusion here is the same as the foregoing.

8. Further, no accident is a principle of substantial difference, because a difference completes a thing's definition, which definition signifies what a thing is.[6] Now powers of a soul are principles of substantial differences, for a thing is said to be sensible in virtue of sense, and to be rational in virtue of reason. Therefore the powers of the soul are not accidents of it, but are the soul itself, which is the form of the body; for the form is the principle of substantial difference.

9. Further, a substantial form is more efficacious than an accidental one. But an accidental form acts by itself and not by some intermediary power. Therefore, so also does a substantial

---

[5] X, 11 (*PL*, XLII, 983).

[6] The type of definition referred to here is the quidditative or essential definition, which is comprised of a genus and a specific difference.

form. Consequently, since the soul is a substantial form, its powers, whereby it operates, do not differ from itself.

10. Further, the principle which gives a thing its act of existing, and that responsible for its operations, are one and the same. Now the soul in itself is the principle that gives a living thing its act of existing, because it is a form according to its very essence. Therefore its essence is a principle of operation. But a power is nothing more than a principle of operation. Consequently the essence of the soul is identical with its powers.

11. Further, the substance of the soul, inasmuch as it is in potency to intelligibles, is the possible intellect. However, inasmuch as the soul is in act with respect to intelligibles, its substance is the agent intellect. But to be in act and to be in potency refer only to the thing itself which is in potency and in act. Therefore the soul is the agent intellect and the possible intellect, and is its other powers for the same reason.

12. Further, just as prime matter is in potency to sensible forms so also is the intellective soul in potency to intelligible forms. But prime matter is its own potency. Therefore the intellective soul is its own powers.

13. Further, the Philosopher says, in the *Ethics*,[7] that man is an intellect. But he is an intellect only by reason of his rational soul. Therefore the soul is the intellect, and, for the same reason, it is also its other powers.

14. Further, the Philosopher says, in the *De anima*,[8] that the soul is a first act, just as any science is. Now a science is the immediate principle of that second act which is cogitation itself.[9] Therefore the soul is the immediate principle of its own opera-

[7] IX, 4 (1166a 16).

[8] II, 1 (412a 20 ff.).

[9] Properly speaking, a science is a "habitus." It is a quality which perfects a power for a definite operation. Consequently it is related to the power which it perfects as an act to a potency, and to the operation which springs from it as a first act to a second act. The current definition of science as a "body of knowledge" is quite inadequate.

tions. But the immediate principle of an operation is called a power. Consequently the soul is its powers.

15. Further, all parts of a whole are consubstantial with the whole, because a whole is composed of its parts. Now the powers of the soul are its parts, as is shown in the *De anima.*[10] Therefore they are substantial parts of the soul and not accidents of it.

16. Further, whatever is a form alone (*simplex*) cannot be a subject.[11] But the soul is a form alone, as we have shown above (Art. VI). Therefore it cannot be a subject of accidents. Consequently the powers which are present in the soul are not accidents of it.

17. Further, if the powers are accidents of the soul, they must flow from its essence; for proper accidents are caused by the principles of a subject. But the essence of the soul, so far as it reveals itself in its powers, cannot be the cause of so great a diversity of accidents, because it is simple. Therefore the powers of the soul are not its accidents. Consequently it is to be concluded that the soul is its powers.

On the contrary, essence is related to the act of existing (*esse*) as power (*posse*) is to action (*agere*). Therefore just as to be and to act are proportionally related to each other, so also are power and essence. Now to exist and to act are one and the same in God alone. Therefore power and essence are one and the same in God alone. Consequently the soul is not its powers.

Further, no quality is a substance. But a natural power is a particular species of quality, as is revealed in the *Categories.*[12] Consequently the natural powers of the soul are not the essence itself of the soul.

I answer: There are different opinions about this question. For some say that the soul is its powers, and others deny this,

---

[10] II, 1 (413a 3).
[11] Boethius, *De Trin.*, II (*PL*, LXIV, 1250).
[12] Aristotle, VIII (9a 13).

holding that the powers of the soul are certain properties of it. In order to see wherein these opinions differ we must understand that a power is nothing but a thing's principle of operation, whether it be an action or a passion [i.e., the undergoing of an action]. Indeed, a principle is not the subject acting or undergoing an action, but that by which an agent acts or a patient undergoes an action; just as the art of building is a power in the builder who builds by means of that power; and as heat is a power of fire, which heats by means of its heat; and as dryness is a power in pieces of wood, because they are combustible in virtue of this dryness. Consequently those who maintain that the soul is its powers, think that the essence itself of the soul is the immediate principle of all its operations. They say that a man understands, senses, and acts, and other things of this sort, by the essence of the soul, and that the soul is referred to by different names inasmuch as its operations differ. It is called sense inasmuch as it is the principle of sensation, intellect inasmuch as it is the principle of intellection, and so on for the other powers; just as if, for example, we were to call the heat of fire its liquifying power, its heating power, and its drying power, because it does all of these.

Now this opinion cannot be maintained. First, indeed, because anything whatever that acts, acts according as it is in act. For fire heats not inasmuch as it is actually bright, but inasmuch as it is actually hot. It is for this reason that every agent produces an effect similar to itself. Wherefore the principle by which an agent acts must be known from its effects (quod agitur), for both must conform. Hence it is said in the *Physics*,[13] that the form and the thing generating are specifically the same.[14] Therefore when an effect does not result from the substantial mode of existing of the one acting, it is impossible that the principle by which such an effect is brought about, belong

[13] II, 7 (198a 25 ff.).
[14] That is, univocal generation. This is most common in living things which produce their like.

in any way to the essence itself of the thing acting. This is quite evident in natural agents. For since a natural agent in generating acts by changing matter with respect to some form (which change occurs inasmuch as matter is first disposed to receive the form, and then acquires it according as generation is the terminus of alteration), the principle which acts immediately on the side of the agent must be an accidental form corresponding to the disposition of the matter. Now an accidental form must act in virtue of a substantial form, and as an instrument of the latter, otherwise it would not induce a substantial form by its activity. For this reason no principles of action appear in the elements except their active and passive qualities,[15] which still act in virtue of their substantial forms; and on account of this their action is terminated not only in accidental dispositions, but in substanial forms as well. For in things made by art the action of an instrument is terminated in the form intended by the artisan. Indeed, if there is an agent that produces a substance directly and immediately by its action (just as we speak of God who produces the substances of things by creating them, and as Avicenna [16] speaks of the Agent Intellect, which, by virtue of its own power, infuses substantial forms into these inferior things [17]), then an agent of this sort acts through its own essence, and thus its active power will not differ from its own essence.

Concerning passive power,[18] it is clear that a passive power which is ordered to substantial act, belongs to the genus of substance, whereas one that is ordered to accidental act, belongs to the genus of accident by reduction as a principle and not as a complete species,[19] because every genus is divided by potency

15 See Art. I, note 20.

16 *Metaph.*, VIII, 7; IX, 5.

17 See Art. XV, note 15.

18 A passive power is one which is disposed to receive a form; whereas an active power is one which is directed to effecting an activity.

19 Only something actual or determined belongs to a species. What is potential belongs to a species "by reduction" inasmuch as the potential may be actualized or determined.

and act. Accordingly a potential man belongs to the genus of substance, and potentially white belongs to the genus of quality. Now it is evident that the powers of the soul, whether active or passive, are spoken of directly with respect to something substantial, but not with respect to something accidental. Similarly, to be understanding or sensing actually, is not a substantial mode of existing, but an accidental one to which the intellect and sense are directed. It is similar with respect to being large or small, to which the augmentative power is ordered. Indeed, the generative and nutritive powers are directed to the production or conservation of a substance, but by changing matter. Wherefore an action of this kind, like that of other natural agents, is performed by a substance through the medium of an accidental principle. Hence it is evident that the essence of the soul is not the immediate principle of its operations, but that it operates through accidental principles. Consequently the powers of the soul are not the essence itself of the soul but are properties of it.

This is also evident from the very diversity of the soul's actions, which differ generically and cannot be attributed to one immediate principle; because some are actions and some are passions, and are distinguished by other differences of this sort which must be attributed to different principles. Consequently, since the essence of the soul is one principle, it cannot be the immediate principle of all its actions, but must have many different powers corresponding to its different actions; for a power is said to be reciprocally related to its act. Hence there must be a diversity of powers in accordance with the diversity of operations. For this reason the Philosopher says, in the *Ethics*,[20] that the scientific power of the soul, which is concerned with necessary things, and the ratiocinative power, which is concerned with contingent things, are different powers, because the necessary and the contingent differ generically.

[20] VI, 1 (1139a 5 ff.).

Answers to objections. 1. This book *De spiritu et anima* was not written by Augustine but is said to have been written by a certain Cistercian monk.[21] Nor is there much to be said for the things which are set forth therein. If it is taken in an orthodox manner, however, it can be said that the soul is its powers or faculties, because they are its natural properties. Wherefore it is said in the same book that all powers are one soul, differing in property it is true, but one power. It would be a similar way of speaking if we were to say that heat, clarity, and brightness are one with fire.

The second, third, and fourth arguments are to be answered in the same way.

5. So far as its act of existing is concerned an accident does not go beyond its subject, but in so far as its operation is concerned it does; for the heat of fire heats something external to fire. It is in this way that the powers of the soul go beyond the soul itself, inasmuch as the soul understands and seeks not only itself but other things as well. Moreover, Augustine introduces this notion when he relates knowledge and love to the mind, not as the thing knowing and loving, but as that known and loved. For if he were to relate them to the soul itself in this way, as an accident to a subject, it would follow that the soul would know and love only itself. Perhaps it is in accordance with this meaning that he said, they are one life, one essence; because actual knowledge is the thing known in a certain respect,[22] and actual love, the thing loved.

6. An image of the Trinity is found in the soul not only with respect to the soul's powers, but also with respect to its essence; for the one essence of the three persons is represented in the soul, although in a very imperfect way.[23] More-

---

[21] Alcher of Clairvaux (Pseudo-Augustine).

[22] See Art. XVIII, note 5.

[23] The human soul is only a very imperfect image of the Trinity, because the essence of the soul is really distinct from its various powers; whereas the divine essence is not really distinct from the three divine Persons. See *Summa theol.*, Ia, q.39, a.1: "Whether in God the essence is the same as the Person?" Also

over, if the soul were its powers, its powers would differ from each other in name only. Consequently the distinction between the Persons which is found in God, is not adequately represented [in the soul].

7. There are three genera of accidents: some are caused by the principles of the species, and are called proper accidents, for example, risibility in man; others are caused by the principles of the individual, and this class is spoken of [in two ways]: first, those that have a permanent cause in their subject, for example, masculine and feminine, and other things of this kind, and these are called inseparable accidents; secondly, those that do not have a permanent cause in their subject, such as to sit and to walk, and these are called separable accidents. Now no accident of any kind ever constitutes part of the essence of a thing, and thus an accident is never found in a thing's definition. Hence we understand the essence (*quod quid est*) of a thing without thinking of any of its accidents. However, the species cannot be understood without the accidents which result from the principles of the species [i.e., the proper accidents], although the species can be understood without the accidents of the individual, even the inseparable accidents. Indeed, there can be not only a species but also an individual without the separable accidents. Now the powers of the soul are accidents in the sense of properties. Therefore, although the essence of the soul is understood without them, still the existence of the soul is neither possible nor intelligible without them.

8. Inasmuch as sensible and rational are essential differences, they are not derived from sense and intellect, but from the sentient and intellective soul.

9. For this reason the substantial form is not the immediate principle of action in inferior agents, as we have shown.

10. The soul is the principle of operation; however, it is

---

*Summa theol.,* Ia, q.93, a.5: "Whether the image of God is in man according to the Trinity of Persons?"

the first principle, not a proximate one, for powers operate by virtue of the soul itself, just as the qualities of the elements operate by virtue of their substantial forms.

11. The soul itself is in potency to the intelligible forms themselves, but this potency is not the essence of the soul; just as the potency to be a statue, which is in the copper, is not the essence of copper. For actual and potential existence do not belong to the essence of a thing, because act is not of the essence.

12. Prime matter is in potency to substantial act which is form; and therefore potency is the very essence of prime matter.

13. Man is said to be an intellect because the intellect is said to be the highest thing in man; just as the state is said to be the governor of the state. However, this does not mean that the essence of the soul is the intellective power itself.

14. The soul is seen to be similar to a science inasmuch as each is a first act, but such similarity does not exist in every respect. Consequently the soul is not necessarily the immediate principle of its operations, just as a science is.

15. The powers of the soul are not essential parts of it as though constituting its essence, but are potential parts, because a virtue of the soul is distinguished by powers of this kind.

16. Whatever is a form in its entirety and is not a subsisting thing, or if it is a subsisting thing that is pure act, cannot be the subject of an accident. Now the soul is a subsisting form and is not pure act, that is, if we speak of the human soul. Therefore it can be the subject of certain powers, such as the intellect and the will. Moreover, the powers of the sentient and nutritive parts are in the composite as a subject; because whatever has an act, has a power, as is shown by the Philosopher in the work *De somno et vigilia.*[24]

[24] I (458b 34).

17. Although the soul is one in essence, yet it contains potency and act and is diversely related to things. It is also related in a different way to the body; and for this reason different powers can proceed from one and the same essence of the soul.

## ARTICLE XIII

## WHETHER THE POWERS OF THE SOUL ARE DISTINGUISHED FROM ONE ANOTHER BY THEIR OBJECTS

The distinction between the powers of the soul is examined in the thirteenth article, that is: Whether the powers of the soul are distinguished from one another by their objects.[1]

Objections. 1. It seems that the powers of the soul are not distinguished in this way. For the things which differ most from one another are contraries. But a contrariety of objects does not diversify powers, because the same power of vision apprehends both white and black. Therefore a difference [i.e., a specific diversity] of objects [2] does not diversify powers.

2. Further, things which differ substantially differ more than those which differ accidentally. Now a man and a stone differ substantially, whereas a sound and something colored differ accidentally. Therefore, since a man and a stone are apprehended by the same power, so much the more so are a sound and something colored. Hence a diversity of objects is not the cause of the diversity of powers.

3. Further, if a difference of objects were the cause of the diversity of powers, one and the same object would necessarily

1 See also *Summa theol.*, Ia, q.77, a.3; *Comm. in De anima*, Bk. II, lect. 6. For a detailed treatment of the various powers of man, see *Summa theol.*, Ia, q.78 to 82 inclusive.

2 That is, "formal objects." Powers are distinguished by their "formal objects" and not by their "material objects." The material object, i.e., the thing perceived, may be the same for all the powers. However, each power grasps a different formal aspect of the thing, and is thereby distinguished from the others. Hence St. Thomas points out in *Summa theol.*, Ia, q.77, a.3: "Not any variety of objects diversify the soul's powers, but a difference in that to which the power of its very nature is directed."

160

cause powers to be identical. Now we see that one and the same object is apprehended by different powers. For the same object is known and desired, because an intelligible good is the object of the will.[3] Consequently a diversity of objects is not the cause of the diversity of powers.

4. Further, wherever the cause is the same, the effect is also the same. Therefore, if different objects diversified some powers, they would necessarily have to cause a diversity of powers in every case. However, we do not observe this. For sometimes different objects are certainly related to different powers, as sound and color are related to hearing and to vision respectively; and, at other times, these same objects are related to one and the same power, namely, to the imagination and to the intellect. Hence it follows that a diversity of objects is not the cause of the diversity of powers.

5. Further, habits (*habitus*)[4] are perfections of powers. Moreover, perfectible things are distinguished from one another by their proper perfections. Consequently powers are distinguished by their habits and not by their objects.

6. Further, whatever exists in a thing exists in it according to the mode of the recipient. But the powers of the soul exist in the organs of the body, for they are the acts of these organs. Therefore the powers of the soul are distinguished by the organs of the body and not by their objects.

7. Further, the powers of the soul are not the essence itself of the soul, but are properties of it. Now the properties of a thing spring from its essence. However, only one thing comes directly from a single thing. Therefore, first of all one single power of the soul comes from its essence, and then the other powers proceed therefrom in a certain order through the medium of this [first] power. Hence the powers of the soul differ according to origin and not according to objects.

[3] The object of the will is a good as known and presented by the intellect. It is in this sense that the intellect moves the will. See *Summa theol.*, Ia, q.82, a.4.

[4] See Art. XII, note 9.

8. Further, if the powers of the soul are diverse, one of them must come from another, for all of them do not come directly from the essence of the soul, because it is one and simple. But it is seen to be impossible for one power of the soul to come from another. First, because all powers of the soul exist simultaneously. Secondly, because accidents have their existence in a subject, and one accident cannot be the subject of another. Therefore the diversity among the soul's powers cannot be a result of the diversity among objects.

9. Further, the higher a substance is, the greater is its power and, as a result, less diversified (*multiplicata*), because every simple power is unlimited more than it is multiplied, as is said in the book *De causis*.[5] Now the soul is the most perfect of all inferior beings.[6] Therefore its power is more unified than theirs, and still extends to many things. Consequently its power is not multiplied because of the diversity among objects.

10. Further, if the diversity among the soul's powers depends on the diversity among objects, the order among the soul's powers must also depend on the order among these objects. However, this is seen not to be the case, for the intellect, whose object is the quiddity (*quod quid est*) and substance, is subsequent to the senses, whose objects are accidents such as color and sound. Furthermore, touch is prior to sight, while the visible is prior to and more common than the tangible. Consequently there is not a diversity of powers merely because there is a difference of objects.

11. Further, every appetible object is either sensible or intelligible. Now the intelligible is the perfection of the intellect, and the sensible is the perfection of sense. Therefore, since any being naturally desires its perfection, it follows that intellect and sense naturally desire every appetible object. Hence

---

[5] *De causis*, XXVII.
[6] Inferior beings are terrestrial beings. According to the classical astronomy, the earth was considered to exist in the lowest of the spheres.

it is unnecessary to admit the existence of any appetitive power other than the sentient.

12. Further, no appetite exists except the will and the irascible and concupiscible appetite. But the will belongs to the intellective order, and the concupiscible and irascible appetites belong to the order of sense, as is pointed out in the *De anima*.[7] Therfore no appetitive power must be held to exist in addition to the sentient and intellective.

13. Further, the Philosopher proves in the *De anima*,[8] that the principles of local motion in an animal are sense or imagination, intellect and appetite. But a power in animals is nothing else than a principle of movement. Therefore there is no motive power except the cognitive and appetitive powers.

14. Further, the powers of the soul are directed to something higher than nature, otherwise there would be powers (*vires*) of the soul in all natural things. But the powers which are assigned to the vegetal soul do not appear to be directed to anything higher than nature. For the vegetal soul is directed to the conservation of the species through generation; to the preservation of the individual through nutrition; and to the [development] of the individual's proper size through augmentation. Now in natural things, nature too performs all of these activities. Consequently the powers of the soul must not be directed to such activities.

15. Further, the higher a power, the greater is its unity and the more numerous are the things to which it extends. But a power of the soul is higher than a power of nature. Therefore, since nature by one and the same power gives existence to a natural body, bestows on it its proper size, and preserves it in existence, it seems a fortiori that the soul does these things through one power. Therefore the generative, nutritive, and augmentative powers are not diverse powers.

16. Further, sense is cognizant of accidents. But certain

7 III, 9 (432b 5).
8 III, 10 (433a 9 ff.).

other accidents differ from one another to a greater degree than do sound and color and the like, which exist not only in the same genus of quality, but also in the same species, namely, the third [kind of quality].[9] Therefore, if powers are distinguished according to the difference of objects, the powers of the soul should not be distinguished by accidents of this kind, but rather by others which differ from each other to a greater degree.

17. Further, there is one first contrary in any genus.[10] Therefore, if the sentient powers are diversified because of the different genera of possible qualities, it seems that there are diverse sentient powers wherever there are diverse contraries. Now in some cases this does occur, for sight apprehends both white and black, and hearing apprehends both low and high notes; but in other cases it does not, for touch apprehends both hot and cold, wet and dry, soft and hard, and so on. Consequently powers are not distinguished from one another by their objects.

18. Further, memory does not appear to be a power distinct from sense. For, according to the Philosopher, memory is a passion of a first sense.[11] However, their objects differ, because the object of sense exists in the present, and the object of memory, in the past. Hence powers are not distinguished from one another by their objects.

19. Further, all things known by the senses are also known by the intellect, which is cognizant of many other things as well. Therefore, if the sentient powers are distinguished from one another by reason of a plurality of objects, the intellect

9 See Aristotle, *Cat.*, VIII (8b 27 ff.). Here quality is divided into four kinds or species: (1) habit or disposition; (2) inborn capacity or incapacity; (3) affective qualities and affections; (4) figure and shape. St. Thomas is referring to affective qualities and affections.

10 A genus must first be divided into two species. The contrary which distinguishes these two species from one another is called the "first contrary." Other contraries form further subdivisions.

11 *De mem. et rem.*, I (449b 24; 450a 14).

must also be distinguished into different powers, just as sense is. This is evidently false.

20. Further, the possible and agent intellect are different powers, as has been shown above (Arts. III, IV, and V). But the object of both is the same. Therefore powers are not distinguished from one another because of a difference of objects.

On the contrary, it is said in the *De anima*,[12] that powers are distinguished by acts, and acts by objects.

Further, perfectible things are distinguished from one another by their perfections. But the objects of powers are the perfections of powers. Therefore powers are distinguished by their objects.

I answer: A power as such is spoken of in relation to an act. Hence a power must be defined by its act, and powers in turn distinguished from one another inasmuch as their acts are different. Now acts derive their species from their objects, because, if they are acts of passive powers, their objects are active. However, if they are the acts of active powers, their objects are as ends. Now the species of an operation must be considered in both of these ways. For the act of heating and that of making cold are distinguished from one another, because the principle of the former is heat, and that of the latter, cold. Besides, both are terminated in similar ends. For an agent acts in order that it may cause something similar to itself to exist in another. It follows, therefore, that the distinction between the powers of the soul is based on a difference [i.e., a specific diversity] of objects.

Now it is necessary to consider the difference between objects in this way and in this way alone, namely, that objects specifically differentiate the actions of the soul. For a species is differentiated in any genus only by the [specific] differences

12 II, 4 (415a 14 ff.).

which essentially divide the genus. The species of "animal," for instance, are not distinguished by white and by black, but by rational and non-rational. Furthermore, it is necessary to consider three grades in the actions of a soul. For the action of a soul transcends that of the nature operating in inanimate things. But this occurs in two ways. First, with respect to the manner of acting; secondly, with respect to what is produced by the action. Now with respect to the manner of acting, every action of a soul must transcend the operation or action of an inanimate nature. For every operation of a soul must proceed from some intrinsic agent, because an action of a soul is a vital action (moreover, every living thing is one that moves itself to operation). However, so far as the effect produced is concerned, not every action of a soul transcends an action of the nature of an inanimate thing. For the effect produced, that is, a natural mode of existing (*esse naturale*), and the things necessary for it, must be present in the case of inanimate bodies just as they are in the case of animate ones. But in the case of inanimate bodies, the effect is brought about by an extrinsic agent, whereas in the case of animate bodies, it is caused by an intrinsic agent. The actions to which the powers of a vegetal soul are directed, are of this sort. For the generative power is directed to giving existence to the individual thing; the augmentative power, to giving the thing its proper size; and the nutritive power, to preserving the thing in existence. But in inanimate things these effects are brought about only by an extrinsic agent. For this reason the aforementioned powers of a soul are said to be natural.

However, there are other higher actions of a soul which transcend the actions of natural forms, and also the effects produced by them, seeing that all things are disposed by nature to exist in the soul with an immaterial existence. For the human soul, in a certain respect, is all things by sensing and understanding. Moreover, there must be different grades of such immaterial existence. For there is one grade inasmuch

as things exist in the soul without their proper matter, but
with the singularity and individuating conditions which are
the result of matter. This is the grade of sense, which is receptive of individual species without matter, yet receives them
in a bodily organ. Now the intellect which receives species
completely abstracted from matter and material conditions,
and without [the aid of] a bodily organ, constitutes a higher
and more perfect grade of immateriality. Furthermore, just as
a thing has a natural inclination toward something, and has
movement and action in order to pursue that toward which it
is inclined through its natural form, so also does the inclination
toward a thing apprehended by sense or by intellect, follow
upon the apprehension of a sensible or intelligible form. This
inclination belongs to the appetitive power. And again, as a
consequence of this, there must be some movement by which
the thing [having sense or intellect] attains the thing desired.
This pertains to the motive power.

Moreover, five things are required for the perfect sense
knowledge which an animal should have. First, that sense receive species from sensible things, and this pertains to the
proper sense.[13] Secondly, that the animal make some judgment
about the sensible qualities received, and distinguish them one
from another, and this must be done by a power to which all
sensible qualities are related. This power is called the common
sense (*sensus communis*).[14] Thirdly, that the species of sensible
things which have been received be retained. Now an animal
needs to apprehend sensible things not only when they are
present, but also after they have disappeared. And it is necessary that this also be attributed to some power. For in corporeal things there is one principle that receives, and another
that retains, because things which are good recipients are some-

[13] A "proper sense" is an external sense, i.e., one which has its own proper
object. For example, sight, whose object is color.
[14] In Thomistic psychology "common sense" is a power of the soul. It is not
to be confused with the current notion of common sense, which designates
the practical judgment or natural sagacity of mankind in general.

times poor retainers. This power is called imagination or "phantasy" (*phantasia*). In the fourth place, the animal must know certain intentions which sense [i.e., the external sense] does not apprehend, such as the harmful, the useful, and so on. Man, indeed, acquires a knowledge of these by investigation and by inference, but other animals, by a certain natural instinct. For example, the sheep flees naturally from the wolf as something harmful. Hence in animals other than man a natural estimative power is directed to this end, but in man there is a cogitative power which collates particular intentions. This is why it is called both particular reason and passive intellect.[15] In the fifth place, it is necessary that those things which were first apprehended by sense and conserved interiorly, be recalled again to actual consideration. This belongs to a memorative power, which operates without any investigation in the case of some animals, but with investigation and study in the case of men. Therefore in men there is not only memory but also reminiscence.[16] Moreover it was necessary that a power distinct from the others be directed to this end, because the activity of the other sentient powers entails a movement from things to the soul, whereas the activity of the memorative power entails an opposite movement from the soul to things. But diverse movements require diverse motive principles, and motive principles are called powers.

Now because the proper sense, which is first in the order of sentient powers, is changed immediately by sensible objects, it was necessary for it to be divided into different powers in accordance with the diversity of sensible modifications. For the grade and order of modifications by which the senses are altered by sensible qualities, must be considered in relation

15 Not to be confused with the "possible intellect." The "passive intellect" compares individual intentions just as the intellect, properly speaking, compares universal intentions. See *Summa theol.*, Ia, q.78, a.4.

16 Man not only has memory, as other animals have, whereby he may recollect the past immediately, but he also possesses reminiscence. That is, he can seek syllogistically for a recollection of the past by the application of individual intentions. See *Summa theol.*, Ia, q.78, a.4.

to immaterial modifications, because sense is receptive of sensible species without matter. Hence there are some sensible objects whose species, although they are received immaterially in the senses, still cause a material modification in sentient animals. Now qualities which are also principles of change in material things are of this sort, for instance, hot and cold, wet and dry, and the like. Hence, because sensible qualities of this kind also modify us by acting upon us, and because material modification is made by contact, it was necessary that such sensible qualities be sensed by making contact with them. This is the reason why the sensory power experiencing such qualities is called touch. However, there are some sensible qualities which do not, indeed, change us materially, although their mutation has a material change connected with it. This occurs in two ways. First, in this way, that the material change affects the sensible quality as well as the one sensing. This pertains to taste. For, although the taste of a thing does not change the sense organ by making it the tasted thing itself, nevertheless this modification does not occur without some change taking place in the thing tasted as well as in the organ of taste, and particularly as a result of moisture. Secondly, in this way, that the material change affects the sensible quality alone. Now change of this sort is caused either by a dissipation and alteration of the sensible object, as occurs, for instance, in the sense of smell, or by a local change only, as occurs in the case of hearing. So it is that hearing and smell sense not by contact with an object, but through an extrinsic medium, because they occur without a material change on the side of the one sensing, although material change does take place in the sensible object. However, taste alone senses by contact, because it requires a material modification in the one sensing. Furthermore, there are other *sensibilia* which modify a sense without a material change being involved, such as light and color, and the sense which apprehends these is sight. Hence sight is the noblest of all the senses and extends to more objects than the other senses do (*universalia*), because the sensible qualities perceived by it are common both to corruptible and incorruptible bodies.[17]

Similarly the appetitive power, which follows the apprehension of the senses, must be divided twofoldly. For a thing is appetible either because it is delightful and suitable to the senses, and the concupiscible power is directed to this; or because the capacity of enjoying things delightful to the senses is made possible through it, which sometimes occurs together with something that is displeasing to sense. For instance, when an animal by fighting makes possible the enjoyment of something properly delightful by driving away anything that hinders this. The irascible power is directed to this end.

Moreover, since the motive power is directed to local movement, it is diversified only with respect to different [local] movements. These movements may differ for different animals, since some of them are able to crawl, some to fly, some to walk, and some to move in other ways; or they may differ for different parts of one and the same animal, because the particular parts of the body have their own movements.

Again, the grades of intellectual powers are similarly distinguished into cognitive and appetitive. Moreover, movement is common to sense and to the intellect, for the same body is moved by each of these powers through one and the same movement. Again intellectual cognition requires two powers, namely, the agent intellect and the possible intellect, as is clear from the previous articles.

Consequently it is obvious that there are three grades of powers in the soul, namely, the vegetal, sentient, and rational. Moreover, there are five genera of powers, i.e., the nutritive, sentient, intellective, appetitive, and locomotive, and each of these contains many powers under itself, as has been pointed out.

[17] The "incorruptible bodies" are the celestial bodies. Their incorruptibility was attributed to their lack of contrary elements.

Answers to objections. 1. Contraries are the things which differ most from each other, but within the same genus. Moreover, generically different objects befit diverse powers [or potencies], because a genus is also potential in a certain respect. Therefore contraries are related to one and the same power [or potency].

2. Although sound and color differ as accidents, yet they differ essentially (*per se*) so far as the alteration which they produce in sense is concerned, as has been explained. However a man and a stone do not, because sense is modified in the same way by them. Therefore a man and a stone differ accidentally so far as they are sensed, although they differ substantially as substances. For nothing prevents a difference from being related substantially to one genus, and accidentally to another, as white and black differ essentially in the genus of color, but not in that of substance.

3. The same thing is not related to different powers of the soul, according to the same formal object (*ratione objecti*), but according to different objects.

4. The higher a power, the more numerous are the things to which it extends. Hence the formal object of such a power has greater scope. This is why certain things that convene in the formal object of a superior power, are separated from each other in the formal object of inferior powers.

5. Habits are not perfections of powers as though powers existed for the sake of habits, but habits exist for the sake of powers in order that powers may better attain their objects. For this reason powers are not distinguished by habits, but by objects, just as things made by art are not distinguished by objects but by ends.

6. Powers do not exist for the sake of organs but vice versa. Consequently organs are distinguished from one another by objects rather than the reverse.

7. A soul has some particular end, just as the human soul has an intelligible good as its end. Besides, it also has other

ends ordered to this ultimate end, just as the sensible is ordered to the intelligible. And because the soul is directed
to its object through its powers, it also follows that in man
the sentient power exists for the sake of the intellective, and
so on. Thus, with respect to the notion of end, one power
arises from another because of the relationship of their objects. Hence the distinction between the powers of the soul
from the point of view of origin and that of objects, involves
no opposition.

8. Although an accident by its very nature cannot be the
subject of another accident, nevertheless a subject is determined by one accident through the intermediary of another,
just as a body is subject to color through the medium of its
surface. Thus one accident proceeds from its subject through
the medium of another accident, and one power of the soul
proceeds from its essence through the medium of another
power.

9. The soul by one power can bring itself to bear on more
objects than a natural thing can, just as sight apprehends all
visible objects. But the soul, by reason of its nobility, performs
many more operations than inanimate things do, and therefore must have several powers.

10. The order among the soul's powers is according to the
order among their objects. But order can be observed in both,
either in relation to perfection, and in this case the intellect
is prior to sense; or in relation to the process of generation,
and in this case sense is prior to the intellect. For in the process
of generation an accidental disposition is induced prior to
the substantial form.

11. The intellect naturally desires the intelligible as such.
For the intellect by nature desires to know, and sense desires
to sense. But there must be an appetitive power in addition
to sense and intellect, because the sensible or intelligible object is desired not merely in order that it may be sensed and
understood, but also for some other end. Therefore there must

be an appetitive power in addition to sense and intellect.

12. The will exists in the intellective order inasmuch as it follows the apprehension of the intellect. Indeed, the will belongs to the same grade of operation, namely, operations of the soul, but not to the same genus. The same thing must be said for the irascible and concupiscible appetite in relation to sense.

13. The intellect and appetite cause movement inasmuch as they command movement. But there must exist a motive power which executes movement according as the members of the body follow the command of appetite, intellect, or sense.

14. The powers of the vegetal soul are called natural powers because they operate only as nature does in bodies. But they are called powers of a soul because such powers do the things that nature does, in a more superior way, as was previously shown.

15. A real inanimate being receives its species and proper size at the same time. This is not possible in living things which require the least possible size at the beginning of generation, because they are generated from semen. Therefore in addition to the generative power which these things possess, there must exist also an augmentative power which produces their proper size. Moreover, this must occur in view of the fact that something is changed within a substance by augmentation and is added to that substance. Furthermore, this change is brought about by heat, which transforms both what is taken in from without, and also what exists within the thing itself. Hence a nutritive power is necessary for the conservation of the individual in order that whatever is lost may be continually restored; that whatever is lacking for the completion of its size may be added; and that whatever is necessary for the generation of semen may be produced. This nutritive power serves both the augmentative and the generative power, and thereby preserves the individual in existence.

16. Sound and color and things of this sort differ accord-

ing to the different way in which they modify sense. However, they are not *sensibilia* of different genera. Therefore the sensory powers are not differentiated by them.

17. In the *De anima*,[18] the Philosopher concludes that touch is not one sense but many, because the contraries which touch experiences are not brought together under one and the same genus, as the different contraries which can be considered in visible things are brought together under one and the same genus of color. Nevertheless all are alike in this respect, that they do not sense through an external medium; and all are called touch, so that there is one sense generically, divided into several species. However, it could be said that there is one sense pure and simple (*simpliciter*), because all the contraries of which touch is cognitive are known of themselves (*per se*); for they are known alternately and brought together under one genus, although this is unnamed, since the proximate genus both of heat and of cold is unnamed.

18. Since the powers of the soul are properties of it, memory is not prevented from being a power distinct from a first sense because memory is said to be a passion of a first sense. This statement shows the way in which memory is related to sense.

19. Sense receives the species of sensible things in the organs of the body and perceives singulars. However, the intellect receives the species of things without a bodily organ and is cognizant of universals. Hence a diversity of objects requires a diversity of powers in the sentient part, which does not require a diversity of powers in the intellective part. For in material things reception and retention are not one and the same, whereas in immaterial things these activities are one and the same. It is also necessary to distinguish the senses from one another with respect to the different modes of change involved. But this is unnecessary in the case of the intellect.

20. The same object, namely, the intelligible species in act,

18 II, 6 (418a 14).

is related to the agent intellect as that which is produced by this intellect; and to the possible intellect as that which moves the possible intellect. Thus it is obvious that the same thing is not related in the same respect both to the agent intellect and to the possible intellect.

# ARTICLE XIV

## WHETHER THE HUMAN SOUL IS INCORRUPTIBLE

The incorruptibility of the human soul is examined in the fourteenth article.[1]

Objections. 1. It seems that the soul is corruptible, for we read: "The death of man and the beast is one and the condition of them both is equal" (Eccles. 3:19). Now when beasts die their soul perishes with them. Consequently when a man dies, his soul perishes along with his body.

2. Further, it is said [2] that the corruptible and the incorruptible are generically diverse. But the human soul and the soul of beasts are not generically diverse, because man belongs to the same genus [animal] as the beast. With respect to corruptibility and incorruptibility, therefore, the soul of man and that of the beasts do not differ. But the soul of the beast is corruptible. Therefore the human soul is not incorruptible.

3. Further, Damascene says,[3] that an angel is endowed with incorruptibility, not by virtue of its own nature but by the gift of grace. The angel, however, is not a soul inferior to the human. Consequently the soul is not incorruptible by its very nature.

4. Further, the Philosopher proves in the *Physics*,[4] that the

[1] The question proposed in this article is also discussed by St. Thomas in *Summa theol.*, Ia, q.75, a.6; *Contra Gentes*, II, 79, 80, 81; *Quodl.*, X, q.3, a.2; *Sent.*, Bk. II, dist. 19, a.1; Bk. IV, dist. 50, q.1, a.1; *op.* II, *Compend. theol.*, chap. 84.

[2] Aristotle, *Metaph.*, X, 10 (1058b 26).

[3] *De fide orth.*, II, 3 (*PG*, XCIV, 865).

[4] VIII, 10 (267b 19).

Prime Mover has infinite power because He moves in infinite time. Hence, if the soul has the power of remaining in existence for an infinite length of time, it follows that this power is itself infinite. But the essence of an infinite power is not finite. Therefore, if the soul is incorruptible, its essence is infinite. But this is impossible, for the divine essence alone is infinite. Consequently the human soul is not incorruptible.

5. It may be objected that the soul is incorruptible, not by virtue of its own essence but by virtue of the power of God. On the other hand, whatever does not belong to a thing by virtue of its own essence is not essential to it; and, as the Philosopher points out in the *Metaphysics*,[5] corruptible and incorruptible are predicated essentially of everything whatever. Hence, if the soul is incorruptible, it must necessarily be incorruptible in virtue of its own essence.

6. Further, everything that exists is either corruptible or incorruptible. Hence, if the human soul is not incorruptible by virtue of its very nature, it follows that it is corruptible by virtue of its very nature.

7. Further, every incorruptible thing has the power of existing forever. Thus, if the human soul is incorruptible, it has the power of existing forever. In that case the human soul did not come into existence but always existed. This is contrary to faith.

8. Further, Augustine says,[6] that as God is the life of the soul, so the soul is the life of the body. But death is the privation of life. Therefore by death the soul is deprived of life and is destroyed.

9. Further, a form has actual existence only in the thing in which it exists. Thus, if the soul is the form of the body, it can exist only in a body. Hence it ceases to exist when the body corrupts.

10. The objection may be raised that, although this argu-

5 X, 10 (1058b 36–1059a 9).
6 *De civit. Dei*, XIX, 26 (*PL*, XLI, 656).

ment truly applies to the soul as a form, it does not hold so far as the essence of the soul is concerned. On the contrary, the soul is not the form of the body in an accidental way, otherwise, since the soul is constitutive of man inasmuch as it is the form of the body, it would follow that man would be a being *per accidens*. But whatever does not belong to a thing accidentally, belongs to it by its very essence. Consequently the soul is a form according to its very essence. Hence, if the soul is corruptible inasmuch as it is a form, it will likewise be corruptible according to its very essence.

11. Further, things having one and the same act of existing (*esse*) in common are so intimately related to each other that, if one of them is corrupted, the other or others are thereby corrupted also. But the soul and the body have one and the same act of existing in common, namely, the act of existing of a man. Therefore, when the body is corrupted, the soul is also corrupted.

12. Further, in man the sentient soul and the rational soul are substantially one and the same. But the sentient soul is corruptible. Therefore the rational soul is also corruptible.

13. Further, a form ought to be proportioned to a matter. But the human soul exists in the body as a form in matter. Therefore, since the body is corruptible, so too is the soul.

14. Further, if the soul can exist in separation from the body, then the soul must be able to perform some operation without the body, for no substance is functionless. Now without the body the soul can do nothing; it cannot even perform an act of knowledge. This is evident from the fact that intellection is impossible without a phantasm, as the Philosopher points out,[7] and there are no phantasms without the body. Consequently the soul cannot exist in separation from the body but ceases to exist when the body corrupts.

15. Further, the argument that the human soul is incor-

---

[7] *De anima*, III, 7 (431a 14 ff.).

ruptible could be based only on the assumption that it is intellective. But it seems that the soul is not intellective. For the
highest part of a being of an inferior nature in some way
strives to imitate the action of the being superior to it. Thus
the ape in some way imitates the action of a man, and yet does
not attain to the human level. Similarly, in view of the fact that
man occupies the highest rank in the order of material things,
it seems that he in some fashion imitates the action of the separate intellectual substances, namely, the act of intellection,
and yet does not really attain to it. Hence there does not seem
to be any necessary reason for holding that the human soul is
immortal.

16. Further, either all or at least most of the members of
any given species participate in the type of activity proper to
that species. But actually very few men succeed in being intelligent. Intellectual operation, therefore, is not the type of operation proper to the human soul. Consequently the human soul
need not be incorruptible simply because it is intellectual.

17. Further, the Philosopher points out in the *Physics*,[8] that
every finite thing comes to an end, since something is always
being taken away from it. But the natural good of the soul is
a finite good. Therefore, since the natural good of the soul is
diminished through sin, it seems that in the end this good
will be totally removed; and hence that the human soul will
at some time cease to exist.

18. Further, it is evident from our observation of the soul's
operations, that when the body grows weak the soul grows
weak also. Therefore, when the body corrupts, the soul also
corrupts.

19. Further, everything that is created can also be annihilated. Now the human soul has been created; therefore it can
be annihilated; and thus it follows that the soul is corruptible.

20. Further, so long as a cause continues to operate, its effect

[8] I, 4 (187b 25 ff.).

continues to exist.[9] Now the soul is the cause of life in the body. Therefore, if the soul always continues to exist, it seems that the body should go on living forever. This is clearly false.

21. Further, everything that subsists of itself is a particular thing (*hoc aliquid*) belonging to some species or genus. Now since the human soul is a form, it appears that it is not a particular thing, and that it does not belong to a species or to a genus as an individual member of the former or as a species of the latter. For to exist in a genus or in a species belongs to a composite [of matter and form], and not to matter or to form taken separately, except by reduction. Therefore the human soul is not a self-subsisting entity, and thus cannot continue to exist once the body has corrupted.

On the contrary, it is written: "God made man inexterminable, and in the image of His own likeness He made him" (Wisd. 2:23); from which it may be inferred that man is inexterminable, that is, incorruptible, inasmuch as he is made in the image of God. But as Augustine says in the book *De Trinitate*,[10] it is with respect to man's soul that he is made in the image of God. Therefore the human soul is incorruptible.

Further, everything that is corrupted has contraries, or is made up of contraries. But the human soul is completely devoid of contrariety, for even those things which are themselves contraries are not contraries in the soul, because the concepts of contraries existing in the soul are not themselves actual contraries. Hence the human soul is incorruptible.

Further, the celestial bodies are said to be incorruptible

---

[9] The principle "manente causa, manet effectus" and "cessante causa, cessat effectus" is frequently misinterpreted by those who think that the "efficient" cause is the only kind of cause. Cause, here, refers to any one of the four causes: efficient, final, formal, and material. The efficacy of the efficient and final causes ceases as soon as the effect is produced, because the thing now exists and depends on its formal and material causes. They are still acting, still causing it to be this thing. In the case of man the "formal cause" is the human soul. It is this cause which St. Thomas is considering here.

[10] X, 12 (*PL*, XLII, 984).

because they do not have matter of the sort found in generable and corruptible things. But the human soul is absolutely immaterial. This is evident from the fact that it receives the species of things immaterially. Hence the soul is incorruptible.

Further, the Philosopher says [11] that the intellect differs [from other powers] as the eternal differs from the perishable. But the intellect is a part of the soul, as he himself points out. Therefore the human soul is incorruptible.

I answer: It must necessarily be granted that the human soul is incorruptible. In proof of this we must take into consideration the fact that whatever belongs to a thing in virtue of its very nature (per se), cannot be taken away from it; for example, animality cannot be taken away from man, nor can the even and odd be taken away from number. Moreover it is evident that the act of existing in itself is a result of a form, for everything has its act of existing from its proper form; wherefore its act of existing can in no way be separated from its form. Therefore things composed of matter and form are corrupted by losing the form that gives them their act of existing. Moreover a form itself cannot be corrupted in itself (per se), but is corrupted accidentally as a result of the disintegration of the composite, inasmuch as the composite, which exists in virtue of its form, ceases to exist as a composite. This, indeed, is the case if the form is one that does not have an act of existing in itself, but is merely that by which a composite exists.

Now if there is a form having an act of existing in itself, then that form must be incorruptible. For a thing having an act of existing (esse) does not cease to exist unless its form is separated from it. Hence if the thing having an act of existing is itself a form, it is impossible for its act of existing to be separated from it. Now it is evident that the principle by which a man understands is a form having its act of existing in itself and is not merely that by which something exists. For, as the

[11] *De anima*, II, 2 (413b 24–29).

Philosopher proves in the *De anima*,[12] intellection is not an act executed by any bodily organ. The main reason why there is no bodily organ capable of receiving the sensible forms of all natural things, is that the recipient must itself be deprived of the nature of the thing received; just as the pupil of the eye does not possess the color that it sees. Now every bodily organ possesses a sensible nature. But the intellect, by which we understand, is capable of apprehending all sensible natures. Therefore its operation, namely, understanding, cannot be carried out by a bodily organ. Thus it is clear that the intellect has an operation of its own in which the body does not share. Now a thing operates in accordance with its nature (*quod est*), for things that exist of themselves have an operation of their own, whereas things that do not exist of themselves have no operation of their own. For example, heat in itself does not produce warmth, but something hot. Consequently it is evident that the intellective principle, by which man understands, has it own mode of existing superior to that of the body and not dependent upon it.

It is also evident that an intellective principle of this sort is not a thing composed of matter and form, because the species of things are received in it in an absolutely immaterial way, as is shown by the fact that the intellect knows universals, which are considered in abstraction from matter and from material conditions. The sole conclusion to be drawn from all this, then, is that the intellective principle, by which man understands, is a form having its act of existing in itself. Therefore this principle must be incorruptible. This indeed agrees with the Philosopher's dictum,[13] that the intellect is something divine and everlasting. Now it was shown in preceding articles (Articles II and V), that the intellective principle, by which man

---

[12] III, 4 (429b 3).

[13] *De anima*, III, 5 (430a 22). Aristotle's exact words are "immortal and perpetual."

understands, is not a substance existing apart from man but is something formally inhering in him which is either the soul or a part of the soul. Thus, from the foregoing considerations we conclude that the human soul is incorruptible.

Now all those who held that the human soul is corruptible missed some of the points we have already made. Some of these people, holding that the soul is a body, declared that it is not a form in its entirety, but a thing composed of matter and form. Others held that the intellect does not differ from the senses, and so they declared that the intellect does not operate except through a bodily organ; that it does not have a higher mode of existence than that of the body, and, therefore, that it is not a form having an act of existing in its own right. Still others held that the intellect, by which man understands, is a separate substance. But the falsity of all these opinions has been demonstrated in preceding articles. It therefore remains that the human soul is incorruptible.

Two additional arguments can be considered as an indication of this: First, respecting the intellect itself, because we see that even those things which are corruptible in themselves are incorruptible so far as they are perceived by the intellect. For the intellect apprehends things in and through universal concepts, and things existing in this [universalized conceptual] mode are not subject to corruption. Secondly, the natural appetite also provides an argument for the incorruptibility of the soul. Natural appetite [desire springing from the nature of man] cannot be frustrated. Now we observe in men the desire for perpetual existence. This desire is grounded in reason. For to exist (*esse*) being desirable in itself, an intelligent being who apprehends existence in the absolute sense, and not merely the here and now, must desire existence in the absolute sense and for all time. Hence it is clear that this desire is not vain, but that man, in virtue of his intellective soul, is incorruptible. .

Answers to objections. 1. In the Book of Ecclesiastes (3:19) Solomon [14] speaks as a popular orator, at one time representing the wisdom of the wise, at another, the stupidity of fools. The text quoted is an example of the latter. Or it may be said that the death of man and that of the beast is one and the same so far as the dissolution of the composite is concerned, since, for the one as for the other, this dissolution is brought about by the separation of the soul from the body. But there is this difference: after that separation occurs, the human soul remains in existence, whereas the soul of the brute does not.

2. Even if the human soul and the soul of brutes were brought under the same [logical] genus, nevertheless they would still exist in different natural genera; for the corruptible and the incorruptible are, of necessity, generically different in reality, although they can be ranged under one common concept; that is, from the standpoint of logic they can be considered under the same generic notion. Moreover, the soul does not exist in a genus as a species thereof, but as a part of a species. Yet both the composites in question are corruptible: the composite of which the human soul is a part, as well as the composite of which the soul of brutes is a part. Hence there is no reason why both types of soul may not belong to one and the same [logical] genus.

3. As Augustine says, true immortality and true immutability are the same. Moreover it is through grace that both the soul and the angel possess that immutability which results from free choice and which prevents them from changing from good to evil.

4. The act of existing (*esse*) is related to a form as something consequent upon the form in virtue of its very nature, and not as an effect to its efficient cause, in the manner in which motion, for example, is related to the power of the thing that produces it. Consequently, although the fact that a thing can move in infinite time may prove that its movement is infinite,

---

[14] The Book of Ecclesiastes is attributed to Solomon.

nevertheless the fact that a thing can exist in infinite time does not prove that the form whereby it exists is infinite; any more than the fact that a given quantity is always equal proves that it is infinite. On the contrary, the fact that a thing exists in infinite time proves the infinite power of that which is the cause of its being.

5. Corruptible and incorruptible are essential predicates because they belong to the essence of a thing as a formal or material principle and not as an active principle. However, the active principle of the perpetual act of existing enjoyed by some things is external to them.

The answer to the sixth objection is clear from what was said above.

7. The soul has the power of existing forever, but it did not always [i.e., before it existed] have that power. Hence the soul need not always have existed, but it must never cease to exist in the future.

8. The soul is called the form of the body inasmuch as it is the cause of life, just as the form is the principle of a thing's act of existing; because for living things, to live (*vivere*) is to exist (*esse*), as the Philosopher says in the *De anima*.[15]

9. The soul is a form of such a kind that its act of existing does not depend on the subject of which it is the form. Its proper operation proves this, as was shown above (Arts. VIII and IX).

10. Although the soul is a form by its very essence, nevertheless inasmuch as it is a form of a particular kind, that is, a subsisting form, it can have a certain character which does not belong to it simply as a form; just as the act of understanding does not belong to man inasmuch as he is an animal, although he is an animal by his very essence.

11. Although the soul and the body of man have one and the same act of existing in common, nevertheless that act of existing is communicated to the body by the soul. Thus the

[15] II, 4 (415b 8).

human soul communicates to the body that very act of existing by which the soul itself subsists. This has been shown in preceding articles. Hence the soul continues to exist when the body has corrupted.

12. The sentient soul in brute animals is corruptible, but since in man the sentient soul is identical in substance with the rational soul, it is incorruptible.

13. The human body is the matter belonging to the human soul and proportioned to the soul's operations. But, as was shown above (Art. VIII), bodily disintegration and other defects occur by reason of the very nature of matter. Or we may reply that the death of the body is the result of [original] sin, and not an original determination of nature.

14. The Philosopher's statement that understanding cannot take place without a phantasm, applies to the state of the present life in which man understands by his soul. However, the separated soul will understand in a different way. (See below, Arts. XVII ff.).

15. Although the human soul does not attain to that mode of understanding which superior substances possess, nevertheless it does attain to understanding in a certain way [i.e., in a way proper to itself], and this suffices to show its incorruptibility.

16. Although few people arrive at perfect understanding, yet all people achieve some kind or degree of understanding. The first principles of demonstration are obviously common conceptions of the soul which are perceived by the intellect.

17. Sin takes away grace totally, but it does not take anything away from the essence of a thing. However, sin does take away something of the inclination toward or aptitude for grace; and inasmuch as every sin stems from a contrary disposition, sin is said to take away some part of that good of nature which is aptitude for grace. But sin never destroys completely the good of nature; because, under contrary dispositions, the potential-

ity for good always remains, though by sin that potentiality is further and further removed from actualization.

18. The soul does not grow feeble when the body grows feeble, not even the sentient soul. For, as the Philosopher observes in the *De anima*,[16] if an old man acquired the eye of a youth, he would see as well as the youth does. From this it is clear that functional debility does not result from a debility of the soul but from that of a bodily organ.

19. Whatever receives existence "from nothing" [i.e., is created] can be reduced to nothing [i.e., annihilated], unless it is conserved in being by a guiding hand. Yet it is not for this reason that a thing is said to be corruptible, but because some principle of corruption exists in the thing itself. So it is clear that corruptible and incorruptible are essential predicates.

20. Although the soul, which is the cause of life, is incorruptible, nevertheless the body, which receives life from the soul, is subject to change; and because of this the body loses that disposition by which it prepared to receive life; and in this way the corruption of man is brought about.

21. Although the soul can exist of itself, yet it does not itself possess a species, for it is part of a species.

[16] I, 4 (408b 20).

## ARTICLE XV

### WHETHER THE SOUL, WHEN SEPARATED FROM THE BODY, IS CAPABLE OF UNDERSTANDING

In the fifteenth article we examine this question: Whether the soul, when separated from the body, is capable of understanding.[1]

Objections. 1. It seems that the soul, when separated from the body, is incapable of understanding. For no operation proper to the human composite remains in the soul when it exists apart from the body. Now understanding is an operation of the composite; for the Philosopher says in the *De anima*,[2] that to say that the soul understands is like saying that it weaves or builds. Therefore the act of understanding does not remain in the soul when it exists in separation from the body.

2. Further, the Philosopher states in the *De anima*,[3] that understanding in no way takes place without a phantasm. Now since phantasms exist in the sense organs, they cannot exist in the separated soul. Hence the soul does not understand when it is separated from the body.

3. But we must say that the Philosopher is speaking of the soul inasmuch as it is united to the body, and not of the separated soul. On the other hand, the separated soul can understand only by means of its intellective faculty. Now understand-

---

[1] This problem is also discussed in *Summa theol.*, Ia, q.89, a.1: IIa IIae, q.67, a.2; *Contra Gentes*, II, 81; *De verit.*, q.19, a.1; *Quodl.*, III, q.9, a.1; *Sent.*, Bk. III, dist. 31, q.2, a.4; Bk. IV, dist. 50, q.1, a.1.

[2] I, 4 (408b 11).

[3] III, 7 (431a 14).

ing is either [a form] of imagination or is impossible without imagination, as the Philosopher says in the *De anima*.[4] But the imagination does not exist without the body. Therefore neither is there any understanding without the body. Consequently the soul does not understand when it is separated from the body.

4. Further, the Philosopher says in the *De anima*,[5] that the intellect is related to phantasms as sight is to colors. But sight cannot see without colors. Therefore the intellect does not understand without the body.

5. Further, the Philosopher says in the *De anima*,[6] that understanding is corrupted when certain things within [the body] are corrupted; for example, the heart or the natural heat of the body. However, this is what occurs after the soul is separated from the body. Therefore the soul is incapable of understanding when it is separated from the body.

6. But it may be argued that the soul does understand when it is separated from the body, although not by abstracting from phantasms as it does in the present life. On the other hand, a form is not united to matter for the sake of the matter but for the sake of the form; for the form is the end and the perfection of the matter. Now a form is united to matter for the sake of fulfilling its own proper operation. Hence a form requires that specific type of matter by which its operation can be carried to completion, just as the form of a saw requires ferrous matter in order to accomplish the work of cutting. Now the soul is the form of the body. Consequently the soul is united to that specific type of body which is adapted to carrying out the soul's proper operation. Now the soul's proper operation consists in understanding. Therefore, if the soul can understand without the body, then the soul is united to the body in vain.

7. Further, if the separated soul is capable of understand-

---

4 I, 1 (403a 8).
5 III, 7 (431a 16).
6 I, 4 (408b 18 ff.).

ing, it understands in a more excellent manner when apart from the body than when united to it. For beings which have no need of phantasms in order to understand, do so in a more excellent way than we, who understand through the medium of phantasms. Now the good of the soul lies in its act of understanding; for the perfection of every substance consists in its own proper operation. Therefore, if the soul is capable of understanding without the aid of phantasms, when separated from the body, then it would be harmful to the soul to be united to a body, and hence would not be natural to it.

8. Further, powers are diversified by their objects. But the objects of the intellective soul are phantasms, as the Philosopher says in the *De anima*.[7] Therefore, if the intellective soul when separated from the body understands without phantasms, it must have powers other than those which it possesses when united to the body. But that is impossible, since the soul's powers are natural to it and inhere in it inseparably.

9. Further, if the separated soul understands, it must understand by means of some power. Now there are only two intellective powers in the soul: the agent intellect and the possible intellect. But it seems that the separated soul cannot understand by means of either of these powers. For the operation of each of them bears on phantasms: the agent intellect renders phantasms actually intelligible, whereas the possible intellect receives the intelligible species abstracted from phantasms. Consequently it seems that the separated soul is incapable of understanding in any way.

10. Further, there is but one proper operation for one thing, just as there is only one perfection for one perfectible thing. Therefore, if the operation of the soul consists in understanding by receiving [intelligible species] from phantasms, it seems that understanding without phantasms cannot be the operation of the soul, and hence that it does not understand when separated from the body.

[7] III, 7 (431a 14).

11. Further, if the separated soul understands, it must understand by means of something, because understanding takes place when the likeness of the thing understood exists in the one understanding. It cannot be said, however, that the separated soul understands by its own essence. This is true only of God; for His essence, being infinite, possesses in itself from eternity every perfection, and thus is the likeness of all things. Nor can it be said that the separated soul understands through the essence of the thing understood, because in that case it would understand only those things which are in the soul in virtue of its essence alone. Moreover it seems that the separated soul cannot understand through any species whether innate or concreated, for this would apparently be a reversion to Plato's theory that we are naturally endowed with all knowledge.[8]

12. Further, species of this sort seem to be needlessly implanted in the soul because, so long as it remains in the body, the soul cannot understand through them. However, intelligible species seem to have no other purpose than this, that the soul may understand through them.

13. Now it may be argued that, considered in itself, the soul is able to understand through innate species but that, as a matter of fact, it is hindered by the body from understanding through them. On the contrary, the more perfect a thing is in its nature, the more perfect it is in its operation. Now the soul is more perfect in its nature when united to the body than when it is separated from the body, just as every part of a whole is more perfect when it exists in that whole than when separated from it. Therefore, if the soul existing in separation from the body is able to understand through innate species, it is even more capable of understanding through them when united to the body.

14. Further, none of the natural properties of a thing are totally impeded by anything which pertains to the nature it-

8 See Plato, the *Phaedo*, chap. 18; also the *Euthydemus*, chaps. 20, 22.

self. Now it pertains to the very nature of the soul to be united to the body, because the soul is the form of the body. Hence, if intelligible species are naturally implanted in the soul, the soul would not be prevented from understanding through them because of its union with the body. But experience shows that the contrary is true.

15. Further, though it seems to be the case, it cannot be said that the separated soul understands through species acquired previously, when united to the body. For many human souls will remain separated from their bodies and will never acquire any intelligible species of things, as is evident in the case of the souls of children, and especially of infants who are still-born. Therefore, if separated souls can understand only through species previously acquired, it would follow that not all separated souls would have understanding.

16. Further, if the separated soul understands only through species previously acquired, it seems to follow that it could understand only those things which it understood in this life while united to the body. This seems untrue, however, for the separated soul knows many things concerning punishments and rewards which it does not know in this life. Hence the separated soul does not understand solely through species acquired before its separation from the body.

17. Further, the intellect is rendered intelligent in act by the intelligible species existing in it. But the intellect existing in act is understanding in act. Therefore the intellect in act understands all those things whose intelligible species actually exist in it. Hence it seems that intelligible species are not retained in the intellect after it ceases to actually understand, and thus that those species through which it is capable of understanding do not remain in the soul after its separation from the body.

18. Further, acquired habits give rise to acts similar to those acts by which the habits were acquired, as is evident from the

Philosopher's observation in the *Ethics*.[9] For by building a man becomes a builder, and the man who thus becomes a builder can in turn engage in building. But the intellect acquires intelligible species by turning to phantasms. Hence it can understand through phantasms only by turning to them. Therefore when the soul is separated from the body it cannot understand through acquired species as seems to be the case.

19. Further, it cannot be said that the intellect understands through species infused by some higher substance. For every receptive entity has its own proper agent by which it is naturally disposed to receive that which it receives. Now the human intellect is naturally disposed to receive [its species] from the senses.

20. Further, in the case of those things which are naturally disposed to be caused by inferior agents, the action of a superior agent alone does not suffice to cause them; thus animals which are disposed by nature to be generated from seed, are not found to be generated by the action of the sun alone.[10] Now the human soul by its very nature is disposed to receive species from sensible things. The influx of higher substances, therefore, does not alone suffice to account for its reception of intelligible species.

21. Further, an agent should be proportioned to a patient, and an inflowing power to a recipient. But the intelligence of a superior substance is not proportioned to the human intellect, since the former has knowledge which is more universal than ours and which is incomprehensible to us. Therefore the separated soul cannot understand through species infused by superior substances as seems to be the case. Consequently there is no way in which the separated soul can understand anything.

9 II, 1 (1103a 30 ff.).

10 It was a common opinion in St. Thomas' day that the sun was capable of producing, by its activity, certain lower species of animal life, but not the higher types.

On the contrary, understanding is the highest and proper operation of the soul. Hence if intellection does not belong to the soul without the body, none of its other operations belong to it either. But if some operation does not belong to the soul without the body, then it is impossible for the soul to exist apart from the body. We maintain, however, that the soul does exist when separated from the body. Hence it is necessary to hold that it understands.

Further, those whom Scripture records as having been brought back to life, possessed the same knowledge after this event that they had possessed before. Therefore the knowledge of those things which a man possesses in this life is not taken away from him after death. Consequently the separated soul can understand through species acquired before death.

Further, the likeness of inferior beings is found in superior ones. Thus mathematicians [11] foretell the future by studying in the celestial bodies the likeness of things which are done here on earth. Now the soul is superior in nature to all corporeal things. Therefore the likeness of all corporeal things exists in the soul, and in an intelligible mode, because the soul is itself an intellective substance. Therefore, it is seen that the soul by its very nature is capable of understanding all corporeal things, even when it will exist in separation from the body.

I answer: The fact that our soul in its present condition needs sensible things in order to understand, is the cause of the difficulty encountered in solving the problem raised in this article. Therefore, to solve this problem, we must consider the various explanations for this need [of sensible things] that have been proposed. For some men (namely, the Platonists,[12]

[11] This reference is to the astrologers who claimed to foretell the future by studying the position of the stars.

[12] See Plato, the *Phaedo*, chaps. 10, 18, and the *Meno*, in which Socrates develops the famous "theory of reminiscence." The following development by St. Thomas is actually a comprehensive summary of the major theses in Pla-

as Aristotle points out [13]) have maintained that, in order for the soul to understand it does not need the senses essentially (*per se*), as though knowledge were caused in us by the senses, but only accidentally inasmuch as our soul is stirred by the senses to recollect things which it knew in a previous existence, and of which it possesses a knowledge naturally endowed. To account for this mode of understanding Plato held that the species of things subsisted apart from them, and were actually intelligible entities. He called them "Ideas" and maintained that our soul knows and understands by participating in them, and by some kind of infusion. Moreover, according to Plato, the soul, prior to its union with the body, was able to use this knowledge freely, but as a result of that union it was so weighed down by the body, and somehow smothered by it, that it seemed to have forgotten the things it had previously known and of which it had possessed connatural knowledge. They also maintained that the soul was in some way stimulated by the senses so that it turned back upon itself and recollected those things which it previously knew and of which it had innate knowledge; just as it sometimes happens that our sense-experiences are the occasion for our recollecting vividly certain things which we seemed to have forgotten.

This position of Plato on knowledge and on sense-objects conforms with his position on the generation of natural things. For he held that the forms of natural things, through which each individual is placed in its proper species, result from a participation in the "Ideas" aforementioned, so that the sole function of inferior agents is to dispose matter for participation in the separated species.

Now if this theory be adopted, the whole problem with which we are dealing becomes simple and easy. For according to this view the soul does not by its essence (*per se*) require

---

tonic philosophy. It is a good example of the Angelic Doctor's ability to scrutinize a doctrine and describe it in the fewest possible words.

[13] *Metaph.*, I, 6 (987b 4 ff.).

sensible things in order to understand; it requires them only accidentally (*per accidens*), and this accidental need ceases to exist as soon as the soul is separated from the body. For the body having ceased to weigh upon the soul, the soul will then have no need of the stimulus of sense. Existing by itself the soul will be, as it were, lightly clad and on the alert for all knowledge.

Now according to this theory, it appears that no explanation can be offered as to why the soul is united to the body. For [according to the Platonic view under consideration] this union is not for the sake of the soul, because when the soul is not united to the body it can still exercise perfectly its own proper operation, whereas its proper operation is impeded by its union with the body. Similarly, according to this view, it cannot be argued that the union of soul and body exists for the sake of the body; for the soul does not exist for the sake of the body, but rather the body for the soul, because the soul is nobler than the body. Then, too, it seems incongruous that the soul should suffer a loss in its own operation for the sake of ennobling the body. It also seems to follow from this view that the union of the soul with the body is not natural, for whatever is natural to a thing does not impede the operation proper to that thing. Hence, if union with a body impeded the soul's understanding, it would not be natural but contrary to the nature of the soul to be united to a body; and in that case man, who is constituted of a soul united to a body, would not be a natural being; which seems absurd.

Likewise, experience shows that our knowledge is not the result of participation in separated species, but is acquired from sensible things, because those who lack one sense lack knowledge of the sensible things apprehended by that sense; just as a person born blind cannot have a knowledge of colors.

Now there is another theory according to which the senses are not accidentally serviceable to the human soul in performing its function of understanding (as the theory just dealt

with supposes), but essentially; not in order that we may acquire knowledge from sense-objects, but because the senses
dispose the soul for acquiring knowledge from some other
source. This is the opinion of Avicenna.[14] For Avicenna maintains that there is a certain separate substance which he calls
the intellect or "the Agent Intelligence"; [15] that the intelligible species through which we understand flow into our intellect from this Agent Intellect, and that by the operation
of the sentient part, the imagination and other things of this
sort, our intellect is prepared for orientating itself toward
the Agent Intellect and for receiving the influx of intelligible
species from it. This theory agrees with Avicenna's view on the
generation of natural things; for he maintains that all substantial forms flow from the Agent Intellect, and that natural
agents only dispose the matter for receiving forms from the
Agent Intellect.

According to this position, as in the preceding, this question
seems to involve little or no difficulty. For if the senses are
necessary for understanding only inasmuch as they dispose the
soul to receive species from the Agent Intellect, because our
soul is thus orientated toward the latter, then when the soul
is separated from the body it will be orientated toward the
Agent Intellect by itself alone, and will receive intelligible
species from that Intellect. Thus the soul will have no need
of the senses in order to understand; just as the ship in which
a person has crossed the sea is no longer needed by him after
the completion of the voyage.

Now it seems to follow from this view, that a man immediately acquires all knowledge, both of things which he per-

---

[14] *Metaph.*, VIII, 7: IX, 4.

[15] According to Avicenna, there is one "Agent Intellect" for all men, and this
intellect exists apart from men, being the last in a series of intelligences emanating from the First Cause. In relation to man and the whole order of terrestrial things, this "Agent Intellect" is a veritable "source of forms" or "giver
of forms" (*dator formarum*) in that it confers intelligible forms or species on
man when he understands, and infuses the substantial forms of things in natural generation.

ceives by his senses and of other things. For if we understand through species which flow into our minds from an Agent Intellect, and if all that is required for the reception of this infusion is the orientating of our soul toward this Intellect, then whenever the soul is so orientated it will be able to receive the infusion of any and every sort of intelligible species; because in that case it cannot be said that the soul is orientated toward the Agent Intellect with respect to one species and not with respect to another; and thus a person born blind will, by imagining sounds, be able to acquire a knowledge of colors, or of any other sensible object; which is manifestly false.

It is also evident that we have need to the sentient powers for understanding, not only in the acquisition of knowledge but also in the utilization of knowledge already acquired. For we cannot even reflect upon the things we know without turning to phantasms, although Avicenna himself is of a contrary opinion. It is for this reason that, even in reflecting upon things which it knows, the soul is impeded in its operation by injuries to the organs of the sentient powers whereby the phantasms are retained and apprehended. It is evident also that we have need of certain phantasms in things divinely revealed to us through the influence of superior substances. Thus Dionysius says: [16] "The divine light cannot shine upon us unless it is screened round about by many sacred veils." Now this would not be so if we needed phantasms only to orientate us toward superior substances.

Consequently a different explanation must be given for the need which the soul has of sensory powers in order to understand. For they are not accidental in the manner of stimuli, as Plato held, nor are they merely dispositive, as Avicenna claimed, but re-present to the intellective soul its proper object, as Aristotle says in the *De anima*: [17] "Phantasms are to

---

[16] *De cael. hier.*, I, 2 (PG, III, 121).
[17] III, 7 (431a 14).

the intellect what sensible things are to sense." Now just as colors are made actually visible by light, so phantasms are made actually intelligible only by the agent intellect. This agrees with what we hold about the generation of natural things. For as we maintain that superior agents produce natural forms by means of natural agents, so we maintain that the agent intellect produces knowledge in our possible intellect through phantasms rendered actually intelligible by the agent intellect. The question whether the agent intellect is a separate substance, as some held, or a light in which our soul participates in the manner of superior substances, has no bearing on this last point.

Now according to this latter theory it seems even more difficult to see how the separated soul can understand. For [on that hypothesis] there will be no phantasms requiring corporeal organs for their apprehension and retention. Yet if these be removed, it is seen that the soul cannot understand; just as the faculty of sight cannot function in the absence of colors. Now in order to solve this problem the fact must be borne in mind that the soul, being lowest in the order of intellectual substances, participates in intellectual light or in intellectual nature, in the lowest and weakest measure. For in the first intelligence, namely, God, intellectual nature is so powerful that He understands all things through one intelligible form, namely, His own essence. Inferior intellectual substances, on the other hand, understand through many species; and the higher each of these substances is, the fewer forms it possesses, and the more potent is its faculty of understanding all things through those few forms. However, even if an inferior intellectual substance possessed forms equally as universal as those of a superior substance, its knowledge would still remain incomplete, since it does not have so great a power of understanding, because that inferior intellectual substance would only know things universally; and, from the few universal forms it apprehends, it could not bring its knowledge to bear on singulars. Therefore, if the human soul, which is lowest in the order of intellectual substances and hence possesses the least intellectual power of them all, received forms abstractly and universally, as separate substances do, then it would have a most imperfect kind of knowledge: that of knowing things in the universal and indistinctly. Hence, in order that the soul's knowledge may be perfect in its kind and bear directly upon singulars, the soul must acquire a knowledge of truth from singular things. However, the light of the agent intellect is necessary in order that those things may be received in the soul and may exist there in a higher mode than that in which they exist materially. Hence it was necessary that the soul be united to a body for the perfection of its intellectual operation.

It is undoubtedly true, however, that bodily movements and the activity of the senses prevent the soul from receiving infused knowledge from separate substances. It is for this reason that certain things are revealed to persons during sleep, and to those who have [momentarily] lost their senses.[18] Therefore, when the soul shall be separated completely from the body, it will be able to receive infused knowledge from superior substances more fully, because, thanks to such knowledge, it will be able to understand without a phantasm, which otherwise it cannot do. Nevertheless an influx of this sort will not produce knowledge as perfect and as directly related to singulars as the knowledge which we acquire here below through the senses, though a much more perfect knowledge will be had in addition to this natural influx by those souls that will enjoy the influx of a supernatural light by which they will know all things most fully and will see God Himself. Moreover, separated souls will have a determinate knowledge of

18 St. Thomas is referring to the revelations made to people in dreams (witness the revelations described in the Old Testament) and to revelations made to people in moments of ecstasy. In both cases the subjects are insensible to the external world and are thereby rendered more capable of receiving infused knowledge of a higher order.

those [singular] things which they had previously known here below, and whose intelligible species they retain in themselves.

Answers to objections. 1. Those words do not represent Aristotle's own opinion, but the opinion of those who said that to understand is to be moved, as the context of his statement shows.

2. The Philosopher is speaking of the intellectual operation of the soul so far as the soul is united to the body; for in that state the soul does not understand without a phantasm, as has been explained.

3. In its present state of union with the body, the soul does not participate in intelligible species flowing from superior substances, but only in intellectual light. Consequently the soul is in need of phantasms as objects from which it may receive intelligible species. But after its separation from the body, the soul will indeed participate more fully in intelligible species, and therefore will have no need of external objects.

This also answers the fourth objection.

5. It is clear from what has been said before that Aristotle refers in this place to the opinion of certain philosophers who held that the intellect has a bodily organ just as a sense faculty does. Now if this were maintained, the separated soul would be entirely incapable of understanding anything. Or we may reply that Aristotle is speaking of that mode of understanding which we possess here and now.

6. The soul is united to the body in virtue of the soul's operation, which is understanding, not because it could in no way understand without the body, but because in the natural order it could not understand perfectly without the body, as has been shown.

Thus, the answer to the seventh objection is evident.

8. Phantasms are objects of the intellect only so far as they are rendered actually intelligible by the light of the agent intellect. Consequently all actually intelligible species which are

received in the intellect, whencesoever they may come, will have no other formal object; and it is by their formal objects that the powers of the soul are differentiated.[19]

9. The operation of the agent intellect and that of the possible intellect bear on phantasms so long as the soul remains united to the body; but when the soul will be separated from the body, it will receive, through its possible intellect, the species that flow into it from superior substances, and it will have the power of understanding through its agent intellect.

10. The proper operation of the soul is to understand things that are actually intelligible. Moreover, intellectual operation is not diversified specifically because actual intelligibles are received from phantasms or elsewhere.

11. The separated soul does not understand things through its own essence, nor through the essences of the things understood, but through species flowing into it from superior substances; nor does it, as the Platonists claimed, understand things from the very beginning of its existence.

Thus the reply to the twelfth objection is evident.

13. If the soul, when united to the body, possessed innate species, it would be able to understand through them, just as it understands through acquired species. Now although it is more perfect in its nature [when united to the body], nevertheless, on account of bodily movements and sense activities, the soul is held in check, so that it cannot be united to superior substances in order to receive infused knowledge from them, as it does when it is separated from the body.

14. To understand through infused species is not natural

---

[19] The various powers of the soul are distinguished by their "formal" objects, that is, that "form" of an object which a power is immediately capable of grasping in virtue of its very nature. The "material" object, that is, the thing itself which is perceived, is common to all faculties or powers and, therefore, they cannot be distinguished so far as this latter kind of object is concerned.

to the soul when united to the body, but only after it has left the body, as we have pointed out.

15. Separated souls will indeed be able to understand through species acquired previously while they existed in the body, but not through them alone. They will also understand through infused species, as we have explained.

Thus the reply to objection sixteen is evident.

17. Intelligible species sometimes exist in the possible intellect only potentially; and when that is the case man knows only potentially, and thus needs to be made actually knowing either by teaching or by discovery. Sometimes, however, intelligible species exist in the possible intellect in a completely actual way, and when that is the case, it knows actually. Sometimes, however, they exist in it in a mode midway between potency and act, that is to say, as a habit; and when that is the case the intellect can understand actually whenever it wishes. Moreover, thanks to this mode of existing, acquired intelligible species exist in the possible intellect even when it is not performing acts of understanding.

18. As has already been pointed out, an intellectual operation, whose actually understood object is received from phantasms, does not differ specifically from an intellectual operation whose object is derived from some other source. For the operation of a power is distinguished and specified by the formal nature of the object, not by its matter.[20] Hence, if the separated soul understands through intelligible species which are retained in the intellect, and which were previously acquired from phantasms, and not by actually turning itself to phantasms, then the operation which results from the species so acquired, and the operation by which those species are acquired, will not be specifically different.

19. The possible intellect is disposed by nature to receive [species] from phantasms only so far as the phantasms are actu-

20 See answer to objection 8, note 19.

alized by the light of the agent intellect, which is a kind of participation of the light of superior substances. Consequently the intellect is not prevented from being able to receive [species] from superior substances.

20. In its present state of union with the body, the soul is disposed by nature to acquire knowledge from phantasms, and in this state its knowledge cannot be caused by superior agents alone. But this will be possible when the soul is separated from the body.

21. From the fact that the knowledge of separate substances is not proportioned to our soul, it does not follow that our soul is incapable of grasping any knowledge from the influx of those substances, but only that it cannot grasp a perfect and distinct knowledge, as has been explained.

## ARTICLE XVI

## WHETHER THE SOUL, WHEN UNITED TO THE BODY, CAN UNDERSTAND SEPARATE SUBSTANCES

In the sixteenth article we examine this question: Whether the soul, when united to the body, can understand separate substances.[1]

Objections. 1. It seems that the soul, when united to the body, can understand separate substances. For no form is prevented from attaining its end by the matter to which it is naturally united. Now the end of the intellective soul seems to consist in knowing separate substances, which are in the highest degree intelligible;[2] for the end of each and every thing is to attain perfection in its operation. Therefore the human soul is not prevented from understanding separate substances by being united to the body, which is the soul's own proper matter.

2. Further, the end of man is happiness. Now according to the Philosopher, in the *Ethics*,[3] ultimate happiness consists in the operation of man's highest power, namely, the intellect, and is related to the noblest object, which seems to be none other than a separate substance. Hence man's last end consists in understanding separate substances. Now it would be

---

[1] The "separate substances" or "pure intelligences" are the angels. St. Thomas also discusses this problem in *Summa theol.*, Ia, q.88, a.1; *Contra Gentes*, II, 60; III, 42, 43, 44, 46; *De verit.*, q.10, a.11; q.18, a.5, ad 7um and 8; *op.* LXX, *De Trin.*, q.6, lect. 3; *Comm. in Metaph.*, Bk. II, lect. 1.

[2] A being is knowable in proportion to its immateriality. Separate substances have no matter and are, therefore, knowable in the highest degree.

[3] X, 7 (1177a 11); 8 (1178b 10 ff.).

incongruous if man failed completely to attain his end; for in that case his life would be meaningless. Therefore man can know separate substances. But it belongs to man's very essence to possess a soul that is united to a body. Therefore the soul, when it is united to the body, can understand separate substances.

3. Further, every generative process reaches a terminus, for no process goes on to infinity. Now there is a certain intellectual generation whereby the intellect is brought from potency to act, that is to say, is made actually knowing. Therefore this process does not go on to infinity but at some time will reach a terminus, that is, it will be completely actualized. But this end can be attained only when the intellect understands all intelligible things, especially separate substances. Therefore the human intellect is capable of attaining a knowledge of separate substances.

4. Further, it seems to be more difficult to separate from matter things which do not exist in separation therefrom, and to apprehend those things, than to apprehend things which exist in themselves apart from matter. But even when united to the body, our intellect separates from matter things which do not in themselves exist apart from matter, inasmuch as it abstracts the intelligible species by which it apprehends material things. Therefore our intellect will be even more capable of apprehending separate substances.

5. Further, sense objects that are excessively intense (*excellentia sensibilia*) [4] are sensed to a lesser degree than others, because they destroy the harmony of a sense organ. However, if there were a sense organ which was not affected adversely by the intensity of its sensible object, then the more intense the sensible object, the more fully would the sense organ experience that object. Now the intellect is not corrupted in any

---

[4] A sense is rendered incapable of adequately perceiving its object when it receives a very intense stimulus, for example, an excessively intense light or sound. This occurs because such a stimulus completely exceeds the normal range of the sense organ.

way by an intelligible object, rather is it perfected by it. Hence the more intelligible things are, the better the intellect knows them. But separate substances which are actually intelligible in themselves, because they are immaterial, are more intelligible than material substances, which are intelligible only potentially. Therefore, since the intellective soul when it is united to the body apprehends material substances, it is even more capable of apprehending separate substances.

6. Further, even when the intellective soul is united to the body it abstracts the quiddity from things having a quiddity; and, since it cannot regress to infinity, it must in this abstractive process eventually attain to a quiddity that is not a thing having a quiddity, but is a quiddity only. Therefore, since separate substances are nothing but certain quiddities existing of themselves, it seems that the intellective soul, when united to the body, is capable of apprehending separate substances.

7. Further, it is natural for us to acquire a knowledge of causes from their effects. However, some of the effects caused by separate substances must be found in sensible and material things; for, as Augustine shows in the *De Trinitate,*[5] all corporeal things are governed by God through the agency of the angels. Therefore the soul, when united to the body, can apprehend separate substances through sensible objects.

8. Further, the soul understands itself when it is united to the body; for, as Augustine says in the *De Trinitate,*[6] the mind understands itself and loves itself. But the mind itself possesses the nature of a separate intellectual substance. Therefore the soul, when united to the body, can apprehend separate substances.

9. Further, in things nothing exists without a purpose. But to be an intelligible seems to be purposeless if the intelligible is not apprehended by any intellect. Therefore, since separate

[5] III, 4 (*PL,* XLII, 873).
[6] IX, 3 (*PL,* XLII, 963).

substances are intelligibles, our intellect can apprehend them.

10. Further, as sight is to visible things, so intelligence is to intelligible things. But our sense of sight can perceive all visible things, even those that are incorruptible, although it is itself corruptible. Therefore, on the assumption that our intellect is corruptible, it would be capable of apprehending incorruptible separate substances because they are intelligibles in themselves.

On the contrary, the soul does not apprehend anything without a phantasm, as the Philosopher says in the *De anima*.[7] Therefore the soul, when united to the body, cannot apprehend separate substances.

I answer: Aristotle set out to solve the problem, posed in this article, in the *De anima*,[8] but the solution is not found in those writings of his which have come down to us.[9] This explains why Aristotle's followers have proceeded to offer various solutions for this problem.

For some have maintained that our soul, even when united to the body, is capable of knowing separate substances, and that man's ultimate happiness actually consists in knowing such substances. However, [these theorists] entertain different opinions as to the way in which we understand such substances. For some have maintained that our soul cannot acquire an understanding of separate substances in the way in which we acquire an understanding of those other intelligible objects which we learn about in the speculative sciences. The latter

[7] III, 7 (1131a 14).
[8] *Ibid.*, (431b 19).
[9] See the Commentary of St. Thomas on Aristotle's *De anima*, Bk. III, lect. 12, where he explains that the Philosopher could not answer the question pertaining to the separated soul's knowledge of separate substances, in that place, because he had not yet solved the antecedent question concerning the existence of separate substances; a question which belongs to metaphysics. St. Thomas was also of the opinion that we do not know Aristotle's solution, either because not all of Book III of the *De anima* was translated, or because death prevented Aristotle from completing this work.

type of knowledge is acquired through definitions and demonstrations, whereas a knowledge of separate substances, these theorists maintained, can be acquired only as a result of the Agent Intellect itself being united to us. For they supposed that the Agent Intellect was a separate substance which by its own nature understands separate substances. Hence, when this Agent Intellect shall be united to us, enabling us thereby to understand through Itself (as we now understand through intellectual habits of scientific knowledge), we shall, consequently, apprehend separate substances.

Moreover, they explain the manner in which this Agent Intellect can be united to us so that we may understand. For it is evident, [they argue], from what the Philosopher says in the *De anima*,[10] that whenever we are said to be so-and-so or to do so-and-so, two things are involved, one having the role of form, the other the role of matter; just as we are said to be made healthy by health and with respect to the body, so that health is related to the body as a form to matter. It is clear also [they say] that we understand by the Agent Intellect and through intelligible objects-known (*speculata*); for we arrive at a knowledge of conclusion through principles known naturally, and through the Agent Intellect. Therefore the Agent Intellect must be related to intelligible objects-known as a principal agent is to an instrument, and as a form is to matter, or as act is to potency. For of two things, the more perfect always has the character of an act with respect to the other. Moreover, whatever receives in itself that which has the character of a form, also receives that which has the character of matter; just as a body having a surface is also receptive of color, which is a kind of form possessed by that surface. Likewise, the pupil of the eye which receives color, also receives light, which is the act of color; for by light color is made actually visible. Consequently, in the same way, so far as the possible intellect receives intelligible objects-known, to that extent does it re-

10 II, 2 (414a 4 ff.).

ceive from the Agent Intellect. Hence, when the possible intellect receives all objects-known, then at that time it will receive the Agent Intellect unto itself completely; and thus the Agent Intellect will assume the character of a form in the possible intellect, and consequently will become one with us. Hence, as we at present understand through the possible intellect, so shall we then understand through the Agent Intellect; and we shall understand not only all natural things but separate substances as well.

On this point, however, there are differences of opinion among those who subscribe to the theory stated above. For some, holding that the possible intellect is corruptible, assert that the possible intellect is in no way able to know either the Agent Intellect or the separate substances; but that as long as we remain in a state of union with the Agent Intellect, we shall know the Agent Intellect and other separate substances as well through the Agent Intellect itself, inasmuch as it will be united to us as a form. But others, holding that the possible intellect is incorruptible, assert that the possible intellect is able to know the Agent Intellect as well as other separate substances.

Now it is impossible to maintain this position. It is gratuitous, and it is contrary to the meaning of Aristotle's doctrine.[11] It is impossible to maintain this position because it premises two contradictory affirmations (*duo impossibilia*): namely, that the Agent Intellect is a separate substance existing apart from us, and that we understand through the Agent Intellect as through a form. Now so far as we carry out an operation by means of something having the character of a form, to that extent do we cause something to exist actually, just as a hot thing heats by its heat inasmuch as it is actually hot. For a thing acts only so far as it is in act. Hence that by which a thing acts or operates formally, must be united to that thing with respect to its very act of existing. Hence in the case of two substances ex-

11 *Ethic.*, I, 9 (1099b 9 ff.).

isting in separation from one another, it is impossible for one of them to operate formally through the other. Thus, if the Agent Intellect is a separate substance existing apart from us, we cannot understand by it formally, although we may be able to understand by it actively, as we are said to see by the light of the sun.

The aforesaid position is likewise gratuitous *(vana)*, because the arguments advanced for it are not conclusive with necessity. Two considerations make this point clear. First, indeed, because if, as the advocates of this view maintain, the Agent Intellect is a separate substance, then this intellect will not be related to intelligible objects-known as light is to colors, but as the sun shining is to colors. Hence, simply because the possible intellect receives intelligible objects-known, that intellect is not thereby brought into substanial union with the Agent Intellect, but is united only to an effect of it; just as the eye by receiving colors is not united to the substance of the sun, but only to the sun's light. Secondly, because (supposing we grant that the possible intellect, being receptive of intelligible objects-known, is in some way united substantially to the Agent Intellect), even though the possible intellect receives all intelligible objects-known, the latter being abstracted from phantasms and known demonstratively through the principles of demonstration, it would not follow that the possible intellect had thus been perfectly united with the Agent Intellect. This could be the case only if it were proved that all those intelligible objects together were equivalent in power and in substance to the power and substance of the Agent Intellect itself. This is obviously untrue, for if the Agent Intellect is a separate substance, it is by that fact alone of a higher order of being than all those objects in the natural order which are rendered intelligible by it.

It is also remarkable that these people did not see the evident error in their reasoning. For, although they maintained that all intelligible objects-known were united by one or two of these objects, still it does not follow for this reason, according to them, that we shall know all the other intelligible objects-known. Now it is evident that separate intelligible substances surpass all those objects which they call intelligible objects-known to a far greater degree than all of the latter taken together exceed one or two or any number of themselves; for these objects are all of one genus and have the same mode of intelligibility, whereas separate substances are of a higher order, and have a higher mode of intelligibility. Hence if the Agent Intellect is brought into union with us as a form, and as the agent of those intelligibles, it does not for this reason follow that it is united to us as a knower of separate substances.

It is likewise clear that this whole position is contrary to the meaning of the doctrine of Aristotle, who says in the *Ethics*,[12] that happiness is a common good which all who are not deprived of virtue may possess. But to understand all those things which these theorists call intelligible objects-known is impossible for any man, or at least is so rare that in this life no man ever did in fact attain such understanding, except Christ Himself, who was both God and man. Hence it is impossible that such knowledge should be required for human happiness. Now the ultimate happiness of man consists in knowing the noblest intelligible objects, as the Philosopher says in the *Ethics*.[13] Thus it is not necessary for a man to know all intelligible objects-known in order to know those substances which are the noblest intelligibles, and in the knowledge of which human happiness consists. In another way this whole position is evidently contrary to the meaning of Aristotle's doctrine. For it is said in *Ethics*,[14] that happiness consists in acting in accordance with perfect virtue. So in order to show clearly and precisely what happiness actually consists in, Aristotle found it necessary, as he says near the end of the *Ethics*,[15] to

[12] I, 9 (1099b 18).
[13] X, 7 (1177a 20).
[14] I, 9 (1099b 25).
[15] I, 13 (1102a 5).

determine the nature of all the virtues. He maintains that
some of these are moral virtues, such as fortitude, temperance,
and the like; however, others are intellectual virtues, which
he held to be five in number: wisdom, understanding, science,
prudence, and art. He says that the chief of these is wisdom,
and that ultimate happiness consists in the exercise of wisdom,
as appears in his text. Moreover, it is clear from his *Metaphysics*,[16] that wisdom is First Philosophy itself.[17] Hence it follows,
according to Aristotle, that the ultimate human happiness
which can be had in this life, consists in such knowledge of
separate substances as can be acquired through the principles
of philosophy, and not through any union [with an Agent In-
tellect] such as some have vainly imagined.

Wherefore there is another theory according to which the
human soul can attain to an understanding of separate substances through the principles of philosophy. The upholders
of this theory proceeded to demonstrate their position as follows. It is evident [they point out], that the human soul can
abstract quiddities from material things and can apprehend
them; for this is precisely what happens whenever we grasp
what (*quid est*) a material thing is. Now if that abstracted
quiddity is not a pure quiddity but is itself a thing having a
quiddity, then even so the intellect must eventually succeed
in grasping the simple quiddity itself alone, because it is impossible to go on to infinity in the process of abstraction. And
by contemplating simply quiddities, our intellect is, in fact,
understanding separate substances because the latter are themselves nothing else than simple quiddities.

However, this argument is entirely inadequate: first of all
because the quiddities of material things are of a different
order from separate quiddities and have a different mode of
existing; so it does not follow that our intellect understands

---

16 I, 2 (982b 7).
17 In the language of Aristotle, "first philosophy" or "theology" designates
the science of being as being. See *Metaphysics*, VI, 1 (1026a 16–33).

separate quiddities simply because it grasps the quiddities of material things. In the second place, the diverse quiddities apprehended by the intellect, themselves differ specifically, so that a person who apprehends the quiddity of one material thing does not thereby apprehend the quiddity of another; for example, to understand what "stone" is, is not to understand what "animal" is. Thus, even if we granted that separate quiddities are of the same formal character (*ratio*) as material quiddities, it would follow that one who understands the latter likewise understands the former, unless one happened to subscribe to Plato's view that separate substances are the species of these sensible things.

Consequently, in opposition to this doctrine, we must maintain that the intellectual soul of man, by being united to the body, has its vision turned toward phantasms, and is informed (*informare*) [18] in its intellection only through species acquired from phantasms. This agrees with the statement of Dionysius in Book I of the *De caelestia hierarchia*,[19] for he says: "The divine light can shine upon us only when screened round about by many sacred veils." Hence the soul, while united to the body, is capable of attaining a knowledge of separate substances only so far as it can be led thereto through species derived from phantasms. But in this way the soul will not attain quidditative knowledge of those substances, because their order of intelligibility transcends completely that of the intelligible species of material things abstracted from phantasms. However, we can in this way attain some [non-quidditative] knowledge of those separate substances, we can know that they exist (*quia sunt*); just as from lowly and deficient effects we proceed to lofty causes, but only to the extent that we know they exist. And while we know that these superior causes exist, at the same time we know that they are not of the same nature

[18] "Informare," i.e., "to inform" in the sense of "to know," literally means to "take in a form," namely, the form of the thing known.
[19] I, 2 (*PG,* III, 121).

as their effects, and this knowledge consists in knowing what they are not, rather than what they are.[20] Consequently it is true to say that, inasmuch as we grasp the quiddities which we abstract from material things, our intellect can, by turning to those quiddities, apprehend separate substances, so that it knows them to be immaterial, just as are the quiddities themselves which are abstracted from matter. Thus, thanks to the reflective power of our intellect, we are brought to a knowledge of intelligible separate substances. Nor is there cause for wonder if in this life we are incapable of knowing separate substances in their very essence, but can know only what they are not. For it is only in this way that we can know even the quiddity and nature of the celestial bodies. Thus in the *De caelo et mundo,*[21] Aristotle shows that the celestial bodies are neither heavy nor light, generable nor corruptible, nor subject to contrariety.[22]

Answers to objections. 1. The end to which the natural power (*possibilitas*) of the human soul is directed is to know separate substances in the manner explained above [in the body of this article], and the soul is not prevented from attaining this end because of its union with the body. Nor does the ultimate happiness of man, so far as it can be attained by his natural powers (*per naturalia*), consists in such knowledge.

Thus the answer to the second objection is evident.

3. Although the possible intellect is continually being brought from potency to act by understanding more and more, nevertheless this reduction or generation will find its term

[20] St. Thomas is contrasting our negative knowledge of the angels with the "positive" or immediate knowledge we have of the essences of things in the natural order, which essences or quiddities are the objects proportionate to our human intellect.

[21] I, 10 (259b 5 ff.).

[22] St. Thomas is, of course, simply following the ancient physics. According to the traditional theory the celestial bodies were of a different nature from the terrestrial, being incorruptible and hence not possessing any contrary qualities, as all corruptible things of the terrestrial order do.

in understanding the supremely intelligible object, namely, the divine essence. But the intellect cannot attain to this understanding by its natural powers, but only by grace.

4. It is more difficult to separate and to understand things [which are not separate] than it is to understand things which are separate, if it is a question of the same things. But in the case of different things, this is not necessarily so; for more difficulty may be experienced merely in understanding one separate thing than in abstracting and understanding others.

5. With respect to sense objects of excessive intensity, a sensory power is subject to a twofold deficiency: one, in that such objects exceed the grasp of sense since they are out of proportion to its powers; another, in that, after the impact of such objects on the sense, the sense is incapable of perceiving sense-objects which are not as intense, because the sense organ has already been made inoperative (corrumpitur). Therefore, although the intellect does not have an organ which can be made inoperative by an intelligible object of great intensity, yet something supremely intelligible can exceed the intellective power of our intelligence. Such an object is a separate substance, which exceeds the power of our intelligence, for our intelligence, inasmuch as it is united to the body, is naturally disposed to be actuated and perfected by species abstracted from phantasms. Nevertheless, if our intelligence did apprehend separate substances, it would have not less but greater understanding of other things.

6. As was shown, the quiddities abstracted from material things do not suffice as means through which we can acquire quidditative knowledge of separate substances.

The same answer applies to the seventh objection; for, as we have said above, effects that do not adequately reflect their causes do not suffice as means through which their causes can be known quidditatively.

8. Our possible intellect does not know itself directly by apprehending its own essence, but through a species abstracted

from phantasms. For this reason the Philosopher says in the *De anima*,[23] that the possible intellect is itself intelligible like other things. The reason for this is that nothing is intelligible so far as it is in potency, but only so far as it is in act, as is said in the *Metaphysics*.[24] Hence, since the possible intellect is only in potency with respect to intelligible being, it can be known only through the form by which it is actuated, namely, by a species abstracted from phantasms; just as everything else is known through the form which it has. That acts are known through objects, powers through acts, and the soul through its powers, is indeed common to all the powers of the soul. So likewise the intellective soul is known through its own act of understanding. However, a species abstracted from phantasms is not the form of a separate substance through which that substance can be known, in the same way as the possible intellect is understood through that form.

9. This argument is entirely ineffective for two reasons: first, because intelligibles do not exist in order that intellects may know them; they rather exist as the ends and perfections of intellects. Consequently, if an intelligible substance existed which was not actually known by any intellect other than itself, this substance would not for that reason exist in vain. For the expression in vain (*frustra*) is said of that which concerns the end that a thing fails to reach. Secondly, the argument of this objection is ineffective because, even if separate substances are not apprehended by our intellect while united to the body, yet they are apprehended by separate substances.

10. The species of which the power of sight is receptive can be the likenesses of any sort of body, whether corruptible or incorruptible. But species abstracted from phantasms, of which the possible intellect is receptive, are not likenesses of separate substances. Hence there is no ground for a comparison between these two cases.

[23] III, 4 (429b 9).
[24] IX, 9 (1051a 30 ff.).

# ARTICLE XVII

## WHETHER THE SOUL, WHEN SEPARATED FROM THE BODY, CAN UNDERSTAND SEPARATE SUBSTANCES

In the seventeenth article we examine this question: Whether the soul, when separated from the body, can understand separate substances.[1]

Objections. 1. It seems that the separated soul cannot understand separate substances. For a more perfect operation is characteristic of a more perfect substance. Now the soul is more perfect when united to the body than when existing apart from it. This is evident, because every part of a whole is more perfect when united to the whole than when separated from it. Therefore, if the soul is unable to understand separate substances when it is actually joined to the body, it seems that the soul cannot understand these substances when it exists apart from the body.

2. Further, our soul can know separate substances either by its nature or by grace alone. If it knows them by its own nature, then, since it is natural to the soul to be united to the body, the soul is not prevented from knowing separate substances by being united to the body. However, if the soul knows them by grace alone, it follows that at least not all separated souls know separate substances, for not all souls existing apart from bodies possess grace.[2]

---

[1] This problem is also discussed in *Summa theol.*, Ia, q.89, a.2; *Contra Gentes*, III, 45; *Quodl.* III, q.9, a.1.

[2] That is to say, the souls of the blessed possess grace; those of the damned do not.

3. Further, the soul is united to the body in order that the soul may be perfected therein by the sciences and the virtues. However, the greatest perfection of the soul consists in knowing separate substances. Therefore, if the soul understands separate substances in virtue of its separation alone, then the soul is united to the body unnecessarily.

4. Further, if the soul, when separated from the body, knows a separate substance, it must know such a substance either through that substance's essence, or through a species of it. But the soul does not know a separate substance through its essence, because the essence of a separate substance is not the same as that of a separated soul. Similarly, the soul cannot know a separate substance through a species of such a substance, for no species can be abstracted by the soul from separate substances, because they are simple. Consequently, when the soul exists apart from the body, it can in no way know separate substances.

5. Further, if the soul, existing in separation from the body, knows a separate substance, the soul apprehends that substance either by its senses or by its intellect. Now it is obvious that the soul does not apprehend a separate substance by its senses, because separate substances are not sensible things. Neither are separate substances apprehended by the soul's intellect, because its intellect does not know singulars,[3] and separate substances are singular substances. Therefore the soul, existing apart from the body, can in no way understand separate substances.

6. Further, our possible intellect differs from an angel to a greater degree than our imagination does from our possible intellect, because our imagination and possible intellect are rooted in one and the same substance of the soul. Now our imagination can in no way understand our possible intellect. Consequently our possible intellect can in no way apprehend a separate substance.

[3] Art. XVIII, note 17.

7. Further, as our will is ordered to good, so is our intellect ordered to truth. But the will of some separated souls, namely, those of the damned, cannot be ordered to good. Therefore neither can their intellect in any way be ordered to truth which the intellect itself pursues above all else in its knowledge of a separate substance. Therefore not every separated soul can know a separate substance.

8. Further, as we have pointed out already, ultimate happiness, according to the philosophers, is thought to consist in the knowledge of separate substances. Now if the souls of the damned understand separate substances, which we here on earth cannot understand, it seems that the damned are nearer to happiness than we are. This is incongruous.

9. Further, one intelligence knows another through knowing its own essence, as is pointed out in the work *De causis*.[4] Now apparently the separated soul cannot know its own essence, because the possible intellect can know itself only through species abstracted from phantasms, as is stated in the *De anima*.[5] Consequently the separated soul cannot know separate substances.

10. Further, there are two ways of acquiring knowledge:[6] first, by proceeding from what is subsequent to what is prior, and thus things which are better known absolutely (*simpliciter*) are known by us through those things which are less known absolutely. Secondly, by proceeding from what is prior to

---

[4] *De causis*, VIII.

[5] III, 8 (432a 6).

[6] The two ways of acquiring knowledge which St. Thomas discusses here are: First, the method of discovery or invention, wherein we proceed from effects to their causes or principles. This demonstration through the effect, or *demonstratio quia*, is called *a posteriori* because the effect is something posterior or subsequent to the cause. It is a demonstration through things which are previously known and prior relatively only to us, so that we go from things which are better known to us to what is absolutely prior and better known in itself. Secondly, the a priori method, or demonstration through the cause, so called because we argue from causes or principles, which are prior absolutely and better known in themselves, to effects. It is sometimes called a *demonstratio propter quid*, because it assigns the "reason for which" of the thing demonstrated. See *Summa theol.*, Ia, q. 2, a. 2.

what is subsequent, and thus things which are better known absolutely are known first by us. Now the first manner of knowing cannot be found in souls existing apart from bodies for that manner of knowing is proper to us so far as we derive our knowledge from the senses. Consequently the separated soul understands in the second manner, namely, by proceeding from what is prior to what is subsequent; and then those things which are better known absolutely are known first by the soul. But that which is best known is the divine essence. Therefore, if the separated soul knows separate substances by its nature, it seems that it can grasp the divine essence, which is life eternal, through natural things alone. This is contrary to the Apostle, who says: "The grace of God is life eternal" (Rom. 4:23).

11. Further, a separate substance of an inferior order understands another separate substance of a higher order by reason of the fact that an impression of the superior substance is present in the inferior one. But the impression of a separate substance is present in the separated soul in a much more imperfect way than it is in the separate substance itself. Therefore the separated soul cannot understand a separate substance.

On the contrary, like things are known by like. Now the separated soul is a separate substance. Consequently it can understand separate substances.

I answer: In view of the things held by faith, it is seen that we must truly maintain that separated souls know separate substances. For the separate substances, to whose society the separated souls of men both good and bad are allotted, are called angels and demons. Now it does not seem credible that the souls of the damned do not know the demons whose society they share, and who are said to terrify the souls. Again, it seems even less likely that the souls of the good do not know the angels whose society they enjoy.

Moreover, the fact that souls existing apart from bodies know separate substances wherever they may be, is in accord with reason. For it is clear that the human soul, when joined to the body, has a direct knowledge of inferior things because of its union with the body. Wherefore the soul is perfected only by what it receives from inferior things, namely, by species abstracted from phantasms. Consequently the soul can acquire a knowledge of itself, and of other things, only inasmuch as it is led thereto through the aforementioned species, as was explained above (Art. XVI).

However, when the soul really will be separated from the body, its vision will not be directed toward inferior beings in order to receive species therefrom, rather will it be independent and capable of receiving infused species from superior substances without turning to phantasms which will then be wholly non-existent. The soul will be actuated by infused species of this kind and thus will know itself directly by understanding its own essence, and not in an *a posteriori* fashion as it does in its present state. Moreover, by its essence the soul belongs to the genus of separate intellectual substances, although it is the lowest in this genus, and possesses the same mode of subsisting: for every separate substance is a subsisting form. Therefore, just as one separate substance knows another by immediately understanding (*intuendo*) [7] its own essence, inasmuch as there is in its own essence some likeness of the other substance which it knows (either because it receives infused species from that substance, or from a superior one that is the common cause of both of them) , so also does the separated soul, by immediately understanding its own essence, know separate substances by reason of the infused species received from them, or from the highest cause, namely, God.

[7] An angel's knowledge is intuitive, not discursive like human knowledge. Man progresses in truth, for he reasons to conclusions from principles acquired as a result of experience. However, the angels possess certain truths connatural to them and are immediately aware of all things that can be known in them. See *Summa theol.*, Ia, q. 55, a. 2; q. 58, a. 3.

However, the soul does not by its natural knowledge understand separate substances as perfectly as they understand themselves, because the soul is the most inferior of all intelligences,
and receives the emanation of intelligible light in the least
degree.

Answers to objections. 1. When the soul is united to the
body, it is in a certain respect more perfect than when it is
separated from the body.[8] However, with respect to its act of
understanding, the soul has a certain perfection, when separated from the body, which it cannot have while united to the
body. Nor is this incongruous, because intellectual operation
is proper to the soul inasmuch as it surpasses the capacity (*proportionem*) of the body, for the intellect is not the act of any
bodily organ.

2. We are speaking here of that knowledge of the separated
souls which belongs to them by their nature; for when we
speak of the knowledge which is given to them by grace, they
are equal to the angels in knowing. Moreover, this knowledge
whereby the soul knows separate substances in the aforesaid
way [i.e., through an influx from separated substances], is not
natural to the soul absolutely, but inasmuch as it is separated
from the body. Therefore the soul is not capable of this knowledge inasmuch as it is united to the body.

3. The highest perfection of the human soul's knowledge
consists in understanding separate substances. But it can ob-
tain possession of this knowledge more perfectly by being
united to the body, because it is disposed to this end by study
and particularly by merit. Consequently it is not united to the
body unnecessarily.

4. When the soul is separated from the body, it does not
know a separate substance through the essence of such a substance, but through a species and likeness of it. Moreover it

8 When the soul is united to the body it is complete in its species and can
perform all the operations of which it is naturally capable. See Art. I.

must be observed that a species through which something is known is not always abstracted from the thing that is known through that species, but only when the knower receives the species from the thing itself. When this is the case the species is received in a simpler and more immaterial way in the knower than it is in the thing that is known through it. Indeed, if the opposite were true, namely, that the thing known is more immaterial and simpler than the knower, then the species of the thing known in the knower is not said to be abstracted, but to be impressed and infused. This is the way it is considered in this argument.

5. To know a singular is incompatible with our intellectual cognition only inasmuch as the singular is individuated by this matter; for our intelligible species must be abstracted from matter. Indeed, if any singulars exist in which the nature of the species is not individuated by matter, but each is a certain nature whose species subsists immaterially, each of them will be intelligible in virtue of its own nature. Separate substances are singulars of this specific type.

6. An imagination and a human possible intellect are more appropriate to the human subject than a human possible intellect and an angelic intellect. However, these are more in keeping with the species and nature (*ratio*), because both of these belong to a thing having an intellective mode of existing. Moreover, an action is the natural effect of the form according to the nature of its species, and not of the subject itself. Therefore, so far as conformity of action is concerned, more attention must be paid to the conformity of two forms that are specifically the same existing in different substances, than to the conformity of specifically different forms existing in the same subject.

7. The damned are diverted from their ultimate end, and for this reason their wills do not tend to a good in keeping with this order [to the ultimate end]. Moreover, their wills do tend toward some good, because even the demons, as Dio-

nysius says,[9] desire what is good and best, to live, to exist, and to understand; but this good is not ordered to the highest good, and hence their wills are perverse. Therefore nothing prevents the souls of the damned from understanding many truths, but they do not understand the First Truth, namely, God, the vision of whom causes happiness.

8. The ultimate happiness of man does not consist in knowing any created thing, but in knowing God alone; wherefore Augustine says, in his *Confessions:* "Happy is he who knoweth Thee, though he knoweth not these," namely, creatures; "but unhappy is he who knoweth these and knoweth not Thee. And whosoever knoweth both Thee and them, is not the happier for them but for Thee only." [10] Therefore, although the damned know some of the things that we know, nevertheless they are much farther away from true happiness than we are, for we can attain it whereas they are unable to do so.

9. The human soul will know itself in one way when it will be separated from the body, and in another way when it is united to the body, as we have explained above (Art. XV).

10. Although that mode of knowing by which the soul knows better the things which are better known in themselves, is proper to the separated soul, nevertheless it does not follow that the separated soul, or any other created separate substance, through its own nature and essence, can understand God; for just as separate substances possess a more excellent mode of existing than material substances do, so does God possess a more excellent mode of existing than all separate substances. For in material beings three things have to be taken into consideration, no one of which is the same as the others; namely, the individual, the specific nature, and the act of existing (*esse*). For we cannot say that this man is his humanity, because humanity is comprised only of the principles of the species; but this man adds individuating principles over and

9 *De div. nom.,* IV, 23 (*PG,* III, 725).
10 V, 4 (*PL,* XXXII, 708).

above the principles of the species inasmuch as the nature of the species is received and individuated in this matter. Likewise humanity is not a man's act of existing. However, in separate substances the nature of the species is not received in any individuating matter, because separate substances are immaterial, but the nature of the species is the nature itself subsisting in virtue of itself. Consequently in them the thing having a quiddity and the quiddity itself are one and the same, although their act of existing and quiddity differ from each other.[11] Only God is His own subsisting act of existing.[12] Therefore, as we cannot know separate substances by knowing material quiddities, neither can separate substances know the divine essence by knowing their own substance.

11. It does not follow, because the impressions of separate substances are received in the separated soul in an imperfect way, that separated souls cannot know separate substances, but only that they know them imperfectly.

[11] Since corporeal things are composed of matter and form, there can be many individuals of one and the same species because of the division of matter which is the principle of individuation. But an angel being a pure intelligence is a pure form. Therefore there cannot be many angels of one and the same species as a result of a division of matter. Each angel is a complete species in itself. However, while there is no composition of matter and form in an angel, there is still a composition of essence and act of existing (esse), for an angel is not its own act of existing. See Summa theol., Ia, q.50, a.2 and 3.

[12] In every finite being the essence (quod est) and act of existing (esse) are really distinct. Things have an act of existing but are not their own act of existing. Only in God are essence and act of existing identical. Hence He is a self-subsisting act of existing (ipsum esse subsistens). See Summa theol., Ia, q.3, a.4.

# ARTICLE XVIII

## WHETHER THE SOUL, WHEN SEPARATED FROM THE BODY, KNOWS ALL NATURAL THINGS

In the eighteenth article we examine this question: Whether the soul, when separated from the body, knows all natural things.[1]

Objections. 1. It seems that the soul does not understand all natural things when it exists apart from the body. For, as Augustine says,[2] the demons know many things through experience over a long time, experience which the soul does not possess as soon as it is separated from the body. Therefore, since the demon possesses a more penetrating intelligence than the soul, because the natural gifts [3] of the demons remain clear and lucid, as Dionysius says,[4] it seems that the soul does not know all natural things when it exists in separation from the body.

2. Further, the souls of men, when united to their bodies, do not know all natural things. Therefore, if souls existing in separation from bodies know all natural things, it seems that they acquire this knowledge after their separation from the body. But some souls acquire a knowledge of some natural

---

[1] See also Summa theol., Ia, q.89, a.3; Contra Gentes, II, 101; De verit., q.8, a.4.

[2] De divinat. daemon., III, (PL, XL, 584).

[3] The demons were not deprived of their natural powers when they fell; for example, their natural knowledge remains undiminished because they are by nature an intellect or a mind. However, their fall did deprive them of the grace in which they were created. See Summa theol., Ia, q. 64, a. 1.

[4] De div. nom., IV, 23 (PG, III, 725).

things in this life. Consequently after separation from their bodies, these souls will possess a twofold knowledge of the same things: one acquired in this life, another, when they exist apart from the body. This seems impossible, for two forms of the same species do not exist in the same subject.

3. Further, no finite power (*virtus*) can extend to infinite things. Now the power of the separated soul is finite, because its essence is finite. Therefore it cannot extend to infinite things. But natural things known by the soul are infinite, for example, the various kinds of numbers, figures, and proportions. Therefore the separated soul does not know all natural things.

4. Further, every cognition is brought about by the one knowing becoming like the thing known.[5] Now it seems impossible for the separated soul to become like natural things, because they are material, whereas it is itself immaterial. Consequently it does not seem possible that the soul can know all natural things.

5. Further, the possible intellect stands in the same relation to intelligible things as prime matter does to sensible things. But prime matter receives only one form at a time. Therefore, since the possible intellect, when it exists apart from the body, has only one order [of objects], because in that state it is not attracted to different things by the senses, it seems that the possible intellect is capable of receiving only one intelligible form, and thus of knowing only one natural thing instead of all natural things.

6. Further, things belonging to different species cannot be like one and the same thing so far as species is concerned. But cognition is brought about by one thing becoming like another so far as species is concerned. Therefore one separated soul

5 That is, knowledge is had when, and only when, a bond of union is established between the knower and the thing known. This bond exists when "the thing understood is in the knower by its own likeness," i.e., when the likeness of the thing understood is the form of the intellect itself. See *Summa theol.*, Ia, q.85, a.2, ad 1um.

cannot know all natural things, since they are specifically diverse.

7. Further, if separated souls know all natural things, they must have in themselves forms which are the likenesses of natural things. Now knowledge of this kind extends either to genera and species alone [or to individuals as well]. In the first case, separated souls will not know individuals, and hence will fail to know all natural things, since individuals above all are seen to exist in reality. In the second case, since individuals are infinite in number,[6] it would follow that an infinite number of likenesses exists in the separated soul. This seems impossible. Therefore the separated soul does not know all natural things.

8. It has been said, however, that only the likenesses of genera and species exist in the separated soul, and that by applying these to singulars it is enabled to apprehend singulars. On the contrary, the intellect can apply the universal knowledge which it has in its possession, only to the particulars which it now knows. For if I know that every [female] mule is sterile, I can apply this knowledge only to this particular mule which I know. Now knowledge of the particular precedes the natural application of the universal to the particular; for an application of this sort cannot be the cause of our knowledge of particulars. Consequently particulars will remain unknown to the soul when it is separated from the body.

9. Further, wherever knowledge exists, there is found a certain order of the knower to the thing known. Now the souls of the damned do not have any order; for it is said that "there," i.e., in hell, "no order dwells, but eternal horror" (Job 10:22). Therefore the souls of the damned, at least, do not know natural things.

10. Further, Augustine says [7] that the souls of the dead can

---

[6] Individuals are potentially, not actually, infinite in number. An actually infinite number or multitude is impossible. See *Summa theol.,* Ia, q.7, a.4.

[7] *De cura pro mort.,* XIII (*PL,* XL, 604 ff.).

have absolutely no knowledge of things that come to pass here below. But natural things are things that come to pass here below. Therefore the souls of the dead have no knowledge of natural things.

11. Further, everything that exists potentially is actualized by that which exists actually. However, it is evident that, so long as it remains united to the body, the human soul is in potency with respect either to all things, or at least to most of the things which can be known naturally, for the intellect does not know all things actually. Therefore if, after its separation from the body, the soul knows all natural things, it must be actuated by something. Now this is apparently none other than the agent intellect, "by which all things are made," as is said in the *De anima*.[8] But the agent intellect cannot actualize the soul with respect to all those intelligibles which it did not apprehend. Thus the Philosopher, in the *De anima*,[9] compares the agent intellect to light, and phantasms to colors. Now light does not suffice to make all visible things actually visible unless colors be present also. Therefore neither will the agent intellect be able to actuate the possible intellect with respect to all intelligibles, for, since phantasms reside in bodily organs, they cannot be present to the separated soul.

12. But it has been said that, so far as all naturally knowable things are concerned, the soul is not actuated by an agent intellect, but by some higher substance. On the other hand, whenever a thing is actuated by an external agent differing generically from itself, such actuation is not natural. Thus if something curable is cured by art or by divine power, the cure will be either artificial [i.e., a work of medical art] or miraculous; however, a cure will be natural only when it is effected through an intrinsic principle. Now the proper and connatural agent so far as the possible intellect of man is concerned, is the agent intellect. Therefore, if the possible intellect is not

8 III, 5 (430a 15).
9 III, 5 (430a 15); 7 (431a 14 ff.).

actuated by an agent intellect but by some higher agent, then the natural knowledge, of which we have been speaking, will not exist. Hence no such knowledge will be had by all separated souls in common, because it is only with respect to natural things that all separated souls are united.

13. Further, if the separated soul is actuated with respect to all naturally intelligible objects, the actualizing agent must either be God or an angel. Now apparently it cannot be an angel, because an angel is not the cause of the nature itself of the soul; hence the natural knowledge of the soul does not seem to be attributable to the action of an angel. Likewise it would appear incongruous if the souls of the damned received from God, after death, such great perfection that they were cognizant of all natural things. Therefore it seems that separated souls do not in any way know all natural things.

14. Further, the ultimate perfection of everything existing in potency lies in this, that it be actualized wth respect to all those things to which it is in potency. But man's possible intellect is in a state of natural potency only with respect to all natural intelligible objects, that is to say, all those things which it is capable of knowing by natural cognition. Therefore, if the separated soul apprehends all natural things, then apparently every separate substance, simply because of the separate existence which it enjoys, truly possesses its own ultimate perfection, namely, happiness. Therefore, if mere separation from the body suffices to confer this perfection upon the soul, then the other helps employed in the effort to attain happiness exist to no purpose. This seems incongruous.

15. Further, delight follows upon knowledge. Therefore, if all separated souls know all natural things, it seems that the souls of the damned enjoy that knowledge thoroughly, taking the greatest delight therein. This seems incongruous.

16. Further, the Gloss [10] on the text in Isaias (63:16),

[10] *Glossa ordinaria*, a Commentary on Holy Scripture attributed to Walafrid Strabo (d. 870). The Gloss is composed of passages from the works of the Fathers of the Church.

"Abraham did not know us," reads: "The dead, even the saints, are ignorant of what the living do; they know not even what their own children do." But the things that are done among the living are natural things. Therefore separated souls do not know all natural things.

Arguments against the conclusions of these objections:

1. The separated soul apprehends separate substances. But the species of all natural things are found in separate substances. Therefore the separated soul does know all natural things.

2. It may be said, however, that he who sees a separate substance need not see all the species existing in its intellect. On the contrary, there is Gregory's saying: "What is there that they, who see Him who sees all things, may not themselves see?" [11] Thus they who see God see all the things that God sees. For the same reason, therefore, those who see the angels see those things that the angels see.

3. Further, the separated soul knows a separate substance so far as the latter is intelligible; for it does not see that substance by corporeal vision. But as the separate substance is intelligible, so also is a species existing in the intellect of that substance. Therefore the separated soul apprehends not only a separate substance but the intelligible species existing in it as well.

4. Further, the object actually known is the form of the knower and is one with him. Therefore, if the separated soul apprehends a separate substance, and if the latter is actually cognizant of all natural things, then apparently the separated soul would itself be cognizant of all natural things.

5. Further, as is said in the *De anima*,[12] he who understands greater intelligible objects, also understands lesser ones. Therefore, if the separated soul apprehends separate substances which are in the highest degree intelligible, as we have said

---

[11] *Dial.*, IV, 33; XII, 13 (*PL*, LXXVII, 376; LXXV, 995).
[12] III, 4 (429b 1–5).

above (see Art. V), then it seems to follow that it apprehends all other intelligible objects.

6. Further, if something is in potency with respect to many things, it is actuated with respect to all of them by an active principle which is all of them actually; just as a matter which is potentially hot and dry, is made actually hot and dry by fire. Now the separated soul's possible intellect is in potency to all intelligibles. However the active principle from which it receives an influx (*influentiam*), namely, a separate substance, is in act with respect to all of those intelligible objects. Consequently the separate substance brings the soul from potentiality to act either with respect to all intelligible objects or to none. But obviously not with respect to none, for separated souls apprehend certain things of which they were not cognizant here below. Therefore it actuates them with respect to all intelligible objects. Consequently the separated soul apprehends all natural things.

7. Further, Dionysius says [13] that superior beings are the exemplars of inferior ones. Now separate substances are superior to natural things; hence they are the exemplars of natural things. Therefore it would seem that separated souls know all natural things in virtue of the intellectual vision that they have of separate substances.

8. Further, separated souls know things through infused forms. But infused forms are said to be forms of the order of the universe. Therefore separated souls know the entire order of the universe, and thus know all natural things.

9. Further, whatever exists in an inferior nature, exists in its entirety in a superior nature. Now the separated soul is superior to natural things. Hence all natural things in a certain respect exist in the soul. But the soul knows itself. Consequently it knows all natural things.

10. Further, as Gregory says,[14] the story of Lazarus and the

[13] *De div. nom.*, V (*PG*, III, 851).
[14] *In Evang.*, hom. 40 (*PL*, LXXIII, 1304).

rich man (Luke 16) is not a mere parable; it clearly related something that actually took place, because the person involved (Lazarus) is explicitly identified by name. Now it is recorded that the rich man in hell knows Abraham, whom he had not known before. Therefore separated souls, even those of the damned, likewise know things which they did not know in this life, and so it seems that they know all natural things.

I answer: The separated soul knows all natural things in a certain respect (*secundum quid*), but does not know them in an absolute sense (*simpliciter*).

In proof of this the fact should be borne in mind that the order among things is such that whatever exists in an inferior nature exists in a higher mode in a superior nature. Thus whatever is found in things susceptible of generation and corruption [terrestrial bodies], exists in a higher mode in celestial bodies as in their universal causes. For example, hot and cold, and other things of this sort, exist in inferior bodies as particular qualities and forms, but exist in celestial bodies as universal powers by which such qualities and forms are conveyed to those inferior bodies. In like manner, whatever exists in a corporeal nature, exists in a higher mode in an intellectual nature. Thus the forms of corporeal things exist materially and particularly in those corporeal things, whereas they exist immaterially and universally in intellectual substances. Wherefore it is said in the book *De causis*,[15] that every intelligence is full of forms. Furthermore, everything that exists in the creature exists in a higher mode in God Himself. For the natures and forms of things exist in creatures in many diverse modes, but in God they exist unitedly, in a simple and undivided way.

This existence of things is expressed in three ways (Gen. 1:6 ff.): First, God said: "Let there be a firmament," by which is understood the existence of things in the Word of God.

15 *De causis*, X.

Secondly, it is said: "And God made the firmament," by which is understood the existence of the firmament in the angelic intelligence. Thirdly, it is said: "And it was made thus," by which is understood the existence of the firmament in its proper nature, as Augustine explains. The same applies to the other creations of God. For just as things flowed from God that they might subsist in their proper nature, so from the divine wisdom the forms of things flowed into intellectual substances so that those things might be understood. Hence it must be borne in mind that the mode in which a thing exists in the order of natural perfection is the mode proper to it in the order of intelligible perfection. Now in the order of natural perfection singulars do not exist on their own account but for the sake of something else, namely, that in them the species to which they belong may be preserved. This indeed is what nature intends. For nature intends to generate man, not this man. Or rather, it generates this man only because the species cannot exist unless the individual man exists. Thus the Philosopher, in his work the *De generatione animalium*,[16] states that in assigning the causes of the accidents of a species we must go back to the final cause. But the accidents of the individual, he says, must be reduced to the efficient or material cause, thus suggesting that only what pertains to the species as such falls under the intention of nature. Thus knowledge of the species of things pertains to intellectual perfection, but not the knowledge of individuals, except perhaps accidentally.[17]

Consequently, although this intellectual perfection is found

[16] V, 1 (778b 10 ff.).

[17] The senses have for their object the individual thing, whereas the proper object of the human intellect is the nature or quiddity of the individual thing. Hence for the intellect to understand actually its proper object, it must of necessity turn to the phantasm in order to perceive the universal nature existing in the individual. Therefore the intellect is perfected in knowledge directly and immediately by the universal through its intelligible species, and indirectly by the individual through the phantasm. See *Summa theol.*, Ia, q.85, a.2; q.86, a.1.

in all intellectual substances, it does not exist in each of them to the same degree. For the intelligible forms of things exist in a more united and more universal mode in superior intellectual substances than they do in inferior [intellectual substances] where they are multiplied to a greater extent and are less universal according as they are further and further removed from the first simple Being [God], and come closer and closer to the particularity of things. But thanks to their greater intellective power, superior substances perfect their intelligence through a few forms, so that they know the natures of things down to their ultimate species.[18] Now even if forms as universal as those existing in superior intellectual substances were possessed by inferior substances, the latter would not thereby attain that ultimate intellectual perfection which consists in knowing things down to their individual species, because inferior intellectual substances have an inferior intellective power. Hence their knowledge of things will remain more or less universal and indistinct; and generality and indistinctness are the marks of imperfect knowledge. For it is evident that the more active the intellect, the greater is its ability to acquire much from little. An indication of this is that things must be explained one by one to uncultivated people and to slow learners, and particular examples introduced for each single thing.

Now the human soul is obviously the lowest among all intellectual substances. Consequently it is capable by nature of receiving the forms of things in the material order. Thus the human soul is united to a body in order that the soul may receive intelligible species from material things through its possible intellect. Nor is its natural intellective power greater than that required for perfecting its knowledge through such forms. Hence the intelligible light in which the human soul participates and which is called the agent intellect, has as its

---

[18] The "ultimate species" is the species which cannot be divided into any subspecies because it contains individuals only.

function to actualize intelligible species of the type referred to. Therefore, since the soul is united to the body, the soul's vision is turned toward inferior things; from these it abstracts intelligible species proportioned to its intellective power; and it is in this way that the soul is perfected in knowledge. But when the soul is separated from the body, its vision is directed toward higher things alone, and from these it receives an influx of universal intelligible species. And although the species thus received have a less universal mode of existence in the separated soul than they enjoy in those higher substances, nevertheless the intellective power of the soul is not so efficacious that it can acquire a perfect knowledge of those intelligibles through this kind of species. That is to say, it cannot apprehend each one of them individually and determinately, but can know them only generally and indistinctly in the manner in which things are known through universal principles. Moreover, separated souls acquire this knowledge all at once by an influx, and not successively by instruction, as Origen says.[19]

Consequently, we must say that separated souls know all natural things in a universal way by natural knowledge, but do not know each of them individually. This is not the case, however, with respect to the knowledge that the souls of the saints possess through grace. For as regards that knowledge the saints are made equal to the angels inasmuch as they, like the angels, see all things in the Word. The answers to the objections are now in order.

Answers to objections. 1. According to Augustine,[20] the demons know things in three ways: First, some demons know things that transcend their natural knowledge through the revelation of the good angels, such as the mystery of Christ and the Church and others of this kind; secondly, some demons

[19] *Peri Archon,* I, 6 (*PG,* XI, 169).
[20] *De divinat. daemon.,* III (*PL,* XL, 584).

know things that are naturally knowable by the native acumen of their own intelligence; thirdly, some demons know the issue of future contingent events in individual cases through experience over a long time. Now as we have pointed out, knowledge of singulars does not pertain essentially to intellectual cognition as such. Consequently the objection is irrelevant, because here there is no question of such knowledge.

2. In those souls which have acquired the science of certain natural things knowable in this life, there will exist a knowledge of those things which bears directly on the individual. Their knowledge of other things, however, will be universal and indistinct, so that they will not have acquired knowledge uselessly in this life. Nor is there any incongruity in their possessing both types of knowledge with respect to the same objects, since those knowledges are formally diverse.

3. That argument is beside the point. For we do not allege that the separated soul knows all natural things in their individuality. Hence the infinity of species that is found in numbers, figures, and proportions, is not out of proportion to the soul's cognitive power. But since that same argument would likewise apply to angelic knowledge, it must be said that the species of figures and numbers and things of this sort are not infinite actually but only potentially.[21] Nor is it improper that the power of a finite intellectual substance should extend to infinites of this kind. For an intellective power in a certain respect is itself infinite inasmuch as it is not limited by matter. This is why it can know the universal, which is also infinite in a certain respect inasmuch as it belongs to the universal by nature to contain infinites potentially.[22]

4. The forms of material things exist in immaterial substances immaterially. Thus immaterial things become like

[21] Mathematical "beings" as such have no real existence, no existence as things (res naturae). Whether continuous or discrete, they are all ideal quantities; hence they are in no way infinite entitatively, but are "infinite" only in the sense of being theoretically addable, multipliable, or divisible without end. See Summa theol., Ia, q. 7, a. 3.

[22] The infinity of "infinites" is that of potentially unlimited denotation.

material ones so far as the intelligible nature of the latter's forms is concerned, not so far as their mode of existing is concerned.

5. Prime matter is related to forms in a twofold manner only, because with respect to them it is either in pure potency or in complete act. For natural forms have their own operations as soon as they exist in matter, unless there be some impediment, because a natural form is directed to one thing only. Thus, as soon as the form fire exists in matter, it causes the matter to move upward. However, the possible intellect is related to intelligible species in a threefold manner: sometimes, as before learning, it is in pure potency; sometimes, as when actually reflecting upon something, it is in complete act; sometimes, as when possessing a *habitus* [23] of science but not actually exercising it, it is in a state midway between potency and act. Therefore an apprehended form so far as it is apprehended actually, but not so far as it exists in the possible intellect "habitually," is related to the possible intellect as a natural form is to prime matter. Hence, as prime matter is informed with but one form at a time, so the possible intellect apprehends but one intelligible object at a time. Nevertheless it can know many things habitually in virtue of its habit of knowledge.

6. There can be a likeness between a thing and a knowing substance in two ways: either according to the thing's real mode of existing, and in this way no likeness exists between things specifically diverse and a knowing substance, since the latter belongs to one species only: or according to the thing's intelligible mode of existing, and in this way there can be a likeness between things specifically diverse and the soul, inasmuch as the knowing substance possesses diverse intelligible species, even though the soul itself belongs only to one species.

7. Separated souls know not only the species but also indi-

[23] In the doctrine of St. Thomas, a "habitus" is a perfectant of a potency or power. The meaning of the term is not properly conveyed by the much looser English word "habit." See *Summa theol.*, IIa IIae, q.49, a.1 and 2.

viduals, although not all individuals but only some. Consequently it is not necessary that an infinite number of species exist in the separated soul.

8. The application of universal knowledge to singulars is not the cause of the knowledge of singulars, but is a natural result of a knowledge of singulars. The problem of how the separated soul knows singulars will be treated later (Art. XX).

9. Since, according to Augustine in his work *De natura boni*,[24] the good consists in mode, species, and order; so far as order is found in a thing, to that extent good is found there. Now the good of grace does not exist in the damned but only the good of nature. Hence in them there exists not the order of grace but the order of nature, and the latter suffices for knowledge of natural things.

10. Augustine is speaking of singulars which come to pass here below. The knowledge of such things, we have said, does not pertain to intellectual cognition.

11. The possible intellect cannot be rendered actually cognizant of all natural things by the light of the agent intellect alone, but only by some superior substance which is actually cognizant of all natural things. And if one considers rightly, he will see that, according to the Philosopher's own treatment of the matter, the agent intellect is not active directly with respect to the possible intellect, but rather with respect to phantasms which the agent intellect makes actually intelligible. And it is by the phantasms thus actualized that the possible intellect is actualized when, as a result of its union with the body, its vision is turned to inferior things. And for the same reason, when, after its separation from the body, the possible intellect turns toward superior things, it is actualized, as by its own proper agent, by the actually intelligible species which exist in superior substances. And such knowledge, therefore, is natural.

Hence the reply to the twelfth objection is evident.

[24] III (*PL*, XLII, 553).

13. Separated souls receive this sort of perfection from God through the mediation of the angels. For, although the substance of the soul is created by God immediately, nevertheless intelligible perfections come from God through the mediation of the angels; and not only natural perfections but also those which pertain to the mysteries of grace, as Dionysius shows.[25]

14. The separated soul, having universal knowledge of natural intelligible objects, is not perfectly actualized. For to know a thing universally is to know it imperfectly and potentially. By such knowledge, therefore, the separated soul does not attain even natural happiness. Consequently it does not follow that the other helps for the attainment of happiness are superfluous.

15. The good of knowledge which the damned possess is itself a cause of sorrow to them, inasmuch as they know that they are deprived of the highest good to which they are directed through other goods.

16. That Gloss refers to particulars which, as was said, do not pertain to intellectual perfection.

Answers to the arguments against the conclusions of the objections.

1. The separated soul does not perfectly comprehend a separate substance. Hence it is not necessary that the separated soul know all the things which are present by their likeness in such a substance.

2. Gregory's statement is true as regards knowledge of that intelligible object which is God: an object which in itself represents all intelligible objects. However, it is not necessary that he who sees God should know all the things that God knows, unless that person should know himself as God knows Himself.[26]

3. The species existing in the angel's intellect are intelligi-

---

[25] De cael. hier., IV, 2 (PG, III, 181).
[26] It is impossible for a created intellect, in seeing the divine essence, to comprehend that essence in its entirety. See Summa theol., Ia, q. 12, a. 8.

ble to the intellect of the one of whom they are the forms, but not to the intellect of the separated soul.

4. Although the intellect is the form of an intellectual substance, it is not necessary that the separated soul, apprehending the separate substance, should apprehend the intellect of that substance, because the separated soul does not comprehend the latter.[27]

5. Although the separated soul does in some way know separated substances, it is not necessary that it know all other things perfectly. For it does not know perfectly the separate substances themselves.

6. The separated soul is actualized with respect to all natural intelligible objects by a superior substance. However, it is not actualized perfectly but universally, as we have pointed out.

7. Although separate substances are in some way the exemplars of all natural things, it does not follow that all these are known when these natural things are known, unless the separate substances themselves are comprehended perfectly.

8. The separated soul knows through infused forms. But these are not forms of the order of the universe in an individual mode, such as superior substances possess, but only in a general mode, as was said.

9. Natural things exist in a certain respect in separate substances and in the soul. However the forms of natural things exist actually in the separate substances, whereas they exist only potentially in the soul inasmuch as they are knowable.

10. The soul of Abraham was a separate substance. Consequently the soul of the rich man was able to know the soul of Abraham, just as it could know other separate substances.

---

[27] That is, the separate substance exists in a higher order of being and so cannot be totally included within the scope of the intellectual power of the separated soul.

# ARTICLE XIX

## WHETHER THE SENTIENT POWERS REMAIN IN THE SOUL WHEN IT EXISTS APART FROM THE BODY

In the nineteenth article we examine this question: Whether the sentient powers remain in the soul when it exists apart from the body.[1]

Objections. 1. It seems this is the case, because the powers of the soul are either essential parts of it or natural properties of it. But the essential parts of a thing cannot be separated from a thing so long as the thing itself remains in existence, and neither can its natural properties be separated from it. Therefore the sentient powers remain in the soul when it exists apart from the body.

2. But it might be said that the sentient powers remain in the [separated] soul as in their root. On the other hand, for a thing to exist in something else as in its root, is for it to exist in that thing potentially, that is, virtually and not actually. Now the essential constituents of a thing and its natural properties must exist in it actually and not just virtually. Therefore the sentient powers do not remain in the separated soul merely as in their root.

3. Further, Augustine says in the book *De spiritu et anima*,[2] that when the soul leaves the body it takes with it sense and imagination, and the concupiscible and irascible appetites which belong to the sentient part. Therefore the sentient

---

[1] See also *Summa theol.*, Ia, q.77, a.8; *Contra Gentes*, II, 81; *Sent.*, Bk. IV, dist. 44, q.3, a.3, q.1 and 2; dist. 50, q.1, a.1; *Quodl.* X, q.4, a.2; *De virt. card.*, a.4, ad 13um.

[2] XV (*PL*, XL, 791).

powers remain in the soul when it exists in separation from the body.

4. Further, a whole from which any of the parts are missing is not a complete one. But the sentient powers are parts of the soul. Hence, if they did not exist in the separated soul, the separated soul would not be a complete whole.

5. Further, as a man is such because of his reason and intellect, so also is an animal such because of its sense, for "rational" is the constitutive difference of "man," "sensible" the constitutive difference of "animal." Therefore, if sense is not one and the same, it will not be one and the same animal. Now if the sentient powers do not remain in the separated soul, the same sense will not be present in man when he arises from the dead as is present in him now, because whatever lapses into nothingness cannot be brought back into existence as numerically the same thing. Therefore when a man rises from the dead he will not be the same animal. This is contrary to what is said: "Whom I myself shall see, and my eyes shall behold, and not another" (Job 19:27).

6. Further, Augustine says in *Super Genesim ad litteram*,[3] that the punishments which souls suffer in hell are similar to the dreams of people asleep, that is to say, according to the [sensible] likenesses of corporeal things. But such dreams of people asleep result from the imagination, which belongs to the sentient part of the soul. Therefore the sentient powers exist in the separated soul.

7. Further, it is evident that joy belongs to the concupiscible appetite, and anger to the irascible appetite. Now there is joy in the separated souls of good men, and sorrow and anger in the souls of evil men, for in hell "there is weeping and gnashing of teeth" (Matt. 8:12). Consequently, since the concupiscible and irascible appetites belong to the sentient part of the soul, as the Philosopher says in the *De anima*,[4] it seems that

[3] XII, 32 (*PL*, XXXIV, 480).
[4] III, 9 (432b 5).

the sentient powers remain in the soul when it is separated from the body.

8. Further, Dionysius says,[5] that the wickedness of the demons is irrational fury, love of concupiscence, and a wanton imagination. But these belong to the sentient powers. Consequently there are sentient powers in the demon and, therefore, even more so in the soul when it is separated from the body.

9. Further, Augustine says in *Super Genesim ad litteram*,[6] that the soul senses certain things without the body, namely, joy and sadness. But whatever belongs to the soul itself without the body, exists in the separated soul. Therefore sense exists in the separated soul.

10. Further, it is said in the book *De causis*,[7] that sensible things exist in every soul. But sensible things are sensed because they are present in the soul. Consequently the separated soul senses sensible things, and thus sense exists in it.

11. Further, Gregory says,[8] that what our Lord relates about the wealthy reveler (Luke 16) is not a parable but a fact. Moreover, it is said there that when the rich man had gone to hell (no doubt so far as he was a separated soul), he saw Lazarus and heard Abraham speaking to him. Therefore the separated soul sees and hears, and thus sense exists in the separated soul.

12. Further, things that are the same so far as their act of existing and substance are concerned, cannot exist without each other. Now in man the sentient and rational soul are the same so far as their act of existing and substance are concerned. Hence it is impossible that sense should cease to remain in the rational soul when it exists in separation from the body.

13. Further, when that which ceases to exist, is brought back into existence again, it is not numerically the same thing as it was when it first existed. But if the sentient powers do

5 *De div. nom.*, IV, 23 (*PG*, III, 725).
6 XII, 32 (*PL*, XXXIV, 480).
7 *De causis*, XIV.
8 *In Evang.*, hom. 40 (*PL*, LXXIII, 1304).

not remain in the separated soul, they must cease to exist. Consequently they will not be numerically the same at the resurrection; and thus, since the sentient powers are the acts of bodily organs, neither will the organs be numerically the same, nor will the whole man be numerically the same. This is incongruous.

14. Further, rewards and punishments are in conformity with a man's merit or lack of merit. Now what a man merits or fails to merit is to a great extent the result of the activities of his sentient powers, for we either give in to our passions or curb them. Therefore justice seems to demand that the acts of the sentient powers exist in separated souls which are either rewarded or punished.

15. Further, a power is nothing more than a principle of action or passion [i.e., being-acted-upon]. Now the soul is the principle of sentient operations. Therefore the sentient powers exist in the soul as their subject. Hence it is impossible that they should cease to exist in the separated soul, for accidents lacking contraries are corrupted only by the corruption of their subject.

16. Further, according to the Philosopher,[9] memory exists in the sentient part [of the soul]. Now memory is present in the soul when it exists apart from the body, as is apparent from what is said to the rich reveler by Abraham: "Remember that you have received good things in your lifetime" (Luke 16:25). Consequently the sentient powers exist in the separated soul.

17. Further, virtues and vices remain in souls when they exist apart from the body. But some virtues and vices exist in the sentient part of the soul, for the Philosopher says in the *Ethics*,[10] that temperance and fortitude belong to the irrational part of the soul. Therefore the sentient powers remain in the soul when it exists apart from the body.

18. Further, it is related of the dead who are brought back

9 *De mem. et rem.*, I (450a 10 ff.).
10 III, 9 (1117b 22).

to life, as we read in many histories of the saints, that they said they saw certain imaginable objects, for example, houses, camps, rivers, and things of this kind. Therefore when souls exist apart from their bodies, they use imagination, which belongs to the sentient part [of the soul].

19. Further, the senses assist in intellectual knowledge, for, if anyone is deprived of one sense, he is deprived of one kind of knowledge. Now intellectual knowledge will be more perfect when the soul is separated from the body than when it is joined thereto. Therefore sense will be required to an even greater extent by the intellect [of the separated soul].

20. Further, the Philosopher says in the *De anima*,[11] that if an old man were to receive the eye of a youth, he would see just as well as a youth. From this it appears that, although the organs are weakened, the sensory powers are not weakened. Therefore neither are they destroyed when their organs cease to exist. Consequently it seems that the sentient powers remain in the separated soul.

On the contrary, the Philosopher says in the *De anima*,[12] when he speaks of the intellect, that "this alone is separate as the perpetual is separate from the corruptible." Consequently the sentient powers do not remain in the soul when it exists apart from the body.

Further, the Philosopher says in the *De generatione animalium*,[13] that "The operations of some powers do not exist without the body, nor do these powers themselves exist without the body." But the operations of the sentient powers do not exist without the body, for they are performed through bodily organs. Therefore the sentient powers do not exist in the soul without the body.

Further, Damascene says [14] that nothing is bereft of its

11 I, 4 (408b 20 ff.).
12 II, 2 (413b 25).
13 II, 3 (736b 21 ff.).
14 *De fide orth.*, II, 23 (*PG*, XCIV, 950).

proper operation. Hence, if the sentient powers remain in the soul when it exists apart from the body, they have their proper operations. This is impossible.

Further, a power which is not exercised is purposeless. Now in the activities of God nothing is done without a purpose. Therefore the sentient powers do not remain in the separated soul, for they cannot be exercised.

I answer: the powers of the soul do not belong to the essence of the soul but are natural properties which flow from its essence, as can be learned from the preceding questions.[15] Now an accident is corrupted in two ways. First, by its contrary, as cold is corrupted by heat. Secondly, by the corruption of its subject, for an accident cannot remain when its subject is corrupted. Consequently what does not have a contrary accident or form, is destroyed only by the destruction of the subject itself. Now it is evident that there is nothing contrary to the powers of the soul. And therefore if they are corrupted, they are corrupted only by the corruption of their subject.

Consequently, in order to discover whether the sentient powers are corrupted when the body is corrupted, or whether they remain in the soul when it exists apart from the body, we must accept the principle of this investigation so that we may learn what the subject of the aforementioned power is. Now it is evident that the subject of a power must be that which is capable of doing something in virtue of its power, for every accident designates its subject. Furthermore, an agent or a patient is nothing more than a thing which can act or undergo some change (*pati*). Hence, whatever is the subject of an action or undergoes a change, must be the subject of a power, the power itself being a principle. And this is what the Philosopher says in the book *De somno et vigilia*,[16] namely,

15 *De spir. creat.*, Art. XI.
16 I (454a 7 ff.).

that an action belongs to the thing to which the power belongs.

Now there has been a diversity of opinion about the operations of the senses. For Plato held that the sentient soul has a proper operation in virtue of its own nature, for he maintained that the sentient soul is a self-mover, and that it moves the body only inasmuch as it is moved by itself. Thus there is a twofold operation in sensing: one by which the soul moves itself, and another by which it moves the body. Wherefore the Platonists defined sense as the movement of the soul through the body. For this reason, certain followers of this position distinguish two operations in the sentient part of the soul, namely, certain interior operations by which the soul senses inasmuch as it moves itself, and certain external operations inasmuch as it moves the body. They also stated that there are two kinds of sentient powers: some which are principles of acts within the soul itself, and which remain together with their activities in the separated soul when the body is corrupted; others, which are principles of external acts, and these are present in the soul and the body simultaneously, and cease to exist when the body corrupts.

But this position cannot be held, for it is evident that anything whatever operates so far as it is a being. Therefore those things which exist of themselves, operate of themselves as individual substances. On the other hand, forms which cannot exist of themselves, but are called beings inasmuch as something exists by them, do not operate of themselves but are said to act inasmuch as their subjects act through them. For just as heat itself is not a thing having existence (*id quod est*), but is that by which something is hot, so heat itself does not heat anything, but is that by which a hot thing heats something. Therefore, if the sentient soul could operate of itself [i.e., without the body], it would follow that it would subsist of itself, and thus would not be corrupted when the body is corrupted; but then the souls of brute animals would also be immortal. This is impossible, yet Plato is said to have conceded this.[17]

It is evident then that no operation of the sentient part can belong to the soul alone in such a way that it can be exercised by the soul alone; but such operations belong to the composite because of the soul, just as the act of heating belongs to the hot thing on account of its heat. Hence the composite sees, hears, and senses all things, but [it does this] through its soul. Consequently the composite is capable of seeing, hearing, and sensing, but [it performs these] because of its soul. Hence it is clear that the powers of the sentient part exist in the composite as their subject, but come from the soul as their principle. Therefore, when the body is corrupted the sentient powers cease to exist, although they remain in the soul as in their principle. This is what the other position maintains, namely, that the sentient powers remain in the separated soul as in their root.

Answers to objections. 1. The sentient powers do not belong to the essence of the soul, but, in fact, are natural properties of the composite as their subject and of the soul as their principle.

2. Powers of this kind are said to remain in the soul as in their root, when it exists apart from the body, not because they are actually present in the soul, but because the separated soul is virtually such that, if it is united to a body, it can again cause these powers in the body, and life as well.

3. We do not have to accept this authority because this false book has authority in name only. For it was not written by Augustine but by some other person.[18] Moreover, that authority can be openly exposed inasmuch as it says that the soul draws with it powers of this kind not actually but virtually.

4. The powers of the soul are neither essential parts nor

17 See *Phaedo*, XXXI.
18 See Art. XII, reply to obj. 1.

integral parts but potential parts. However, some of these belong to the soul in virtue of itself, and others belong to the
composite.

5. Sense is spoken of in two ways. In one way as the sentient
soul itself which is the principle of powers of this kind, and
in this way the animal is an animal by sense as by its proper
form. For in this way "sensible" is taken from sense inasmuch
as it is the constitutive difference of "animal." Sense is spoken
of in another way as the sentient power itself, which, since it
is a natural property, as has been pointed out, is not a constitutive part of the species, but is the natural effect of the
species. Therefore sense does not remain in the separated soul
in the latter way, but sense does remain in the first way spoken
of, for in man the essence of the rational soul and that of
the sentient soul is one and the same. Consequently nothing
prevents a man who rises from the dead from being the same
man numerically, for, in order that something be numerically the same, it is enough that the essential principles remain
numerically the same. However, it is not necessary that the
properties and accidents be numerically the same.

6. Augustine seems to have revoked this in his *Retrac-
tiones.*[19] For he says in *Super Genesim ad litteram,*[20] that the
punishments of hell exist by reason of imaginary vision, and
that this place hell is not corporeal but imaginary. Whereupon
this view was withdrawn to conform with the reason that if hell
is not a corporeal place, why is it said that hell is underground.
And he reproves himself for this, saying: "Concerning the
damned, it seems to me that it should be taught that they are
under the earth rather than question why they are believed
to be or are said to be under the earth, as if this were not so."
However, what he said about the place of hell has been retracted, and all other things which pertain to this seem to be
retracted.

19 II, 24 (*PL,* XXXII, 640).
20 II, 32 (*PL,* XXXIV, 480).

7. In separated souls there is neither joy nor sorrow so far as these are acts of the irascible and concupiscible appetites which belong to the sentient part of the soul, but so far as the movement of the will, which is in the intellective part, is signified by these.

8. Because human evil is a result of one of three things, namely, a wanton imagination which is the principle of error, a love of concupiscence, and irrational anger, Dionysius describes the evil of the demons in likeness to human evil; not that it is to be understood that there is imagination in the demons, or irascible and concupiscible appetites which are in the sentient part of the soul, but that in them there is something proportionate to these as becomes their intellective nature.

9. We must not understand by these words of Augustine that the soul senses something without a bodily organ, but that it senses something without sensible bodies themselves, for instance, fear and sorrow. Again it senses other things through the body itself, for example, heat and cold.

10. Whatever exists in another, exists in that thing according to the mode of the recipient. Consequently sensible things do not exist in the separated soul according to a sensible mode but according to an intelligible one.

11. Nothing prevents us from speaking of certain facts metaphorically, for, although the story related in the Gospel about Lazarus and the rich man is a fact, still it is said metaphorically that Lazarus saw and heard, just as it is also said metaphorically that he had a tongue.

12. The substance of the sentient soul remains in man after death. However, the sentient powers do not.

13. Just as sense, inasmuch as it is called a power, is not the form of the whole body but the sentient soul itself (moreover, sense is a property of the composite), so neither is the power of vision the act of the eye, but that of the soul itself as the principle of such a power; just as it may be said that the visive

soul is the act of the eye as the sentient soul is the act of the body. Moreover the power of vision is a property consequent on this. Therefore it is not necessary that there be a different eye for the resurrected individual, although there is a different sentient power.

14. Reward does not correspond to merit as rewarding, but as that on account of which some reward is given. Consequently it is not necessary that all the acts by which some one merits reward, should be brought back into existence again when the reward is actually given. It is sufficient that they exist in the divine memory. Otherwise it would be necessary for the saints to die a second time, which is absurd.

15. The soul is a principle of sensing, not as a thing that senses, but as that by which a sensing thing senses. Consequently the sentient powers do not exist in the soul as a subject, but come from the soul as a principle.

16. The separated soul does not remember through the memory which belongs to its sentient part, but through that which belongs to its intellective part, inasmuch as Augustine considers this to be part of the image [of God in us].

17. The virtues and vices which belong to the irrational part of the soul remain in the soul only in principle, for the seeds of all the virtues are found in the will and the reason.

18. The soul does not understand in the same manner when it exists apart from the body as it does when it exists in the body, as is evident from the preceding articles (Arts. XVII and XVIII). Therefore, concerning those things which the separated soul apprehends in the manner proper to it without phantasms, this knowledge remains in the soul after it returns to its former state. Having been joined to the body again, the soul now understands in a manner befitting it, that is, by turning to phantasms. And for this reason things grasped intelligibly are narrated imaginatively.

19. The intellect requires the aid of the senses because of the imperfect kind of knowledge which it has, that is, inasmuch

as it receives [species] from phantasms. But this is not true with respect to the more perfect mode of knowledge possessed by the separated soul; just as a man requires milk in infancy but not when fully grown.

20. The sentient powers are not weakened absolutely because their organs are weakened, but only accidentally. Consequently they are corrupted accidentally when their organs are corrupted.

## ARTICLE XX

## WHETHER THE SOUL, WHEN SEPARATED
## FROM THE BODY, KNOWS
## SINGULAR THINGS

In the twentieth article we examine this question: Whether the soul, when separated from the body, knows singular things.[1]

Objections. 1. It seems that the separated soul does not know singular things, because of all the soul's powers, only the intellect remains in the soul when it exists apart from the body. Now the object of the intellect is the universal and not the singular, for science has to do with the universal, whereas the senses are directed to singulars, as is stated in the *De anima*.[2] Therefore the separated soul does not know singulars but only universals.

2. Further, if the separated soul knows singulars, it does so either through the forms which it acquired previously while it existed in the body, or through infused forms. Now it does not know singulars through forms acquired previously, for some of the forms which the soul acquired through the senses while it existed in the body, are individual intentions, which are conserved in the sentient part [of the soul]; but these cannot remain in the soul when it is separated from the body, because powers of this kind do not remain in the soul, as has been shown (Art. XIX). Some intentions, however, that is, those which are in the intellect, are universal; therefore these

---

[1] See also *Summa theol.,* Ia, q. 89, a. 4; *Contra Gentes,* II, 100; *Sent.,* Bk. IV, dist. 50, q. 1, a. 3; *De ver.,* q. 19, a. 2.
[2] III, 5 (430a 10 ff.).

alone can remain in the separated soul. But singulars cannot be known through universal intentions. Therefore the separated soul cannot know singulars through the species acquired while it existed in the body. Similarly, it cannot know singulars through infused forms, because such forms represent all singulars equally. Therefore it would follow that the separated soul knows all singulars. This does not appear to be the case.

3. Further, the separated soul is prevented from knowing a thing that is located in a different place from itself. For Augustine says in the book *De cura pro mortuis agenda*,[3] that the souls of the dead are in a place where they cannot know in any way whatever the things that occur here. But knowledge that is caused through infused species is not prevented because of a difference of place. Therefore the soul does not know singulars through infused species.

4. Further, infused species are related equally both to the present and to the future, for the infusion of intelligible species is not affected by time. Therefore, if the separated soul knows singulars through infused species, it seems that it does not know the present or the past, but only the future. However, it appears that this cannot be the case, because knowledge of the future belongs to God alone; for it is said: "Show the things that are to come hereafter, and we shall know that ye are gods" (Isa. 41:23).

5. Further, singular things are infinite.[4] Infused species, however, are not infinite. Therefore the separated soul cannot know singulars through infused species.

6. Further, whatever is indistinct cannot be a principle of a distinct knowledge. But the knowledge of singulars is distinct. Therefore, since infused species are indistinct inasmuch as they are universal, it seems that the separated soul cannot know singular things through infused species.

---

[3] XIII (*PL*, XL, 604).

[4] Singulars are "potentially" infinite, not "actually" infinite. See Art. XVIII, note 6.

7. Further, whatever is received in a thing is received according to the mode of the recipient. Now the separated soul is immaterial. Therefore infused forms are received in it immaterially. But what is immaterial cannot be the principle of a knowledge of singular things which are individuated by matter. Therefore the separated soul cannot know singulars through infused forms.

8. But it may be said that singular things can be known by infused forms, even though they are immaterial, because singulars are likenesses of the ideal exemplars by which God knows both universals and singulars. On the contrary, God knows singulars through the ideal exemplars inasmuch as they are productive of matter, which is the principle of individuation. But the forms infused in the separated soul are not productive of matter, because they do not create, for creation belongs to God alone. Therefore the separated soul cannot know singulars through infused forms.

9. Further, the likeness which any creature bears to God cannot be a univocal likeness, but only an analogous one. Now a knowledge that is acquired because of some analogous similarity [between things] is the most imperfect sort of knowledge; for example, if one thing is known through something else inasmuch as it conforms with it in being. Therefore, if the separated soul knows singulars through infused species, inasmuch as they are like the ideal exemplars, it seems that it knows singulars in a most imperfect manner.

10. Further, it was shown in a preceding article (Art. XVIII), that the separated soul knows natural things through infused forms only indistinctly and in the universal. Now this is not to know them. Therefore the separated soul does not know singulars through infused species.

11. Further, those infused species through which the separated soul admittedly knows singular things, are not caused immediately by God; because, according to Dionysius, the divine law (*lex divinitatis*) is to change the lowest thing

through an intermediary. On the other hand, neither are in-fused species caused by an angel; because an angel cannot cause species of this kind, either by creating them, since it never creates anything; or by changing something, because this re-quires a communicating medium. Therefore it seems that the separated soul does not possess infused species through which it may know singulars.

12. Further, if the separated soul knows singular things through infused species, this can occur only in one of two ways: either by applying species to singulars, or by turning itself toward the species themselves. If the soul knows singu-lars by applying species to singulars, it follows that such an application is not made by deriving something from singular things themselves, because the separated soul does not have sentient powers naturally disposed to receive [species] from singulars. Therefore it remains that this application is made by premising something about singulars; and thus the soul will not know singulars themselves, but only what it premises about them. However, if the separated soul knows singulars through the aforesaid species by turning itself toward them, it follows that it will know singulars only so far as they exist in the species themselves. But singulars exist only universally in the aforesaid species. Therefore the separated soul knows singulars only in the universal.

13. Further, nothing finite can be superior to infinite things. But singulars are infinite. Therefore, since the power of the separated soul is finite, it seems that the separated soul does not know singulars.

14. Further, the separated soul can know a thing only by intellectual vision. Now Augustine says in the *De Genesi ad litteram*,[5] that separated souls by their intellectual vision know neither bodies nor the likenesses of bodies. Therefore, since singular things are bodies, it seems that they cannot be known by the separated soul.

5 XII, 24 (*PL*, XXXIV, 474).

15. Further, wherever the nature is the same, the mode of operation is also the same. Now a separated soul possesses the same nature as a soul that is joined to a body. Therefore, since the soul by its intellect cannot know singulars when it is joined to the body, it seems that it cannot know singulars when it exists apart from the body.

16. Further, powers are distinguished by their objects. But the cause [in this case, the object] possesses that which it produces [viz., distinction] in a higher degree. Therefore the diversity among objects is greater than that found among powers. But a sense never becomes an intellect. Hence the singular, which is the object of sense, never becomes an object of the intellect.

17. Further, a cognitive power of a superior order is less complex (*multiplicatur*), with respect to the same cognizable object, than a power of an inferior order; for the common sense knows all things apprehended by the five external senses; and likewise an angel, by one cognitive power, namely, by its intellect, knows both the universals and singulars which a man apprehends by his senses and his intellect. Now no power of an inferior order can apprehend the object of another power which differs [specifically] from itself, just as sight can never apprehend the object of hearing. Therefore a man's intellect can never apprehend a singular which is the object of sense, although an angel's intellect knows and apprehends both.

18. Further, it is said in the work *De causis*,[6] that an intelligence knows things inasmuch as it causes them or directs them. But the separated soul can neither cause singulars nor direct them. Therefore it does not know singulars.

Arguments against the conclusions of these objections.

1. On the contrary, to form propositions belongs to the intellect alone. Now the soul, when still joined to the body, forms propositions, the subject of which is a singular, and the predicate of which is a universal; for example, when I say: Socrates

6 *De causis*, XXIII.

is a man; but I cannot do this unless I know the singular and its relationship to the universal. Therefore the separated soul really knows singulars by its intellect.

2. Further, the soul is inferior in nature to every angel. Now the angels of a lower hierarchy receive illuminations about singular effects. In this way they are distinguished from the angels of an intermediary hierarchy, who receive illuminations according to the universal likenesses (*rationes*) of these effects. They are also distinguished from the angels of a supreme hierarchy, who receive their illuminations according to the universal likenesses existing in their cause [i.e., God]. Therefore, since the more particular in nature a knowledge is, the lower is the order of existence of the substance possessing such knowledge, it seems that the soul knows singulars in a much more desirable way when it exists apart from the body.

3. Further, whatever an inferior power can do, a superior power can do. Now sense, which is inferior to the intellect, can know singulars. Therefore the separated soul can know singulars by its intellect.

I answer: We must say that, when the soul exists apart from the body it knows some singulars, but not all of them. Now it knows some of the singulars of which it first acquired knowledge while united to the body, otherwise it would not remember the things which it did in this life, and thus remorse of conscience would vanish from the separated soul. It knows also those singulars of which it acquires knowledge after being separated from the body, otherwise it would not be punished by the fire of hell and by the other corporeal punishments which are said to exist in hell. However, that the separated soul does not know all singulars by its natural knowledge, is shown by the fact that the souls of the dead are not aware of things that occur here, as Augustine says.[7]

Therefore this inquiry involves two difficulties: one com-

[7] *De cura pro mort.*, XIII (*PL*, XL, 604).

mon [to intellectual nature as such] and one proper [to human nature]. The difficulty common to intellectual nature as such arises from the fact that our intellect does not seem to be capable of knowing singulars, but only universals. Therefore, since intelligence is the only cognitive power proper to God, to the angels, and to the separated soul, it appears difficult to see how they can possess a knowledge of singulars. For this reason some men made the mistake of denying any knowledge of singulars to God and the angels; but this is altogether impossible. For if this position were adopted, divine providence would be excluded from things, the judgment of God concerning human acts would disappear, and the ministering of the angels would also be removed, for we believe that the angels are solicitous of the safety of man, as the Apostle says: "Are they not all ministering spirits, sent to minister for them, who shall receive the inheritance of salvation?" (Heb. 1:14.)

For this reason some said that God, the angels, and separated souls as well, know the whole order of the universe through a knowledge of universal causes; for there is nothing in singular things that is not derived from these universal causes. They offer the example that, if anyone should know the whole order of the stars and the heavens, and their measure and movement, he would know, by means of his intellect, all future eclipses, both their number, in what places they would occur, and at what time they would take place in the future. But this is insufficient for a true knowledge of singulars. For it is clear that, no matter how closely universals may be united, a complete singular never results from their union: just as if I say man, white, musical, and will have added whatever others are possible, a singular will never result from them; since it is possible for all these universals, which are joined together, to belong to many men. Therefore anyone who knows all causes universally, never knows expressly any singular effect as a result of such knowledge. Nor does one who knows the whole order of the heavens know this eclipse inasmuch as it is this [i.e., as a singular], for although he knows that a future eclipse will occur at such a postion of the sun and moon, at such an hour, and whatever else is to be observed in eclipses of this kind, yet it is possible for an eclipse of this specific kind to occur frequently.

Therefore others, that they might ascribe a true knowledge of singulars to the angels, maintained that knowledge of this sort is derived from singulars themselves. But this is quite incongruous; for, since the greatest difference exists between an intelligible mode of existing and a material and sensible mode of existing, the form of a material thing is not received immediately by the intellect, but is carried to it through a number of intermediaries; for example, the form of a sensible thing first exists in a medium wherein it is more spiritual [8] than in the sensible thing itself; next it exists in a sense organ; and from there is drawn into the imagination and the other inferior [sense] powers; and finally it is carried to the intellect. Now it is inconceivable that such media should play any role either in the knowledge of an angel or in that of a separated soul.

Therefore it must be said, on the contrary, that the forms of things through which the intellect knows, are related to things in a twofold manner: for some forms are productive of things, while others are derived from them; and forms which are productive of things lead to a knowledge of a thing inasmuch as they are productive of it. Thus the artisan who gives the form to the thing made, or gives some disposition to matter, knows the thing made by the form of his art as regards that which he causes in the thing. And because no human art causes matter, which is the principle of individuation, but receives matter already in existence, therefore the artisan, for example, a builder, knows the house in a universal way by its form, but he does not know this house as this house, except so far as he acquires knowledge of it through the senses.

[8] I.e., less distant from the intelligible being that it has in the intellect.

Now God, by His intellect, not only produces the form from which the universal notion (*ratio*) is derived, but also produces matter which is the principle of individuation. Consequently He knows by His art, both universals and singulars; for, as material things flow from the divine art, with the result that they subsist with their proper natures, so also by the same art do the likenesses of intelligible things flow into the separate intellectual substances, and these substances know the things produced by God, through these likenesses. Therefore the separate substances know not only universals, but singulars as well, inasmuch as the intelligible species which are infused in them by the divine art are the likenesses of things as regards both their form and their matter.

Nor is it improper for a form which is productive of a thing, even though the form itself is immaterial, to be the likeness of a thing as regards both its form and its matter, because a thing always exists more simply in a superior nature than it does in an inferior one. Therefore, although form and matter are diverse in the sensible nature, nevertheless that which is higher and the cause of both, is related to both as one existing thing; and for this reason superior substances know material things immaterially, and diverse things unitedly, as Dionysius says.[9] However, intelligible forms that are derived from things are acquired by abstraction. Hence they do not give rise to knowledge of the thing as such, but only to a knowledge of what is abstracted from the thing. Therefore, since the forms in our intellect, which are derived from things, are abstracted from matter and from all material conditions, they do not lead to a knowledge of singulars, but to a knowledge of universals alone. This, therefore, is the reason why separate substances can know singulars by their intellect, whereas, on the other hand, our intellect knows only universals.

Now an angelic intellect and a separated soul are differently situated so far as the knowledge of singulars is concerned. For

[9] *De div. nom.*, VII, 2 (*PG*, III, 868).

we explained in a previous article (Art. XVIII) that the efficacy
of the angels' intellective power is proportioned to the universality of the intelligible forms which they possess; and
therefore they know through universal forms of this kind all
the things to which these forms extend. Therefore, just as they
know all the species of natural things existing under their
genera, so they know all the singular natural things contained
under their species. However, the efficacy of the separated
soul's intellective power is not proportioned to the universality of infused forms, but, on the contrary, is proportioned
to forms abstracted from things. For this reason it is natural
for the soul to be united to a body. Therefore it was said
above that the separated soul does not know all natural things
determinately and completely, even with regard to their species, but that it can know them in a certain general and in-
determinate manner. Consequently the infused species [which
separated souls possess] are not sufficient for a knowledge of
singulars to the point of enabling those souls to know all singulars as the angels do.

Nevertheless these infused species in the soul are limited
to a knowledge of those singulars to which the soul is specifically ordered or inclined, for example, those things which act
upon it, either things afflicting it, or things which leave impressions and traces upon it. For whatever is received is limited
[or determined] in the recipient in accordance with the condition of the recipient's mode of being. Hence it is evident that
the separated soul knows singulars; not all singulars, however,
but only some of them.

Answers to objections. 1. In this life our intellect knows
through species derived from things, which species are abstracted from matter and from all material conditions; and
therefore it cannot know singulars, the principle of which is
matter, but only universals. However, the separated soul's

intellect has infused forms through which it can know singulars, for the reason just given.

2. When the soul exists apart from the body, it does not know singulars by the species which it previously acquired while united to the body, but by infused forms. However, it does not follow that it knows all singulars, as has been shown.

3. Separated souls are prevented from knowing things that occur here, not because they exist in a different place, but because they do not possess a sufficiently efficacious intellectual power whereby they can know all singulars through infused species.

4. The angels do not know all future contingent things, for they know singulars through infused species inasmuch as they participate in these species. Hence future things, in whose species the angels do not yet participate, are not known by the angels inasmuch as they are future, but are known only inasmuch as they are present in their causes [i.e., as possibles].

5. The angels who know all singular natural things do not have as many intelligible species as there are singulars known through these species; but they know many things through one species, as we have shown above. Separated souls do not know all singulars. Consequently this objection does not apply so far as they are concerned.

6. If [infused] species were derived from things, they could not be the proper [intellectual] likenesses of the singulars from which they are abstracted; but the infused species, since they are the likenesses of the ideal forms which are in the divine mind, can distinctly represent singulars, especially those which the soul is somehow determined to know by its nature.

7. Although an infused species is immaterial and distinct, yet it is the likeness of a thing as regards its form as well as its matter, which matter is the principle of distinction and individuation, as we have shown.

8. Although intelligible forms are not creative of things,

nevertheless they are similar to creative forms, not indeed because they create, but because they represent created things.
For an artisan by his art can communicate something to the
thing which he makes, although the virtue [of the artisan]
which perfects the thing, is not itself present to that thing.

9. Because infused forms are only analogously similar to
the ideal exemplars existing in the divine mind, it follows
that these ideal exemplars cannot be known perfectly through
forms of this kind. However, it does not follow that the things
of which these are the ideal exemplars, are known imperfectly
by the infused forms; for things of this sort are not more excellent than infused forms, but rather the reverse. Consequently they can be understood perfectly through infused
forms.

10. The infused forms in the separated soul are limited to a
knowledge of certain singular things because of the soul's own
disposition, as we have shown.

11. Infused species are caused in the separated soul by God
through the intervention of the angels. Nor does this prevent
some of the separated souls from being superior to some of
the angels. For we are not speaking now of the knowledge of
glory, in accordance with which the soul can be either similar,
or equal, or even superior to an angel, but we are speaking of
that natural knowledge [of the soul] wherein the soul is inferior to an angel. Moreover, forms of this kind are caused in
the separated soul by an angel, not in a creative manner, but
as something actual brings something in its genus from potentiality to actuality. And because such action is not spatial, it is
unnecessary here to examine a conveying spatial medium.
But the order of nature operates here in the same was as the
order of place (*situs*) does in corporeal things.

12. The separated soul knows singulars through infused
species inasmuch as they are the likenesses of singulars in the
manner just described. Moreover, application and conversion,

mention of which is made in the objection, accompany knowledge of this kind rather than cause it.

13. Singulars are not actually infinite but potentially infinite. Nor is the intellect of an angel or that of a separated soul prevented from knowing an infinite number of singulars one after another, because sense can also do this. And our intellect, in this way, knows infinite species of numbers, for the infinite exists in knowledge only successively, and according as act is allied with potency, as the infinite in material things is also considered to be.

14. Augustine did not intend to say that bodies and the likenesses of bodies are not known by the intellect, but that the intellect is not moved in its vision by bodies in the same way as the senses are, nor by the likenesses of bodies as the imagination is, but by intelligible truth.

15. Although a separated soul is of the same nature as a soul which is joined to a body, nevertheless, because of its separation from the body, the soul has the character proper to superior substances, so that it can receive from them the infused intelligible forms through which it knows singulars; which it cannot do while it is united to a body, as we have shown above (Art. XVII).

16. The singular inasmuch as it is sensible, that is, so far as it is subject to corporeal change, never becomes intelligible; but it becomes intelligible so far as an immaterial form can represent it, as has been shown.

17. The separated soul receives intelligible species by means of its intellect, after the manner of a superior substance which knows by one power what man knows by two, namely, by his sense and his intellect. And thus the separated soul can know both.

18. Although the separated soul does not direct or cause those things, nevertheless it possesses forms similar to those which do cause and direct; for a being that causes and directs,

knows what it directs and causes only inasmuch as it possesses the likeness of that thing.

We must also answer those arguments which are raised as contrary objections, because they are false.

1. When the soul is joined to the body, it does not know singulars by its intellect directly, but by a certain reflection; that is, inasmuch as it apprehends its intelligible, it turns back to consider its act, the intelligible species (which is the principle of its operation) and the origin of its species; and in this way it proceeds to consider phantasms, and the singulars of which they are the phantasms. But this reflection can be completed only with the cooperation of the cogitative power (*ratio particularis*) and the imagination, which are not present in the separated soul. Hence the intellect does not know singulars in this way.

2. The angels of an inferior hierarchy receive illumination regarding the natures of singular effects, not through singular species, but through universal likenesses by which they can know singulars by reason of the efficacy of their intellectual power, wherein they surpass the separated soul; and although the likenesses perceived by them are universals absolutely, yet they are said to be particular in comparison to the more universal species, which superior angels receive.

3. Whatever an inferior power can do, a superior power can also do; not in the same way, however, but in a more excellent manner. Consequently those things which the senses perceive materially and singularly, the intellect knows immaterially and universally.

# ARTICLE XXI

## WHETHER THE SOUL, WHEN SEPARATED FROM THE BODY, CAN SUFFER PUNISHMENT BY CORPOREAL FIRE

In the twenty-first article we examine this question: Whether the soul, when separated from the body, can suffer punishment by corporeal fire.[1]

Objections. 1. It seems that the separated soul cannot suffer punishment by corporeal fire. For a thing suffers (*patitur*) [i.e., is acted upon or undergoes a change] only so far as it is in potency. But when the soul exists in separation from the body it is in potency only so far as the intellect is concerned, because the sentient powers do not exist in the soul, as we have shown above (Art. XIX). Consequently the separated soul can be acted upon by corporeal fire with respect to the intellect alone, namely, by understanding this fire. Now this is not punitive, but is, in fact, delightful. Therefore the separated soul cannot suffer punishment by corporeal fire.

2. Further, an agent and a patient have the same matter, as is stated in the *De generatione et corruptione*.[2] But since the soul is immaterial it does not have any matter in common with corporeal fire. Therefore, when the soul exists in separation from the body, it cannot be acted upon by corporeal fire.

3. Further, whatever does not make contact with a thing does not act upon that thing. Now corporeal fire cannot make contact with the soul, either by the elemental [contact] of

[1] See also *De veritate*, q. 26, a. 1; *Quodl.*, II, q. 7, a. 1; III, q. 9, a. 21.
[2] I, 7 (324a 34). See Art. VI, note 9.

quantity, because the soul is incorporeal, or by contact of power,[3] because the power of a body cannot make an impression upon an incorporeal substance, but rather the reverse. Therefore the separated soul cannot be acted upon in any way whatever by corporeal fire.

4. Further, a thing is said to be acted upon in two ways: either as an object, as when wood is acted upon by fire, or as a contrary, as when something hot is acted upon by something cold. Now the soul cannot be acted upon by corporeal fire as the subject of a passion, because in that case the form fire would have to arise in the soul, and, as a consequence, the soul would be made hot and would burn, which is impossible. In like manner, we cannot say that the soul is acted upon by corporeal fire as one contrary is acted upon by another: first, because the soul has no contrary, and secondly, because it would follow that the soul would be destroyed by corporeal fire; which is impossible. Therefore the soul cannot be acted upon by corporeal fire.

5. Further, there must be some proportion between an agent and a patient. Now there does not seem to be any proportion between the soul and corporeal fire, because they belong to different genera. Therefore the soul cannot be acted upon by corporeal fire.

6. Further, whatever is acted upon is moved [i.e., passes from potency to act]. Now the soul is not moved, because it is not a body. Therefore the soul cannot be acted upon by fire.

7. Further, the soul is nobler than a body composed of the fifth essence.[4] But a body composed of the fifth essence is al-

---

[3] One being cannot act upon another unless there is some contact between them. In the *Summa theologica,* St. Thomas points out that "No action of an agent, however powerful it may be, acts at a distance, except through a medium" (*Summa theol.,* Ia, q.8, a.1). The two ways in which such contact may be made are by quantity and by power.

[4] According to the traditional physics, the celestial bodies were perfect and unchangeable, and therefore had to be composed of a different element from the four elements of which terrestrial beings are constituted. Consequently this element made a fifth body, or "fifth essence." See Aristotle, *De caelo,* I, 2 (269a 5 ff.).

together unchangeable. Consequently the soul is even more unchangeable.

8. Further, Augustine says in the *De Genesi ad litteram*,[5] that an agent is nobler than a patient. But corporeal fire is not nobler than the soul. Therefore corporeal fire cannot act upon the soul.

9. But it was said that fire does not act upon the soul in virtue of what is proper and natural to fire, but inasmuch as it is the instrument of divine justice. On the contrary, it is characteristic of a wise builder to use suitable instruments for the end which he intends. Now corporeal fire does not seem to be an adequate instrument for punishing the soul, because this is not proper to fire by reason of its form; and it is by its form that an instrument is adapted to its effect, as an axe for chopping and a saw for cutting, for a builder will not act with greater wisdom if he should use a saw for chopping and an axe for cutting. Therefore even less will God, who is most wise, use corporeal fire as an instrument for punishing the soul.

10. Further, since God is the Author of nature, He does nothing contrary to nature, as it says in a certain Gloss [6] on the text: "It is implanted contrary to nature" (Rom. 11:24). But it is contrary to nature for the corporeal to act upon the incorporeal. Therefore God does not permit this.

11. Further, God cannot cause contradictories to be true simultaneously.[7] Now this would occur if He were to withdraw from a thing a constitutive part of its essence; for example, if a man were not rational, it would follow that he would be a man and not be a man at the same time. Therefore God cannot cause a thing to be deprived of any of its essential parts. Now to be unchangeable is essential to the soul, for this is proper to

[5] XII, 16 (*PL*, XXXIV 467).

[6] *Glossa ordinaria*. See Art. XVIII, note 10.

[7] In the *Summa*, St. Thomas explains that whatever implies a contradiction does not come within the scope of divine omnipotence, because it cannot have the aspect of possibility. He adds, however, that "It is more appropriate to say that such things cannot be done, than to say that God cannot do them." See *Summa theol.*, Ia, q.25, a.3.

it by reason of its immateriality. Consequently God cannot cause the soul to be acted upon by corporeal fire.

12. Further, everything possesses the power of acting in accordance with its nature. Therefore a thing cannot receive a power of acting which is not proper to itself but to something else instead, unless its proper nature is changed into some other nature; water, for example, will not heat unless it is changed [i.e., made hot] by fire. Now it is not proper to fire by nature to have the power of acting upon immaterial things, as we have already shown. Therefore, if God gives fire, as the instrument of divine justice, the power of acting upon the separated soul, it now seems that it is not corporeal fire, but fire of a different nature.

13. Further, what is done by the divine power is in accord with the proper and true specific nature of a thing existing in reality. For when by divine power a blind man is given the power of vision, he receives sight according to the true and proper natural notion of sight. Therefore, if the soul is acted upon by fire, as the instrument of divine justice, by virtue of the divine power itself, it follows that the soul really is acted upon in the true sense of "passion." Now passion [i.e., being acted upon] is used in two ways. First, to signify merely the reception of something [by a patient], as when the intellect is acted upon by an intelligible, and a sense by a sensible. Secondly, to signify the loss of something on the side of the substance of the thing being acted upon, as when wood is acted upon by fire. Therefore, if the separated soul is acted upon by corporeal fire, in virtue of the divine power, inasmuch as the nature of passion consists merely in receiving something, it follows that the separated soul is receptive of corporeal fire in an immaterial and incorporeal way in keeping with the soul's own mode; because whatever is received in something is received according to the mode of the recipient. However, a reception of this sort does not punish the soul, but perfects it.

Consequently this will not be a punishment for the soul. Similarly the soul cannot be acted upon by corporeal fire so far as passion consists in the loss of something on the side of the substance being acted upon, because then the substance of the soul would be corrupted. Therefore the soul cannot be acted upon by corporeal fire as the instrument of divine justice.

14. Further, an instrument acts as an instrument only by exercising its proper operation, just as a saw, by cutting, acts instrumentally in the production of a chest. Now fire by its proper natural operation cannot act upon the soul, because it cannot make the soul hot. Consequently fire as the instrument of divine justice cannot act upon the soul.

15. But it has been said that fire acts upon the soul by a proper action inasmuch as it confines the soul in such a way as to imprison the latter. On the other hand, if the soul is imprisoned by fire and detained by it, the soul must be united to fire in some way. However, the soul is not united as a form to fire, because then the soul would give life to fire. Nor is the soul united as a mover to fire, because then fire would be acted upon by the soul, and not vice versa. Now there is no other way in which an incorporeal substance can be united to a body, so it follows that the separated soul cannot be detained by fire, nor be imprisoned by it.

16. Further, whatever is fettered by something cannot be separated from it. But the spirits of the damned are sometimes separated from the corporeal fire of hell, for the demons are said to be in this misty atmosphere, and the souls of the damned have occasionally appeared to certain individuals here, as well. Therefore the soul is not acted upon by corporeal fire, as though imprisoned by it.

17. Further, whatever is fettered to something and detained by it, is thereby prevented from performing its proper operation. Now the proper operation of the soul is intellection; but the soul cannot be prevented from exercising this activity

by being bound to something corporeal, because the soul contains its intelligibles within itself, as is said in the *De anima*.[8]
Consequently it is not necessary for the soul to seek these things
outside itself. Therefore the separated soul is not punished by
being fettered to corporeal fire.

18. Further, just as fire can detain the soul in this way, so
also can other bodies, or to an even greater extent inasmuch
as they are larger and heavier. Therefore, if the soul is punished only by being detained and fettered, its punishment
should be attributed not only to fire, but even more so to other
bodies.

19. Further, Augustine says in the *De Genesi ad litteram*,[9]
that the substance of hell is not believed to be corporeal, but
spiritual. Damascene also says that the fire of hell is not corporeal. Therefore it seems that the soul is not acted upon by
corporeal fire.

20. Further, Gregory says in the *De moralibus*,[10] that the
delinquent servant is punished by his master in order that he
may be corrected. But the damned in hell are incorrigible.
Therefore they should not be punished by the corporeal fire
of hell.

21. Further, punishments are inflicted by means of contraries. Now the soul sinned by subjecting itself to corporeal
things, under the influence of passion. Therefore it should
not be punished by being united to corporeal things, but rather
by being separated from corporeal things.

22. Further, just as punishments are allotted to sinners by
divine justice, so also are rewards to the just. Now corporeal
rewards are not given to the just, but spiritual rewards only.
Consequently, if in Scripture any rewards of a corporeal nature
are said to be given to the just, they are to be understood metaphorically; for example, it is said: "That you may eat and

---

8 III, 4 (429b 5 ff.).
9 XII, 32 (*PL*, XXXIV, 480).
10 XXXIV, 19 (*PL*, LXXVI, 738).

drink at My table, in My kingdom" (Luke 22:30). Therefore corporeal punishments are not inflicted on sinners, but spiritual punishments only; and whatever is related in the Scriptures about corporeal punishments, is to be understood metaphorically. Consequently the soul is not acted upon by corporeal fire.

On the contrary, the fire by which the demons and the bodies and souls of the damned are punished, is the same, as is evident from this text: "Depart from Me ye cursed, into everlasting fire, which was prepared for the devil and his angels" (Matt. 25:41). But the bodies of the damned must be punished by corporeal fire. So likewise their separated souls must be punished by corporeal fire.

I answer: Men have spoken in many ways about the suffering (*passio*) of the soul by fire.

For some said that the soul did not suffer punishment by corporeal fire, but by a spiritual affliction which is referred to metaphorically in the Scriptures by the name of fire. This was the opinion of Origen.[11] But, such as it is, it does not seem satisfactory, because as Augustine says in the *De civitate Dei*,[12] we must understand that the fire by which the bodies of the damned are tormented, is corporeal; as is also the fire by which both the demons and the souls are tormented, inasmuch as this conclusion is inferred from it.

Wherefore it seemed to others that, although this fire is corporeal, nevertheless the soul does not suffer punishment by it directly, but by its likeness in the imagination; just as happens to people asleep who are truly tormented by the appearance of certain terrible things which they see themselves suffer, although the things by which they are tormented are not real bodies, but merely the likeness of bodies. But this

---

[11] *Peri Archon*, II, 11 (*PG*, XI, 236).
[12] XXI, 10 (*PL*, XLI, 724).

position cannot be maintained, because we have shown above (Art. XIX, ans. obj. 6) that the powers of the sentient part of the soul, of which one is the imaginative power itself, do not remain in the soul when it is separated from the body.

Therefore it must be said that the separated soul is acted upon by corporeal fire itself. However, it seems difficult to determine in what way it is acted upon by fire.

For some said that the separated soul suffers by the very fire which it sees. Gregory mentions this in his *Dialogues*,[13] for he says: "The soul suffers by fire in the very things which it sees." However, since the act of seeing is a perfection of the one seeing, every vision is delightful inasmuch as it is of this sort. Hence nothing is painful inasmuch as it is seen, but inasmuch as it is apprehended as harmful.

Wherefore others said that when the soul sees this fire and understands that fire is harmful to it, it is tormented by this fact. Gregory mentions this is his *Dialogues*,[14] for he says that the soul is consumed by fire, because it sees itself being consumed by fire. But then we still have to discover whether fire by its very nature is harmful to the soul or not. Indeed, if it is not by its very nature harmful to the soul, then it follows that the soul is deceived in that judgment wherein it apprehends fire as harmful. This seems unlikely, particularly so far as the demons are concerned, because they possess an extensive knowledge of the natural order by reason of their intellectual acumen.

Therefore it must be said that corporeal fire in virtue of its true nature is harmful to the soul. Hence Gregory concludes by saying: "We can gather from the aforesaid Gospels that the soul suffers not only by seeing fire but by experiencing it."[15] Therefore to discover how corporeal fire can be harmful to the soul or to a demon, we must bear in mind that harm does

---

[13] IV, 29 (*PL*, LXXVII, 368).
[14] *Ibid.*
[15] *Ibid.*

not befall a thing inasmuch as it receives something by which
it is perfected, but inasmuch as it is hindered by its contrary.
Hence the suffering of the soul by fire does not consist simply
in its receiving something, as the intellect suffers by an intelligible and sense by a sensible, but in this, that one thing is acted
upon by another by way of contrariety and as an obstacle.

Now this happens in two ways. For sometimes a thing is
hindered in one way by its contrary as regards its very act of
existing which it receives from some inhering form; and in
this way something is acted upon by its contrary through alteration and corruption, as wood, for example, is consumed by
fire. Secondly, a thing is hindered by an obstacle or a contrary
with respect to its inclination, just as the natural inclination
of a stone is to tend downward, but it is hindered in this by
some obstacle and opposing power so that it is brought to rest
or is moved contrary to its nature.

However, neither of these ways of suffering punishment
exists in a thing that lacks knowledge. For where sorrow and
sadness cannot exist, the nature of affliction and punishment
is not found. However, in a being which possesses knowledge,
torment and punishment are the natural effects of both kinds
of suffering, although in different ways. For the suffering [or
being-acted-upon] which is the effect of change by a contrary,
results in affliction and punishment by sensible pain, as when
a sensible object of the greatest intensity corrupts the harmony of a sense.[16] Therefore when *sensibilia* are of too great intensity, particularly those of touch, they inflict sensible pain;
but when moderate they cause delight, because then they are
proportioned to sense. However, the second kind of suffering
does not inflict punishment by sensible pain, but by that sadness which arises in a man or in an animal because something
is apprehended by an interior power as being repugnant to
the will or to some appetite. Hence things which are opposed
to the will and to the appetite inflict punishment, and some-

16 See Art. XVI, note 4.

times even more than those which are painful to sense. For some choose beforehand to be whipped and to undergo severe physical punishment rather than be scolded or the like, which is repugnant to the will.

Consequently the soul cannot suffer punishment by corporeal fire according to the first kind of suffering [i.e., being-acted-upon], because it is impossible for the soul to be altered and corrupted by suffering of this specific kind. Hence the soul is not afflicted by fire in this way, namely, that it suffers sensible pain thereby. However, the soul can suffer by corporeal fire according to the second kind of suffering, inasmuch as it is hindered from its inclination or volition by fire of this kind. This is evident. For the soul and any incorporeal substance, inasmuch as this belongs to it by nature, is not physically confined in any place, but transcends the whole corporeal order. Consequently it is contrary to its nature and to its natural appetite for it to be fettered to anything and be confined in a place by some necessity; and I maintain that this is the case except inasmuch as the soul is united to the body whose natural form it is, and in which there follows some perfection.

Moreover, the binding of a spiritual substance to a body is not brought about by any power which a body has for detaining an incorporeal substance; but is the result of the power of some superior substance which unites a spiritual substance to such a body; just as by the magic arts, and with divine permission, some spirits are bound to certain things by the power of superior demons, either by signs or imaginary visions or other things of this kind. It is in this way, through the divine power, that the souls and the demons are confined in their punishment by corporeal fire. Wherefore Augustine says in the *De civitate Dei:* "If men's souls, having been created incorporeal, are now in this life incarnate in bodily members, and shall one day be bound thereto forever, then why cannot we truly say, though you may marvel at it, that even incor-

poreal spirits may be afflicted by corporeal fire? Therefore
these spirits, even though incorporeal, shall dwell in tormenting corporeal fires . . . and, instead of giving life to these
fires, they shall receive punishment from them." [17]

Thus it is true that this fire, inasmuch as it detains the fettered soul, as a result of the divine power, acts upon the soul
as the instrument of divine justice; and inasmuch as the soul
apprehends that this fire is harmful to it, it is afflicted by interior sadness. Indeed, this sadness is greatest because the soul,
which was born to be united to God through possession, medi-
tates on the fact that it occupies a place below the lowest things
in existence. Therefore the greatest affliction of the damned
will be caused by the fact that they are separated from God;
secondly, by the fact that they are situated below corporeal
things, and in the lowest and meanest place.

Answers to objections.

As a result of this the solution to the first seven objections
is evident. For we do not say that the soul is acted upon by
corporeal fire in the manner of reception only or according
to change by a contrary, as the preceding objections maintain.

8. An instrument does not act by its own power but by that
of the principal agent. Therefore, when fire as the instrument
of divine justice acts upon the soul, the dignity of fire is not
considered, but that of divine justice.

9. Bodies are appropriate instruments for punishing the
damned, because it is proper for those who are unwilling to be
subject to their superior, that is, to God, to be made subject
to inferior things as a punishment.

10. Although God does not act contrary to nature, yet He
acts in a way superior to that of nature when He does what
nature cannot do.

11. To be incapable of being changed by a corporeal thing
after the manner of an alteration, is proper to the soul by

[17] XXI, 10 (*PL*, XLI, 724).

reason of its very essence. However, the soul does not suffer in this way through the divine power, but as we have explained above (the body of this article).

12. Fire does not possess the power of acting upon the soul inasmuch as it acts in virtue of its proper power, as those things do which act naturally; it acts only in an instrumental way. Therefore it does not follow that its nature is changed.

13. The soul is not acted upon by corporeal fire in any of these ways, but as we have explained.

14. Although corporeal fire does not make the soul hot, nevertheless it has another operation or relationship to the soul; which relationship bodies are naturally disposed to have toward spirits in order that bodies may be united to them in some way.

15. The soul is not united as a form to the fire which punishes it, because the soul does not give life to fire, as Augustine says; [18] but it is united to fire in the way in which spirits are united to corporeal places by contact of power, although they are not the movers of these.

16. The soul is afflicted by corporeal fire inasmuch as the soul apprehends that fire is harmful to it as binding and confining it, as we have already pointed out. Moreover, this apprehension can torment the soul even when it is not actually confined by fire, simply because it sees that it is capable of being so confined; and for this reason the demons are said to bring hell-fire with them wherever they go.

17. Although the soul is not prevented from performing its intellectual operation by being detained in this way, yet it is deprived of a certain natural liberty whereby it is wholly freed from being physically confined to a corporeal place.

18. The punishment of hell-fire (*gehenna*) belongs not only to the soul but also to the body. For this reason this fire above all is said to be the punishment of hell, because fire is particularly capable of tormenting bodies. However, there will also

[18] *De civit. Dei*, XXI, 2 (*PL*, XLI, 710).

be other torments, according to this: "Fire and brimstone and the storms of winds shall be the portion of their cup" (Ps.10:7). It is also appropriate to that inordinate love which is the principle of sin, so that as the empyrean heaven [19] rewards the fire of charity, so does the fire of hell reward inordinate desire.

19. Augustine says this not by way of an answer but by way of an inquiry, or if he stated this as an opinion, he expressly revoked it afterward in the *De civitate Dei*.[20] Or we can say that the substance of hell is said to be spiritual as to the proximate effect produced, namely, that fire is apprehended as harmful inasmuch as it confines and binds the soul.

20. Gregory introduces this as an objection against certain people who believed that all punishments inflicted by God belong to purgatory and are not perpetual; which indeed is false. For some punishments are inflicted by God, either in this life or after this life, for correction and purgation; others, indeed, for ultimate damnation. Nor are such punishments inflicted by God because He delights in punishment, but because He delights in justice inasmuch as punishment is due to sinners. This is the way it is among men, because some punishments are inflicted for the correction of the one who is punished, as when a father chastises his son, whereas others are inflicted as a final condemnation, as when a judge hangs a bandit.

21. Punishments take place by means of contraries so far as the intention of the sinner is concerned, for the sinner intends properly to satisfy his will. Punishment is also contrary to the will itself inasmuch as punishment results from the divine wisdom, so that that wherein someone seeks to satisfy his will is turned into its contrary, as is said in the Book of Wisdom: "That by which a man sins, by the same also is he tormented"

---

[19] The "empyrean heaven" was the highest heaven, completely outside the realm of change. It was regarded, by certain authors, as the abode of the blessed. St. Thomas maintains that this conception rests solely on the authority of Walafrid Strabo, Venerable Bede, and St. Basil. See *Summa theol.*, Ia, q.66, a.3.

[20] XXI, 2 (*PL*, XL, 710).

(Wisd. 11:17). Wherefore, because the soul sins by adhering to corporeal things, it is consistent with the divine wisdom that it be punished by corporeal things.

22. The soul is rewarded by enjoying things which are superior to it, but is punished by being subjected to things which are inferior to it. Therefore the rewards of the soul are fittingly understood only when regarded spiritually; punishments, however, are understood to be corporeal.

# INDEX

Accidents
  corruption of, 248
  genera of, 157
  nature of, 1, 67, 156, 162, 172
  not substantial principles, 139
  properties of, 150
  relation to material and efficient
    cause, 235
  relation to matter, 115
Act: God pure, 69, 74; a principle of
  movable things, 73; soul an, 118
Act of existing
  analogous, 82
  desirable in itself, 183
  distinct from essence in created
    beings, 74, 225
  form and matter have common, 5
  given by form, 73, 181, 184
  highest act, 74
  individuation and, 11
  most communicable, 15
  most formal principle, 15
  not participating in anything, 74
  relation to essential principles of
    species, 15
  relation to substance of soul, 5
  soul and body have a common, 5,
    11, 21
  supreme in soul, 5
  vital activity (vivere) is a living be-
    ing's, 9
Act of sensing: accidental mode of existing, 155; belongs to animated
  organ, 77; belongs to soul and
  body, 250
Activity, agent and patient required
  for, 56
Adam, nature of his body before sin,
  95, 104
Agent
  action of, 76, 154
  nature of, 49, 153, 248

Agent (continued)
  nobler than patient, 57
  power of finite, 137
  relation to instrument, 279
  relation to patient, 36, 193, 270
Alexander of Aphrodisias on the intellect, 68 f.
Anaxagoras: on agent intellect, 103;
  on celestial bodies, 103
Angel
  changeable through choice, 77
  a complete species, 84-92, 226
  difference in knowledge of man
    and, 222
  nature of, 83-85
  nobler than soul, 91
  not properly definable, 91
  our knowledge of, 90
  singulars known by, 261 ff.
  specifically different from soul, 84-
    92
Animal: generation of, 145 f.; movements in, 120; nature of, 119;
  sensory knowledge in, 167
Animal, imperfect: how generated,
  39
Animal spirits, ancient theory of, 95
Appetite: causes movement, 173; nature of, 167, 172; objects of, 170;
  twofold division of, 170
Aristotle: man an intellect, 151, 158;
  one agent intellect contrary to
  doctrine of, 210, 212; versus
  Plato, 44, 50
Aristotle, views on
  accidents, 235
  action, 248 f.
  agent and patient, 68, 69, 153, 269
  agent intellect, 47, 49, 55-57, 62, 67,
    230
  animal movements, 138 f.
  animal nature, 125

283

Soul of man (continued)
  similar to a science, 158
  simplicity of, 70, 72, 124, 135, 152,
    162
  substantial form of body, 7, 9, 72,
    135
  three grades of actions in, 166
  transcends the body, 8, 11 f., 15, 25,
    29, 31, 93, 194
  union of body and, 13, 16-31, 45, 93,
    98, 113-23, 132
  united to body for intellection, 6,
    106, 201, 222, 236
  in whole body and each part, 128-
    36
Soul, sentient: corruptible in ani-
    mals, 186; in the embryo, 145-47;
    reception of species in, 8
Soul, separated
  how it knows, 188-204, 218-27, 253
  joy and sadness in, 252
  knowledge of natural things, 229-
    37
  knowledge of separate substances,
    218-27
  knowledge of singulars, 259-64
  relation of virtues and vices to, 253
  sentient powers not in, 247-54
  two kinds of knowledge in, 238
Soul, vegetal: in embryo, 145 f.; from
    an intrinsic principle, 147; op-
    erations of, 163, 166; surpasses
    operations of elements, 8
Species
  basis of, 2, 71, 81, 130, 148
  has character of form, 69
  kinds of, 86
  known from operations, 40
  not diversified by more and less, 79

Species (continued)
  relation of accidents to, 157
  relation to genus, 165
State of innocence, 105
Subject, nature of a, 248
Substance: Aristotle on first and sec-
    ond, 7; nature of composite, 73;
    threefold division of, 4

Taste, 169
Terrestial sphere, relation of celestial
    bodies to, 58 f.
"To live" is to exist, 185
Totality, threefold, 129 f.
Touch, 99 f., 169, 174
Transparency, 13, 75
Trinity, soul imperfect image of, 156,
    157
Truth: acquired through senses, 3;
    nature of, 41

Unity: convertible with being, 36;
    nature of substantial, 143 f.
Universals
  abstraction of, 35 f.
  nature of, 17, 33 f., 49 f., 182, 261
  no real existence, 1, 11
  Platonists on, 43, 50, 142
  relation to singulars, 240, 256
Universe, diversity required for per-
    fection of, 84

Vegetal powers, 173

Whole, relation of parts to, 152, 218,
    244
Wisdom is first philosophy, 213
Wisdom, divine: relates secondary
    and primary beings, 6
Word, the: intellection of, 89